IMAGES
of America

JORDAN LAKE

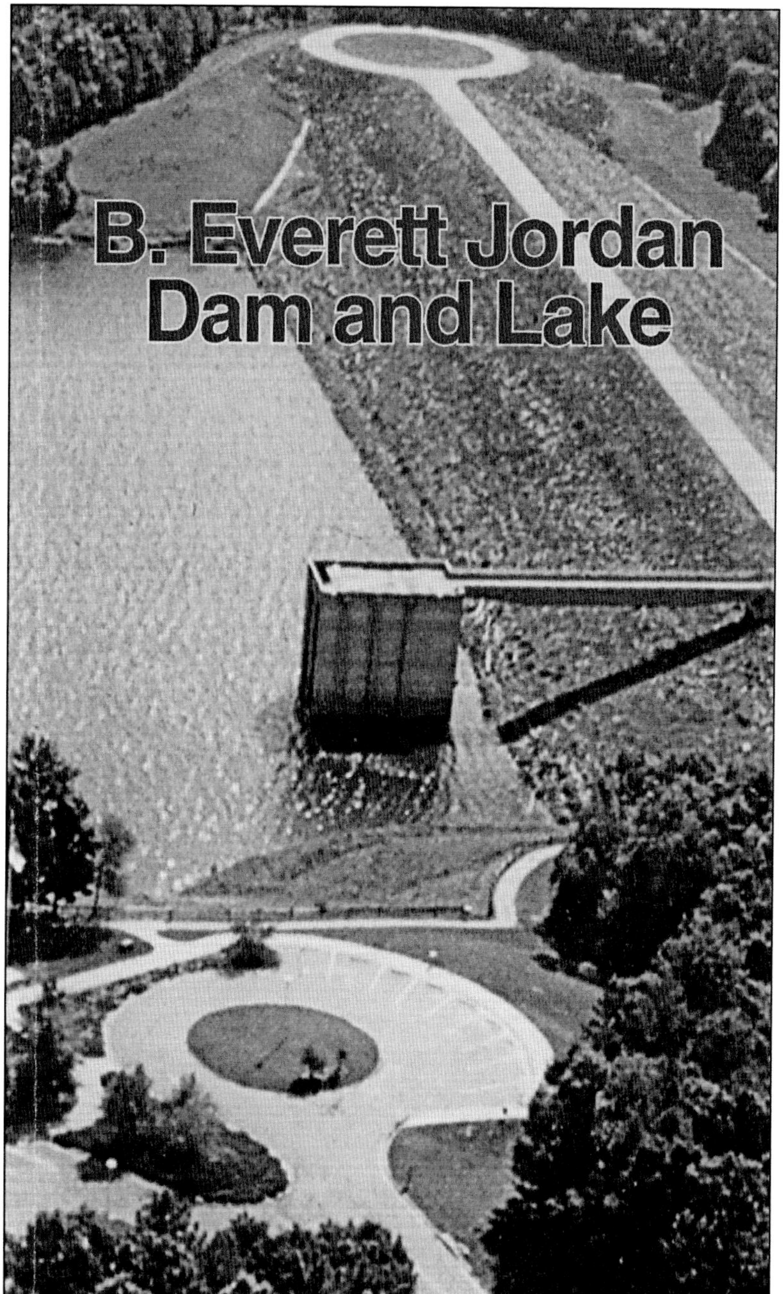

This is a beautiful view of the dam from the dam overlook platform at the U.S. Army Corps of Engineers Visitor Assistance Center. (Author's collection.)

On the Cover: This is news coverage of the New Hope Project on August 9, 1971, before the lake was renamed after the late Senator B. Everett Jordan. The television reporter is with WFMY Channel 2. The story of Jordan Lake and Dam has made news headlines for many decades. This photograph was taken after the announcement of recreation plans for the lake. (Courtesy of U.S. Army Corps of Engineers.)

IMAGES
of America

JORDAN LAKE

Heather Leigh Wallace

ARCADIA
PUBLISHING

ISBN 978-0-7385-8594-9

Published by Arcadia Publishing
Charleston, South Carolina

Printed in the United States of America

Library of Congress Control Number: 2009942546

For all general information contact Arcadia Publishing at:
Telephone 843-853-2070
Fax 843-853-0044
E-mail sales@arcadiapublishing.com
For customer service and orders:
Toll-Free 1-888-313-2665

Visit us on the Internet at www.arcadiapublishing.com

This book is dedicated to all the men and women of the U.S. Army Corps of Engineers and to my grandfather Adolph Chek for standing guard as his comrades raised the flag at Iwo Jima.

Contents

Acknowledgments

It is impossible to thank every individual here who has made this effort to preserve history feasible. My most indebted gratitude goes to the people listed below.

U.S. Army Corps of Engineers, for whom I have gained enormous respect.

R. C. "Duck" Duckson, assistant operations manager of the U.S. Army Corps of Engineers at Jordan Lake and Dam, has been very professional, patient, and insightful and kept me on the right civilian track with my research. Duck has been at Jordan Lake since February 1979, which was two and a half years prior to the start of impoundment. His dedication, experience, and knowledge have proven beneficial to such an important project as Jordan Lake and Dam.

Pittsboro mayor Randy Voller, for truly being active with the welfare of his community.

Nicholas Macaulay, who probably loves Jordan Lake even more than I do.

Sue Dayton with the Blue Ridge Environmental Defense League. May your environmental awareness reach from sea to sea.

The Haw River Assembly (HRA), a nonprofit citizens group formed in 1982 to protect and restore the Haw River and Jordan Lake. Your voice is being heard.

Dr. Tom Colson, of the Clean Jordan Lake organization, for sharing the same goals and grassroots quality of life.

Chatham County Historical Association (CCHA), for their support and ongoing preservation.

Patrick Barnes, former Chatham County commissioner, for knowing all things great and small.

The Friends of Chris Matheus (FOCM) professional networking group, for introducing me (and countless others) to Jordan Lake.

Dr. John and Bunny Shillito for providing great photography for the book.

Jeff Starkweather, please write that book (or many)!

Joyce Jones Cotten, for sharing the history of the lost Pea Ridge. Keep up the great work preserving Pittsboro High School's history and the Pea Ridge family heritage.

Joan Wilson Frazier, for being a darling and making me laugh through hours of scanning materials.

Anthony Esquivel of Middleman Photography (middlemanphotography.com), for providing priceless photographs of baptisms at Jordan Lake.

Ivan Watkins of Ivan Watkins Photography (ivanwatkins.com), for sharing his heartfelt stories of family trips to the lake.

Adolph Chek for always reminding me that I am just like him.

Most importantly, my editor Lindsay Harris, for being excited about Jordan Lake, being very patient, and providing guidance when needed.

INTRODUCTION

Jordan Lake was conceived generations ago as a means of flood control for the Cape Fear watershed. The Lake's placid waters and bucolic charm obscure the controversy that impacted its conception and construction. Today, it serves as a wonderful park and an important source of drinking water for the burgeoning Triangle area. Understanding its singular importance as a source of regional drinking water will help citizens and businesses to continue to protect its natural buffers and keep its tributaries healthy. To enjoy the unique qualities and charms of Jordan Lake please visit Chatham County and Pittsboro.

—Randolph Voller, Pittsboro mayor

Some of the most breathtaking and relaxing views in North Carolina can be found while driving across Jordan Lake on Route 64. This view, and the endless recreational activities the lake provides, will make people understand why so many are gravitating to Chatham County. The U.S. Army Corps of Engineers skillfully designed this human luxury and wildlife sanctuary.

Since the 1820s, the U.S. Army Corps of Engineers has aided and protected the development of North Carolina by dredging rivers, ocean bars, and inlets; clearing rivers of debris; and building locks and dams.

The Jordan Lake recreation area encompasses 46,798 acres, of which 13,900 acres are flooded to form a reservoir 216 feet above mean sea level. This vast, much-needed preserved area is surrounded by endlessly expanding urban areas. The lake, which is mostly a feature of Chatham County, is a placid area for boating, canoeing, camping, fishing, hiking, and much more. The lake also supplies water to local communities. There is a dedicated reserve for bald eagles that attracts one of the largest concentrations of bald eagles in the southeast. The locale provides mature trees and large undisturbed private areas.

Jordan Lake is a young lake with a long history. The story of Jordan Lake has made the cover of newspapers countless times. The stories range from beautiful sailing events and triathlons to remorseful stories from former landowners and local activists urging business owners to stop polluting the waterways.

The New Hope River Valley, where Jordan Lake resides, is now also home to the corporate world of Research Triangle Park (RTP), which was originally settled by Scottish highlanders in the 1740s and saw action in both the Revolutionary and Civil Wars. When explorer John Lawson visited the Piedmont area, he referred to the Haw River in his journal as "the famous Haw River." The RTP area is growing at an alarming rate and would have seen issues with scarcity of water if not for Jordan Lake and Dam. This valley was historically flooded by storms. Local roads and the original Norfolk Southern Railroad frequently succumbed to high waters that made it difficult for cars to pass.

In 1933, the chief of the U.S. Army Corps of Engineers developed three plans for multiple areas to receive lakes for power and/or flood control. The plans were found to be too costly at the time and were put aside.

In 1945, a devastating hurricane rocked the Carolinas and hovered over the New Hope River Valley, severely flooding and incapacitating the area. This storm, called Hurricane No. 9, was one of the last before hurricanes were properly named in the 1950s. The impact of Hurricane No. 9 significantly increased government interest in protecting the area, and Congress directed the U.S. Army Corps of Engineers to undertake a comprehensive study of water resource needs and to review the plans from 1933.

The New Hope Valley area was chosen, and thus the vast undertaking was named the New Hope Project. North Carolina senator B. Everett Jordan (senator from 1958 to 1973) was very passionate about the lake and dam project and secured funding for its development in 1963, with construction beginning in 1967. Legal battles impeded construction off and on through the 1960s and 1970s. Additionally, during the construction period, Native American artifacts were found and a special archeological dig took place, delaying the lake progress. Local business owner Vossie Horton, of the original Wilsonville General Store, sold T-shirts during the 1970s that said "swim Jordan Lake, you will never drown" and showed people swimming and boating in dirt. Senator Jordan's good friend Ben Bulla and son John Jordan share stories of the late Senator Jordan, who chafed over the delays and said that he would wind up one day being the first person to be named after a mud puddle. Senator Jordan passed away in 1973, and the lake and dam project were renamed in his honor in 1974. The senator never got to see the lake finished, as it was not filled until 1982.

Local land acquisitions to build the lake began in the 1970s; they started in Moncure and then moved upriver. Several families were displaced by the acquisitions; some were very satisfied with the money the government paid them, and some settled in court. Some felt their land was useless, swampy, and frequently flooded. For others, their land was a way of life and provided a means for income. Landowners would rent out a portion of their land to tenant farmers, who might farm and reside on the land. The farmers would pay for their area with a portion of their produced crops, cash, or both. Many families had parcels of land that were greater than 200 acres and were handed down from original land grants in the 1700s. Their land was so large that they were able to grow crops and hunt game on their property to feed their whole family for the year.

Former Chatham County commissioner Patrick Barnes lost 177 acres of his land to the lake at a cost of $651 per acre. This left Barnes with 32 of his family's original 209 acres. Barnes shared the story of the time he found a land surveyor on his property and politely asked the stranger why he was trespassing. The surveyor informed him that his land was being acquired and his property lines were being surveyed. After being nicely asked, the surveyor refused to leave. Barnes went into his home and after waiting and growing impatient with the stranger tooling around on his property, Barnes came out with a shotgun and shot a leg off of the surveyor's tripod. The surveyor packed his things and left the property. Barnes was sent before a magistrate, found guilty, and required to pay a fine, but contrary to newspaper sensationalism, he did not go to jail. The irony is that Barnes went on to become president of Chatham County United, an organization formed to protect Jordan Lake. He spent four years as Chatham County commissioner fighting the development of new construction by the town of Cary that was infringing upon Jordan Lake's boundaries and causing concern for pollution in the very water that is provided to the local communities. Several recent developments caused severely muddy waters at the lake. Barnes still resides by Jordan Lake. After he lost his land, he purchased 13 acres adjacent to his remaining 32 acres for tenfold more than what he was paid for his previous land. A beautiful aerial photograph of Barnes's land is provided within this book.

Land Beneath the Waters and *Our Land Our Lives* is a combination DVD produced and sold by the Chatham County Historical Association that traces the history of the New Hope River Valley. The DVD covers native population, early settlers, both the Civil and Revolutionary Wars, land acquisitions through eminent domain, the construction of Jordan Dam, and present-day recreational activities. The historical society gathered many original locals and interviewed them for the DVD.

A typical day at the lake includes striper fishing. North Carolina's Wildlife Resources Commission provides an astonishing stocking program within Jordan Lake for which they release upwards of 70,000 stripers each year. Striper season is from April to December, and several striper tournaments are held during this time. To date, the largest striper caught at Jordan Lake was 16 pounds. The Jordan Lake Striper Club can be contacted for guides and tournament schedules. It also monitors VHF Channel 68 on Jordan's waters.

There are many groups and political figures that are very passionate about Jordan Lake, including the Haw River Assembly (HRA), a nonprofit organization founded in 1982 to restore the Haw River and to protect Jordan Lake. The Haw River is 110 miles of scenic waterway that peaks at the Cape Fear River Basin and stretches from Greensboro to Wilmington, all of which finds its way into the Jordan Lake Reservoir. Almost 1 million people are part of this regional watershed, a number that is rapidly increasing. The HRA is dedicated to educating those individuals and businesses whose wastewater, sedimentation, and runoff impairs these waters. For the past 20 years, HRA has been holding a Learning Celebration camp for fourth graders that is a solar-powered environmental educational extravaganza. The HRA also holds field trips and yearly lake clean up projects. In 2008, there were 250 bags of trash removed from the shores of Jordan Lake during a one-day HRA-led volunteer program. Photographs from the HRA's first year are provided within this book.

Clean Jordan Lake is an environmental protection organization and grassroots team of volunteers headed up by Dr. Tom Colson, a faculty member at North Carolina State University. Clean Jordan Lake was incorporated in July 2009 in the state of North Carolina with the aims of developing several new and innovative programs for litter removal on Jordan Lake and fostering elimination of the sources of litter in the future. These efforts are complementary to those of the Haw River Assembly. The two organizations have agreed to work cooperatively on future clean ups, with the lead taken by Clean Jordan Lake, which in turn will coordinate with the U.S. Army Corps of Engineers and Chatham County Waste Management.

Another regional organization that protects our environment is the Blue Ridge Environmental Defense League (BREDL), a nonprofit that works with communities threatened by polluting industries. The league's humble beginnings started in 1984, when 50 citizens of Ashe and Watauga Counties met in the Mission House of the Holy Trinity Church in Glendale Springs, North Carolina. Teachers, homemakers, merchants, and farmers listened to the report of the Episcopal Church Women on the federal government's search to find a site for the nation's first high-level nuclear waste dump in Western North Carolina. Recognizing that the Blue Ridge Mountains were a region at risk, the Blue Ridge Environmental Defense League was formed with Executive Director Janet Marsh at the helm to protect air and water quality in their backyards. Since then, the league has successfully worked with many communities threatened by industrial pollution and toxic waste. One of the many environmental protection goals for BREDL is trying to educate and work with local farmers about spraying sludge (human waste products) on their crops. Wastewater treatment plants give the free sludge to farmers, who use it as fertilizer and are not told of the toxic effects. Rainwater causes this sludge to run off into the local watershed. Sludge was originally disposed of into the ocean until scientists found that is was killing marine life. A photograph of sludge from a farmer's land can be found in the environment chapter.

The Jordan Lake Visitor Assistance Center, managed by the U.S. Army Corps of Engineers, is a great place for anyone who wants to learn more about the creation of Jordan Lake and what the lake and corps have to offer. The U.S. Army Corps of Engineers at the lake is constantly monitoring the lake's water level for flood control and drought control. It is a task that is taken very seriously and carried out with precision. The corps' other main concern is for the safety of the one to two million visitors each year. In addition to its daily activities, each year the center holds a Junior Rangers camp, which includes fun and adventurous learning activities such as hiking, environmental games, crafts, and much more. The center also provides water safety and environmental classes and seminars that can be tailored to an organization's needs.

It takes 10 to 20 years for a plastic bag to decompose and 450 years for a plastic soda bottle to decompose, so please, before leaving Jordan Lake, clean up the area so it will still be beautiful upon return.

The story of Pea Ridge is about a community that forever changed as a result of Jordan Lake. The Pea Ridge Road ran north and south and crossed the New Hope Valley approximately 5 miles northeast of the junction of the New Hope Creek and the Haw River. It was a major thoroughfare for travel from the southern part of Chatham County to points north such as Chapel Hill and Durham. The land on either side of Pea Ridge was extremely fertile from years of deposits left from the flooding of the New Hope Valley.

The people who lived along the Pea Ridge Road were mostly farmers who had an immense love of the land. They were self-sufficient people who raised most of their own food—chickens and eggs, milk and beef from their own cows, and vegetables from their gardens—and they always had flowers blooming in the summer. Most of these people were born and raised in and around the Pea Ridge Road. They knew what the flooding of the valley could do, but they learned to live with it and sustained. These people had survived the Depression—many had been sharecroppers and sawmill workers and had purchased or inherited their farms through blood, sweat, and tears.

Electricity and indoor bathrooms were unknowns until the late 1940s and early 1950s. Their heat source as well as their cooking source was a wood stove. Life was good, however; they worked hard, played hard, and helped their neighbors in time of need. Farm families got together with neighbors at school events, church dinners, or corn shuckings. Children and adults found ways to have fun for free—playing hopscotch, listening to the Lone Ranger on the radio, or enjoying a hot afternoon at the favorite swimming hole in the New Hope Creek.

The Sam and Pansy Jones family's farm bordered the Pea Ridge Road, and the eastern side of the farm ran along the New Hope Creek. It was a fertile farm that grew an abundance of vegetables, tobacco, corn, and wheat. Sam and Pansy purchased the farm in 1940 and built a new home there in 1942. It was a dream come true for them to have a farm of their own on which to raise their five children—Betty, Patsy, Marie, Joyce, and Stanley. They taught their children to love God and country, to take pride in their work, and to get a good education.

It was in the midst of this setting that they learned that the government wanted to take their land for flood control and recreation, something that they and many other families never quite understood. When the locals moved to their new homes after the government purchased their original homesteads for Jordan Lake, their barns were looted and farm equipment was stolen. Even 16-inch beams designated for moving to the new locations were taken. Outsiders from all around thought the barns were abandoned, but the folks were just moving, and it could not be done in one day. Many family treasures were lost.

A number of small, less traveled roads were lost to the lake, but none were as major or as populated as the Pea Ridge Road. There was no major crossroad along the Pea Ridge and no popular gathering place such as a store. As a result, the Pea Ridge Road got lost in the maze of road closings as the Jordan Lake Project became a reality. It is these circumstances that Joyce Jones Cotten, the fourth daughter of Sam and Pansy Jones, wanted to share a little of with the story of Pea Ridge found in chapter seven.

One

The Making of Jordan Lake

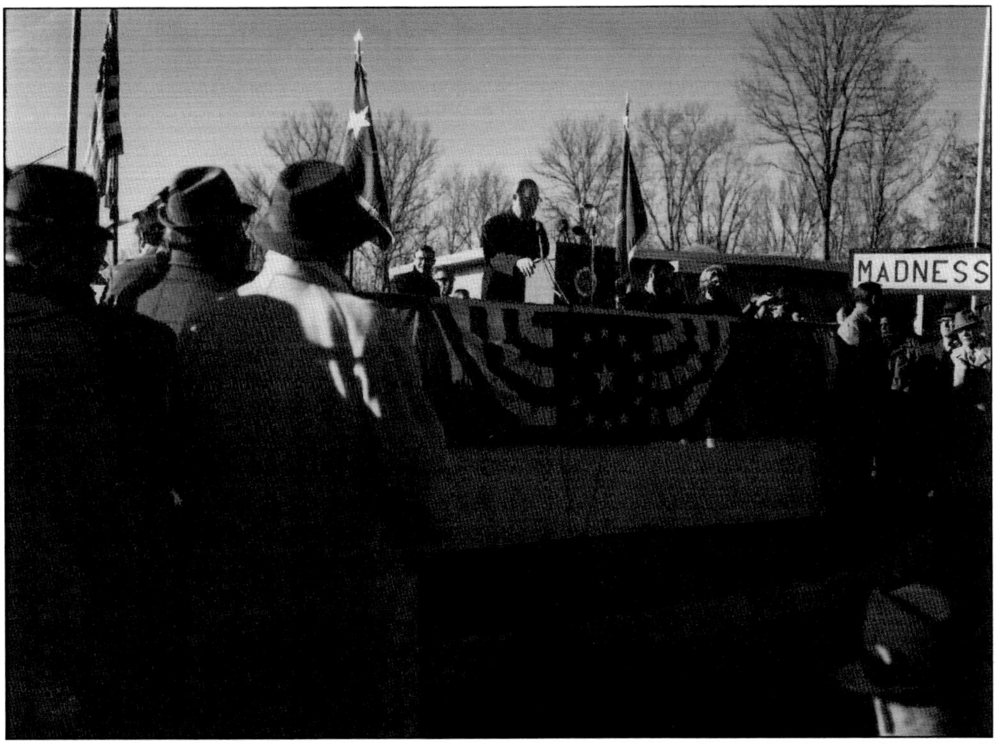

The late senator B. Everett Jordan stands at the podium in December 1970 during the groundbreaking ceremony at Jordan Lake. Freedom of speech allowed the protestors to raise the "madness" sign; some of those protestors are now very involved in protecting the lake. (Courtesy of U.S. Army Corps of Engineers.)

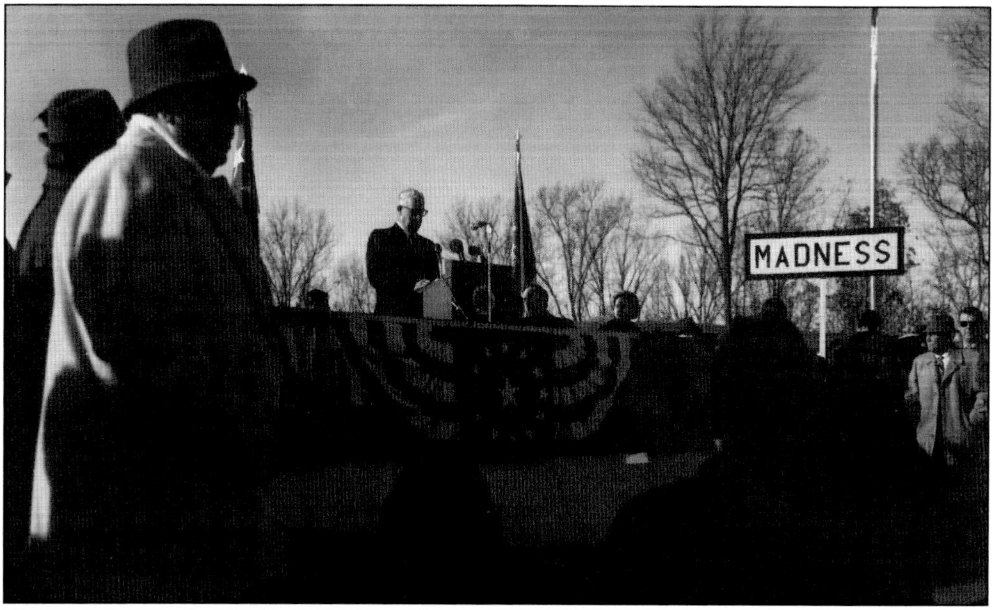

Former politician Ike Andrews stands at the podium in 1970 and gives a speech about his support of the lake. (Courtesy of U.S. Army Corps of Engineers.)

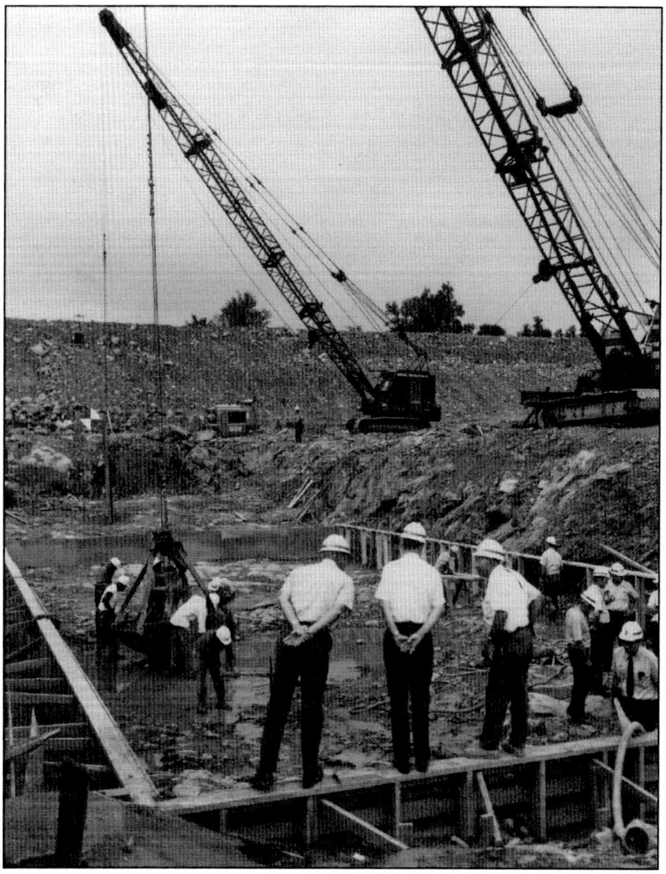

This photograph of construction on the outlet structure was taken on September 15, 1971. Executives from the Sanford Construction Company oversee the progress. (Courtesy of U.S. Army Corps of Engineers.)

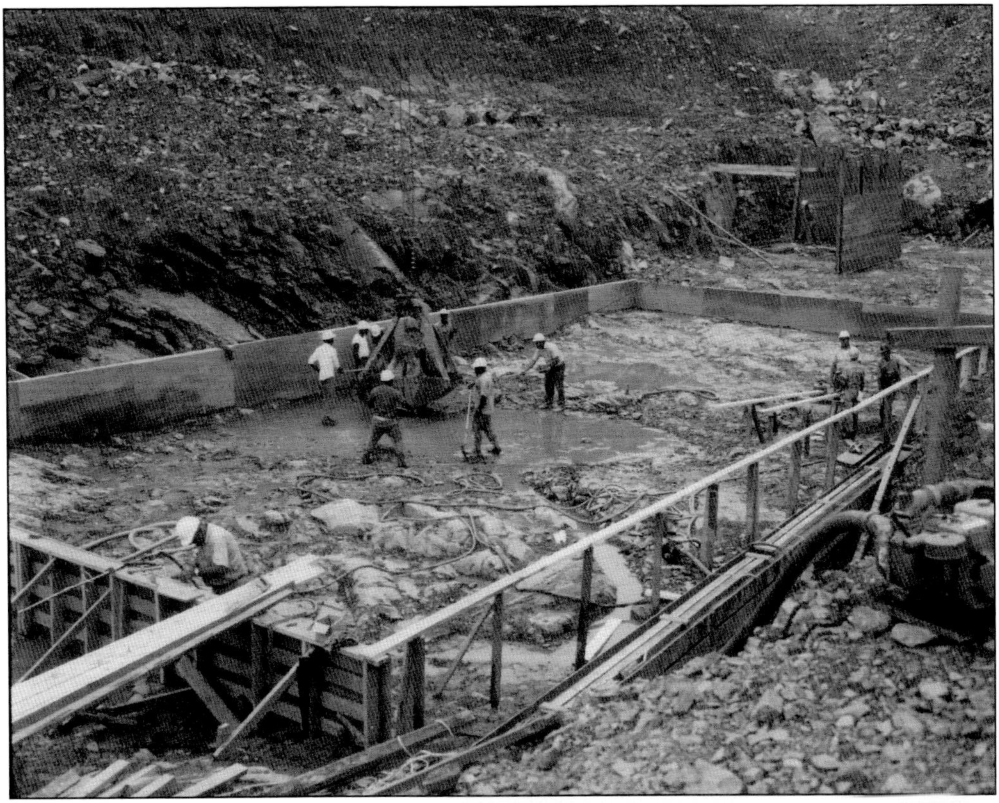

Pictured is construction on the outlet structure, most of which will remain permanently underwater. The photograph was taken on September 15, 1971. (Courtesy of U.S. Army Corps of Engineers.)

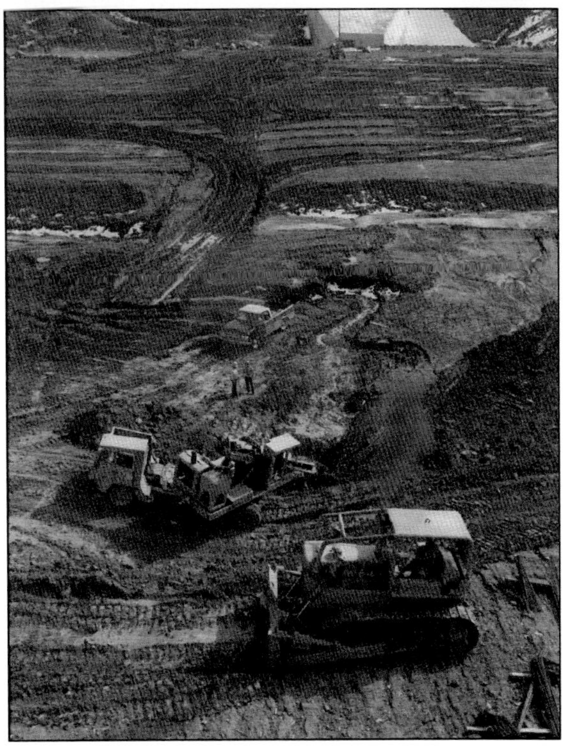

The spillway to the dam and intake structure can be seen at the top of the photograph in 1971. The machines were preparing the ground for the intake tower construction to begin. (Courtesy of U.S. Army Corps of Engineers.)

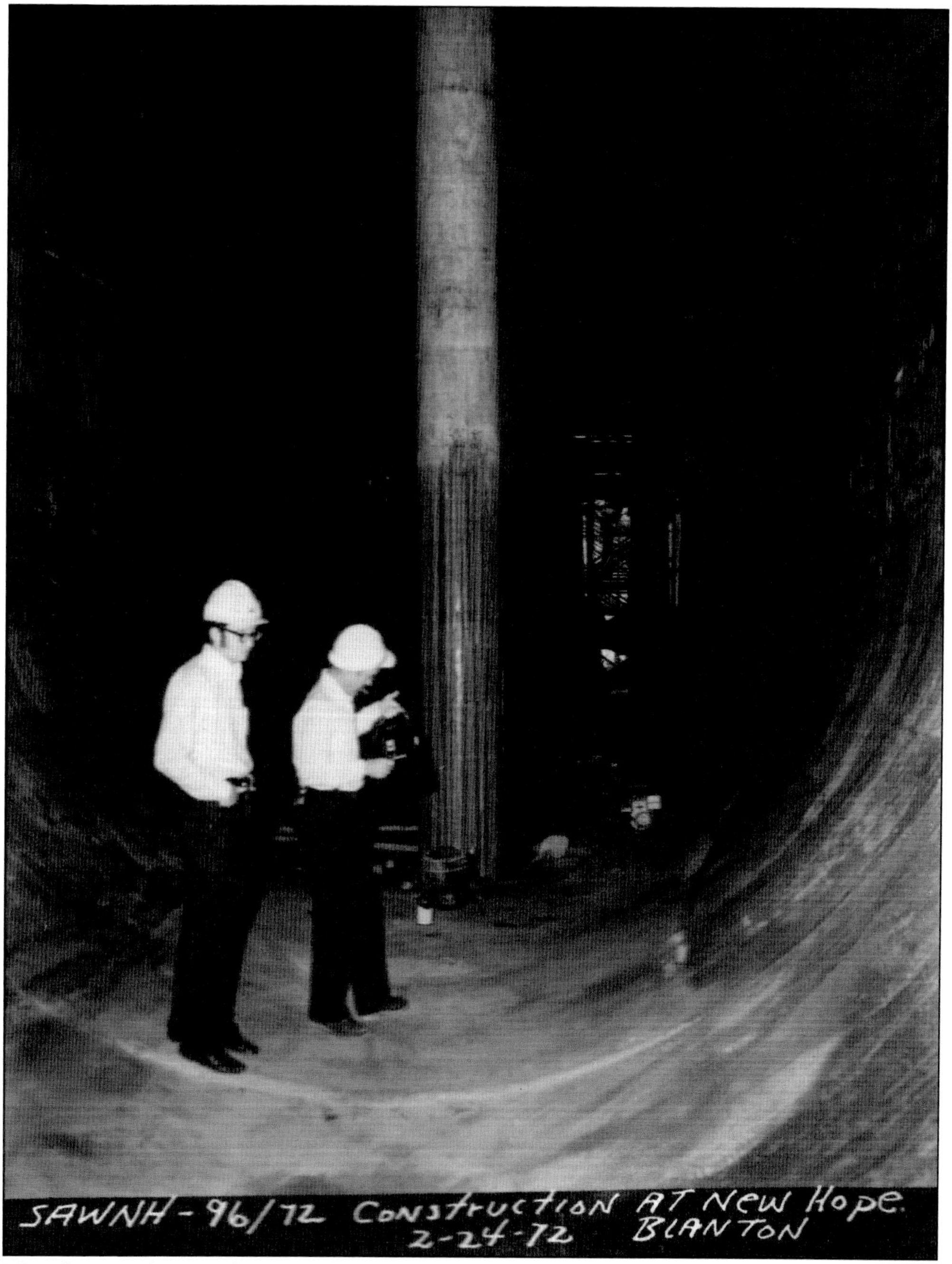

The photograph was taken on February 24, 1972, and reads "construction at New Hope." The two engineers are inside of the intake tower, which is now fully underwater. (Courtesy of U.S. Army Corps of Engineers.)

On June 14, 1972, the Sanford Construction Company and the U.S. Army Corps of Engineers are having a discussion inside of the dam intake tower. The U.S. Army Corps of Engineers has both military and civil works missions and is responsible for military engineering and for the development, utilization, management, and conservation of water resources. (Courtesy of U.S. Army Corps of Engineers.)

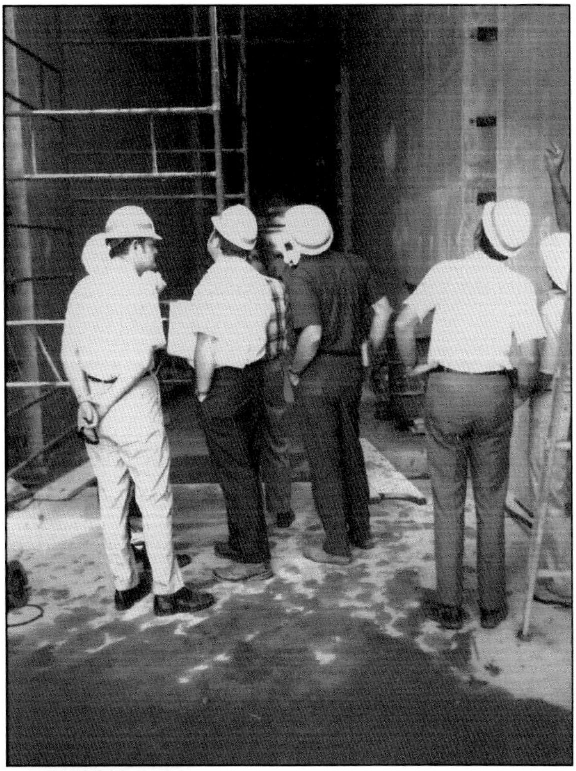

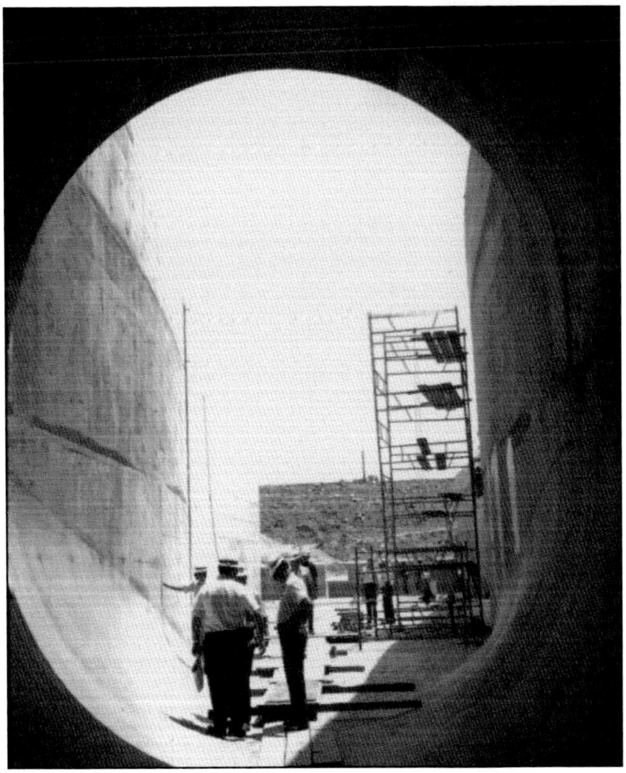

This is a construction image of the New Hope Dam (Jordan Dam) conduit taken on June 14, 1972. The U.S. Army Corps of Engineers is the largest engineering organization in the free world. (Courtesy of U.S. Army Corps of Engineers.)

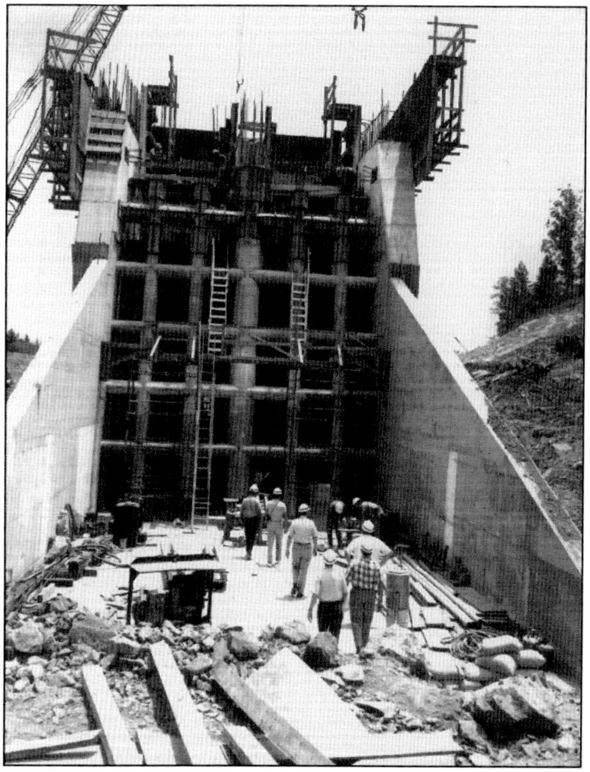

This photograph was taken on June 14, 1972, at the New Hope Dam (now Jordan Dam) construction site. The area of Jordan Lake where the dam resides is very placid and quite breathtaking. (Courtesy of U.S. Army Corps of Engineers.)

The intake tower is being constructed on November 2, 1972. The intake tower is a square concrete structure divided into two halves with a total of 12 metal sluice gates. Each half of the structure is equipped with six gates: one emergency gate, one service gate, one 6-foot-by-6-foot water quality control gate, and three 8-foot-by-8-foot water quality control gates. Each gate is operated by a hydraulic cylinder that is connected to a hydraulic system. The hydraulic system and the gates are operator-controlled at a local control panel. (Courtesy of U.S. Army Corps of Engineers.)

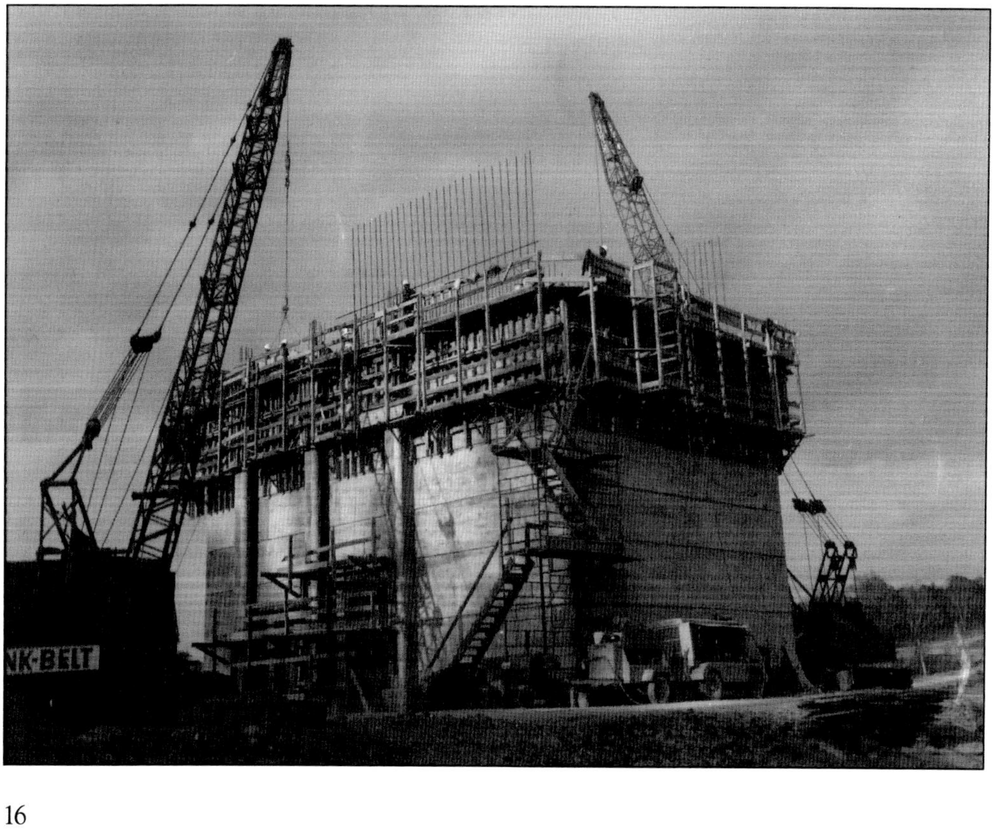

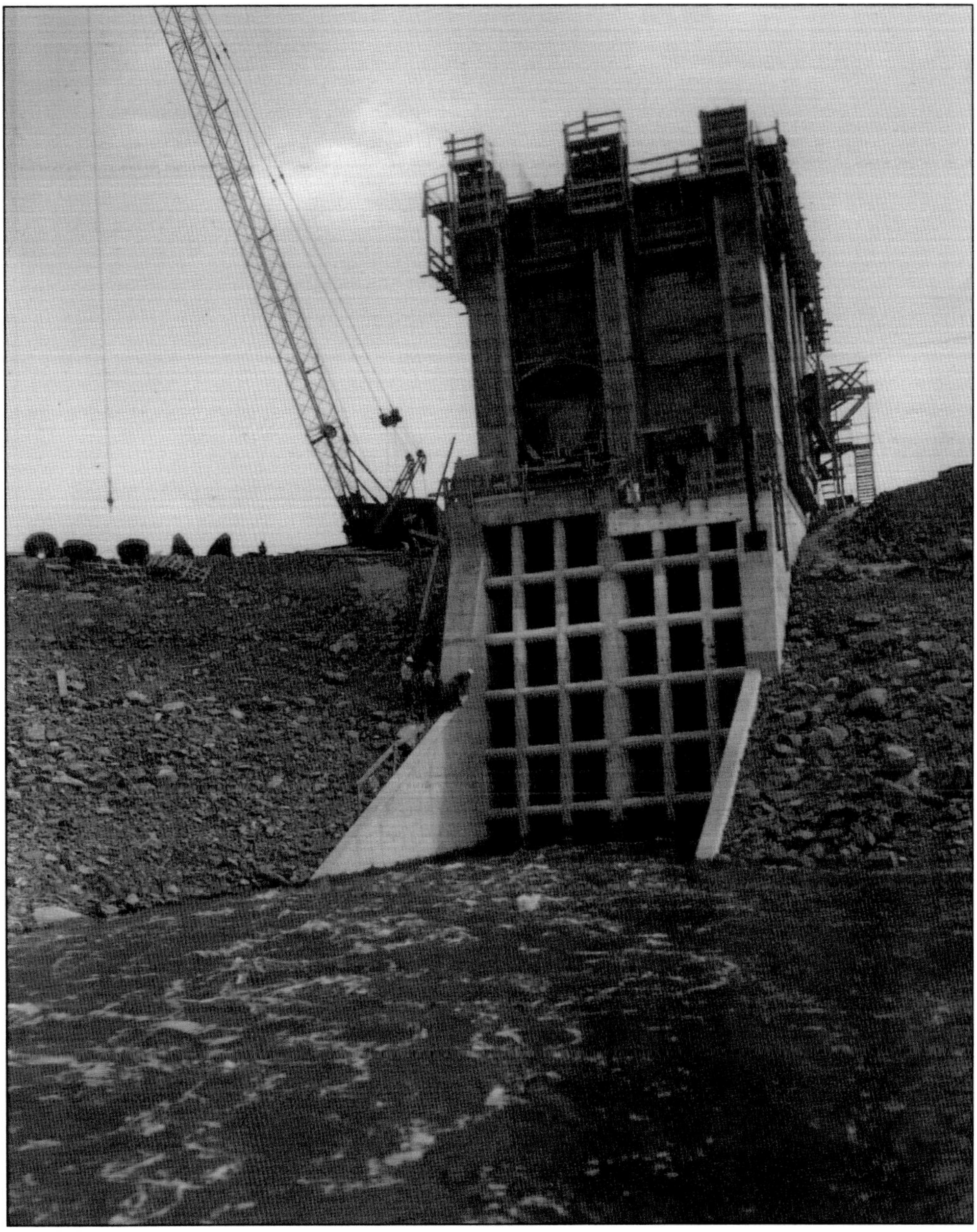

Water is entering the dam intake structure in November 1972. Most of this structure is now underwater. The structure provides water quality control through gates that are used to allow flow into the structure from different depths, while the service gates are used to control the water discharge from B. Everett Jordan Lake. (Courtesy of U.S. Army Corps of Engineers.)

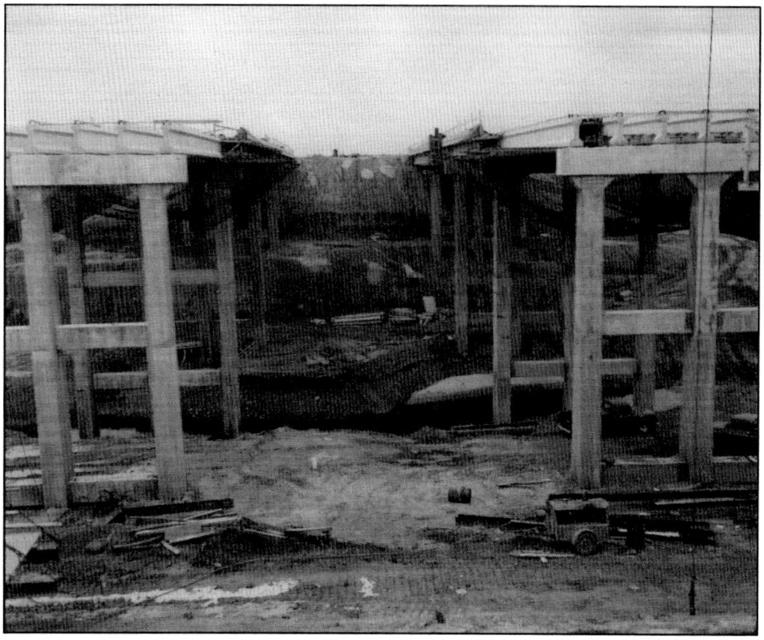

Pictured are the U.S. Route 64 relocation bridges at New Hope River looking east on November 3, 1972. U.S. Route 64 is an east-to-west highway that runs 2,326 miles from eastern North Carolina to just southwest of the Four Corners in northeast Arizona. (Courtesy of U.S. Army Corps of Engineers.)

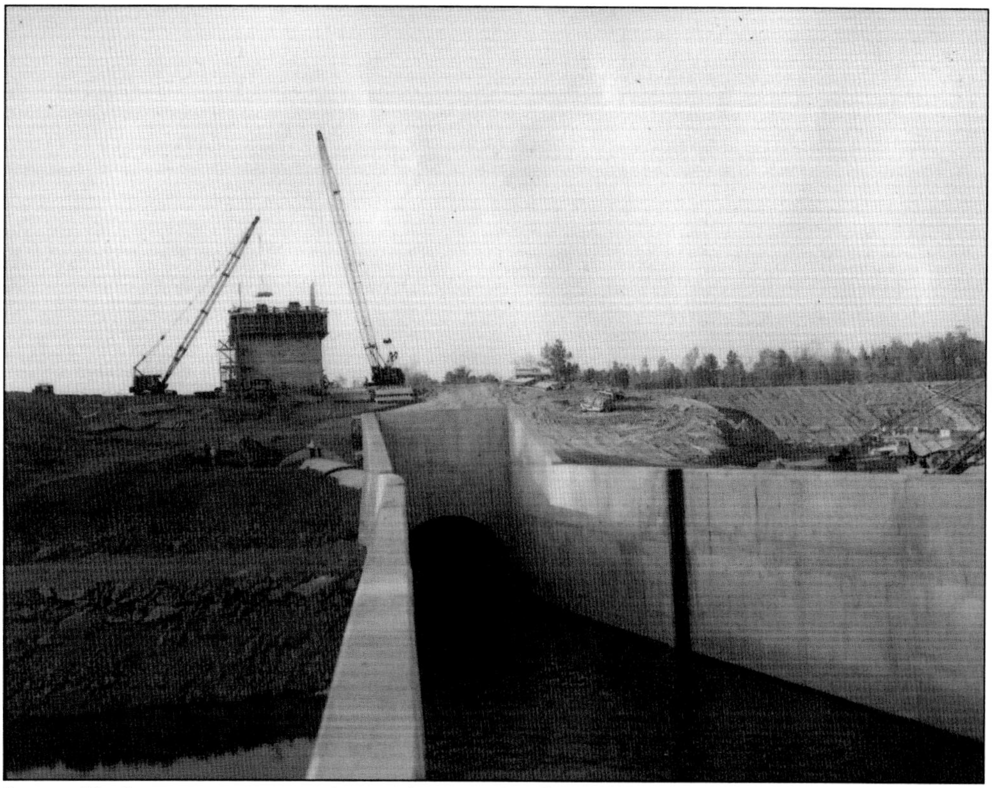

Pictured looking upstream into the conduit in 1972, this site is now a popular place for fishermen who enjoy fishing from the shoreline into the water that runs downstream. For comfort, public restrooms and picnic benches have also been provided by the U.S. Army Corps of Engineers in this location. (Courtesy of U.S. Army Corps of Engineers.)

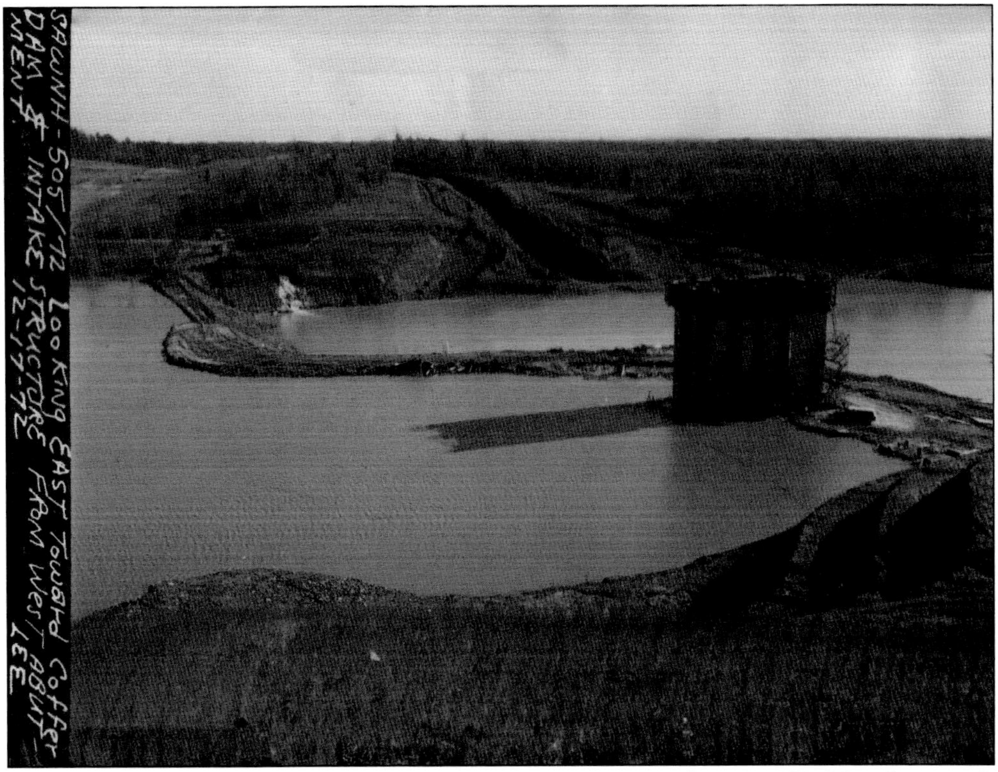

This is a photograph of the dam construction progress on December 12, 1972. The photograph reads "looking east toward coffer dam and intake structure from West abutment." (Courtesy of U.S. Army Corps of Engineers.)

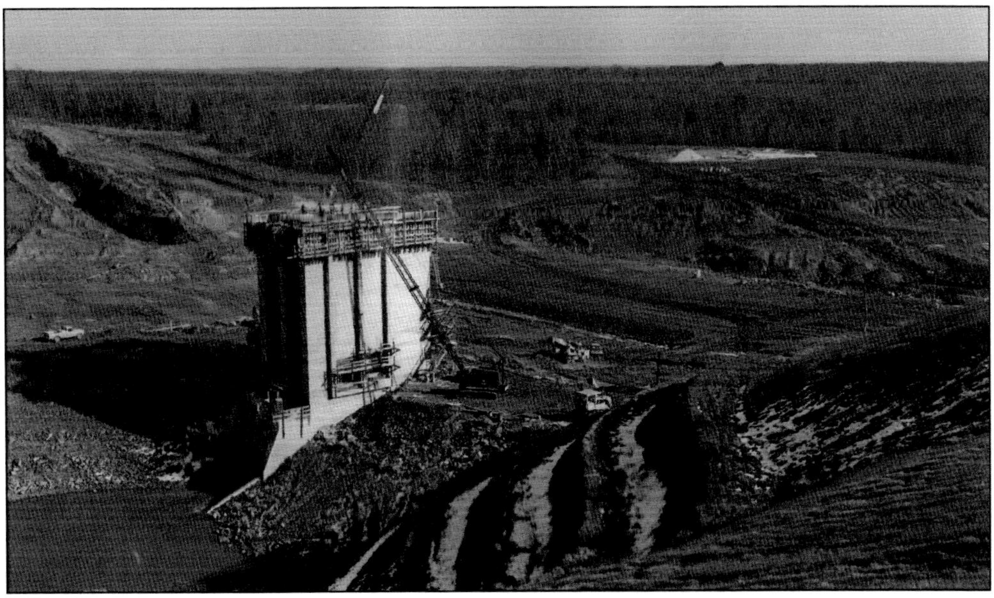

This is a photograph of the intake tower and construction prior to a rainstorm that impacted development efforts. The photograph was taken on January 18, 1973. (Courtesy of U.S. Army Corps of Engineers)

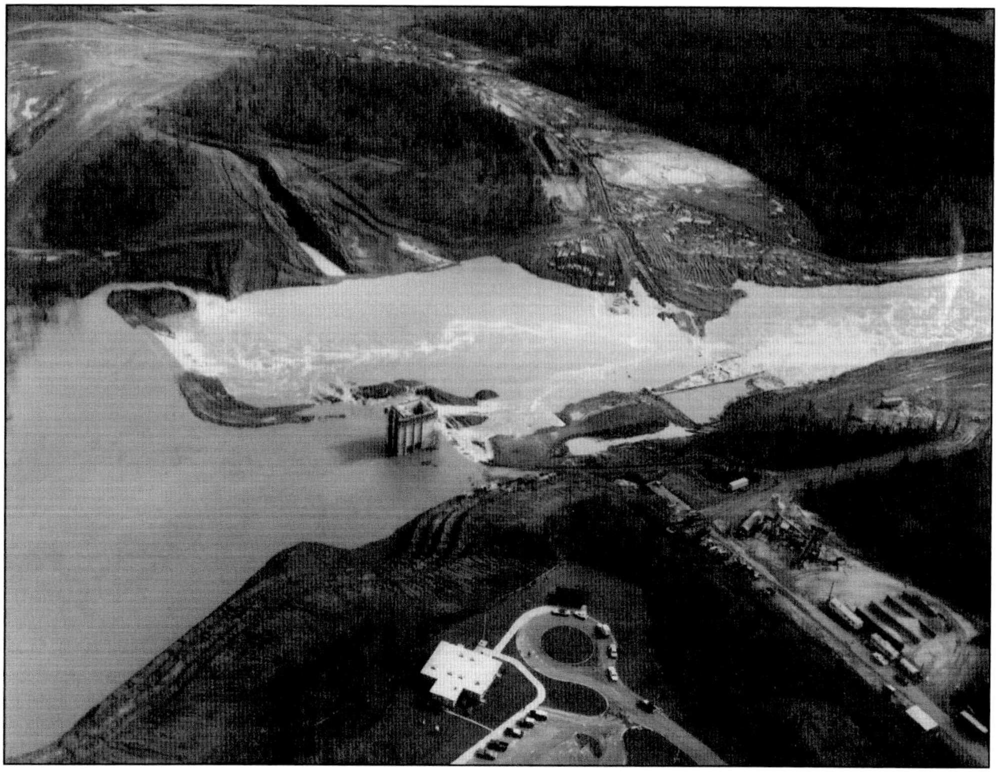

The intake tower is pictured during flooding after a storm in February 1973. This was nine years before the dam was even finished. The area at the bottom of the photograph is the U.S. Army Corps of Engineers Visitor Assistance Center, which is actually higher than the dam and intake tower. The view at the visitor center is breathtaking. An overlook platform and public restrooms are provided in this area with picnic tables for that perfect lunch. (Courtesy of U.S. Army Corps of Engineers.)

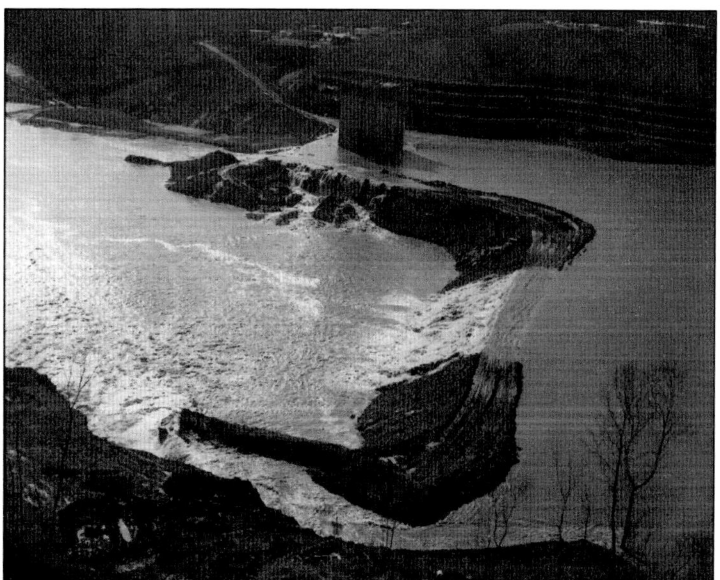

This is a rare photograph of the dam intake tower construction efforts from the opposite side of the tower. The U.S. Army Corps of Engineers visitor center building and parking lot can be seen in the upper right corner of the photograph. (Courtesy of U.S. Army Corps of Engineers.)

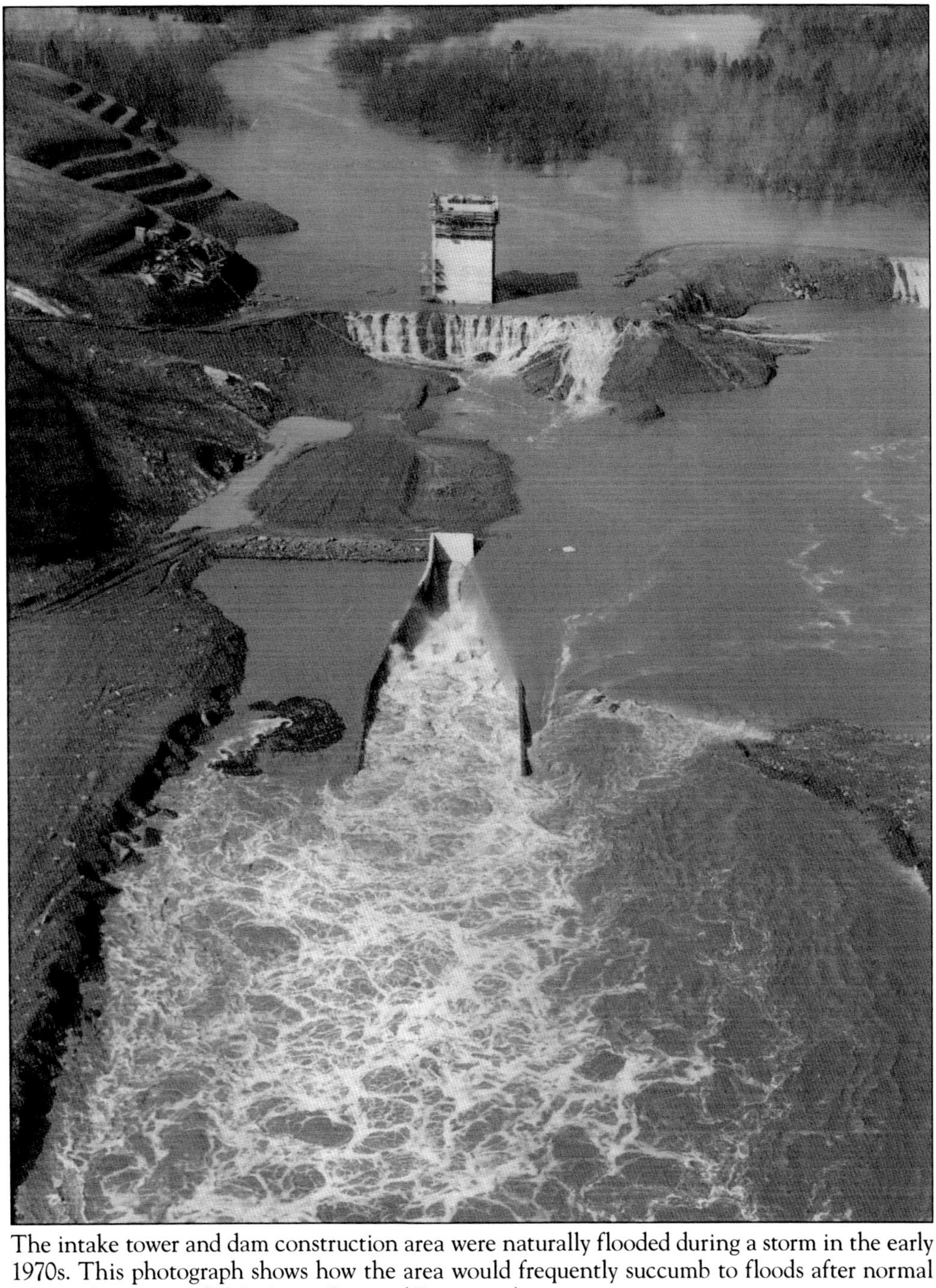

The intake tower and dam construction area were naturally flooded during a storm in the early 1970s. This photograph shows how the area would frequently succumb to floods after normal storms. (Courtesy of U.S. Army Corps of Engineers.)

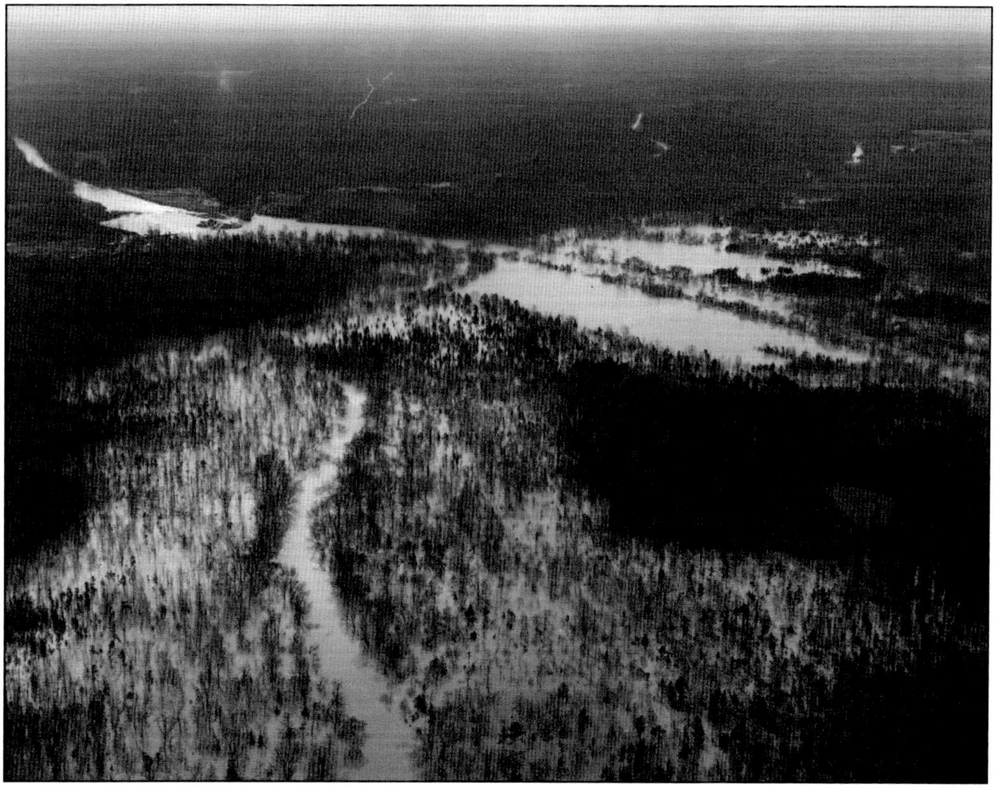

This is a photograph from 1973 after a storm caused the area to naturally flood in the location that would eventually be Jordan Lake. It is no wonder that this area was chosen for the lake. (Courtesy of U.S. Army Corps of Engineers.)

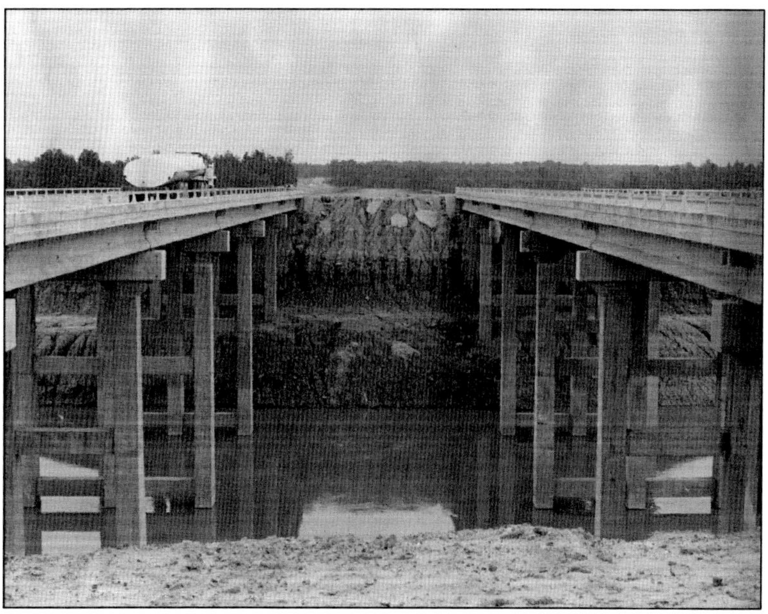

Pictured in 1973, the U.S. Route 64 relocation bridges at New Hope River are just about done. (Courtesy of U.S. Army Corps of Engineers.)

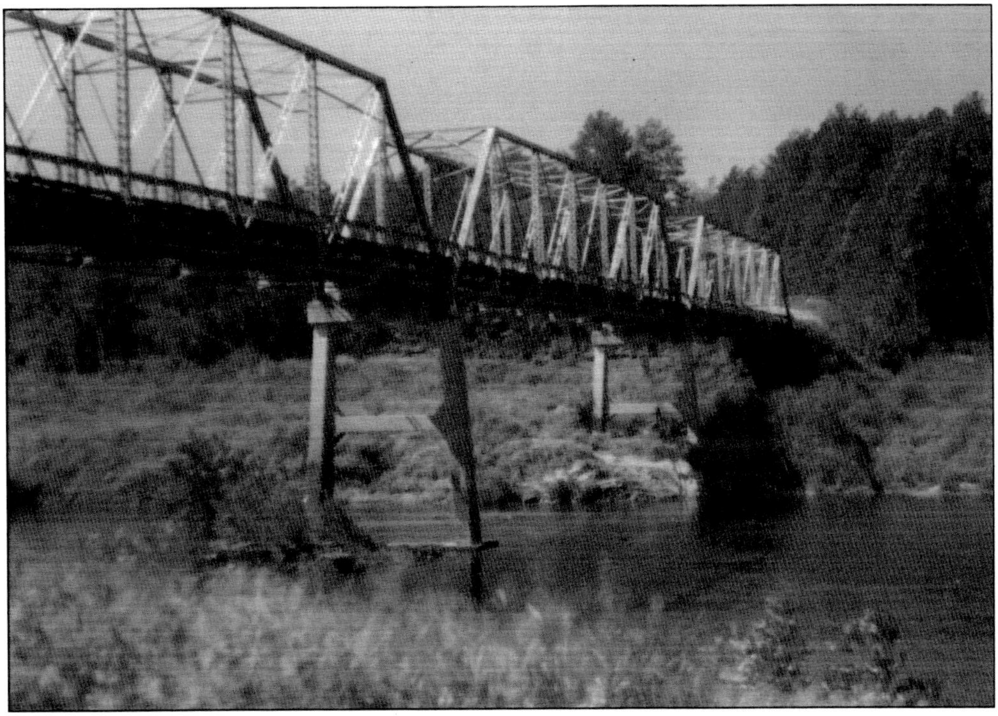

This is what the Haw River Steel Bridge looked like 21 days before being torn down in October 1979. (Courtesy of Joyce Jones Cotten.)

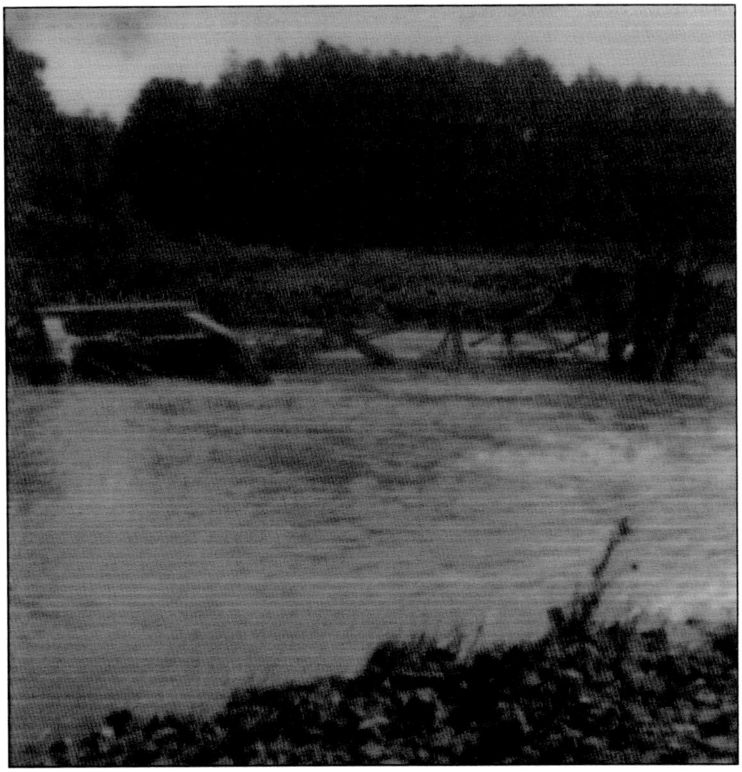

This photograph was taken on October 9, 1979, showing the debris after the Haw River Steel Bridge was demolished. (Courtesy of U.S. Army Corps of Engineers.)

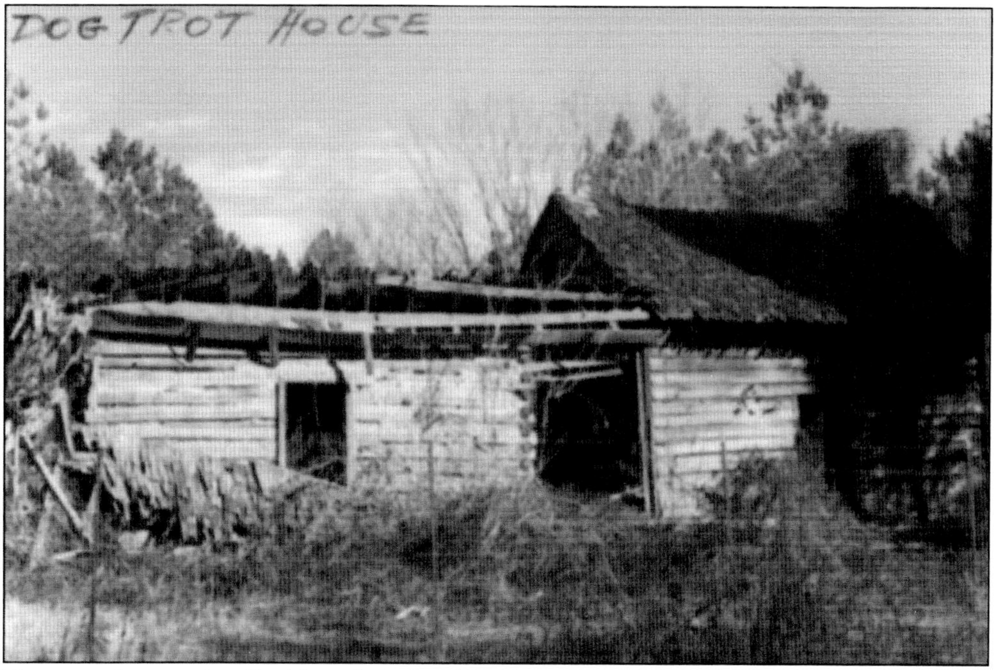

These are photographs of buildings from the 1800s that were found on the land that the government purchased for the Jordan Lake Project. The buildings were in bad condition, and squatters were apparently using them and weakening their structure, so the U.S. Army Corps of Engineers had to put fences around the buildings until they could properly be removed. Above is a dogtrot house, and below is the original Ebenezer Church with a stick chimney. (Both, courtesy of U.S. Army Corps of Engineers.)

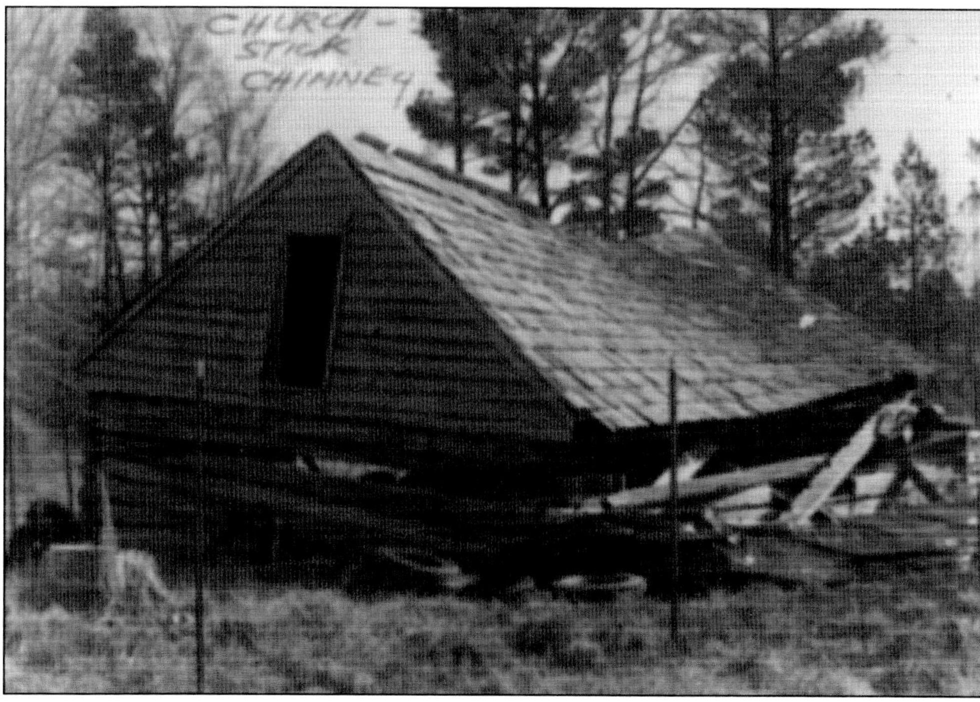

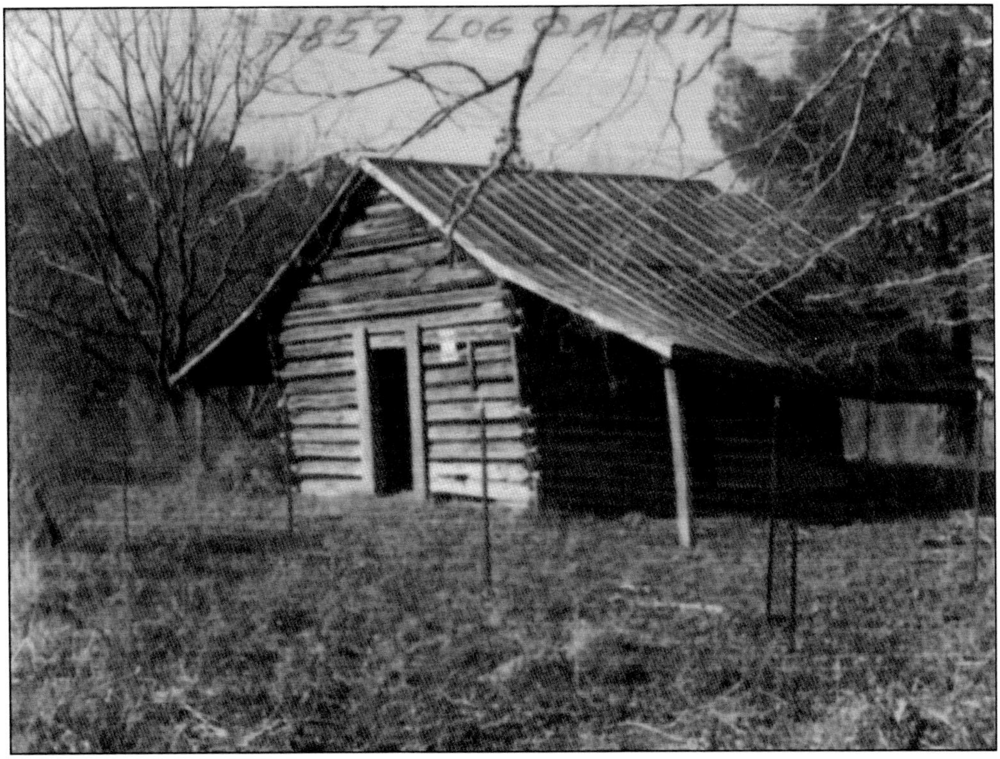

Above is an 1859 log cabin that was left behind by the previous owners and destroyed by vandals. Below is the original Ebenezer Church. This 21-foot-by-18-foot wooden structure was used as a church, house, and storage building, and it was being used by locals as a dumping ground. (Both, courtesy of U.S. Army Corps of Engineers.)

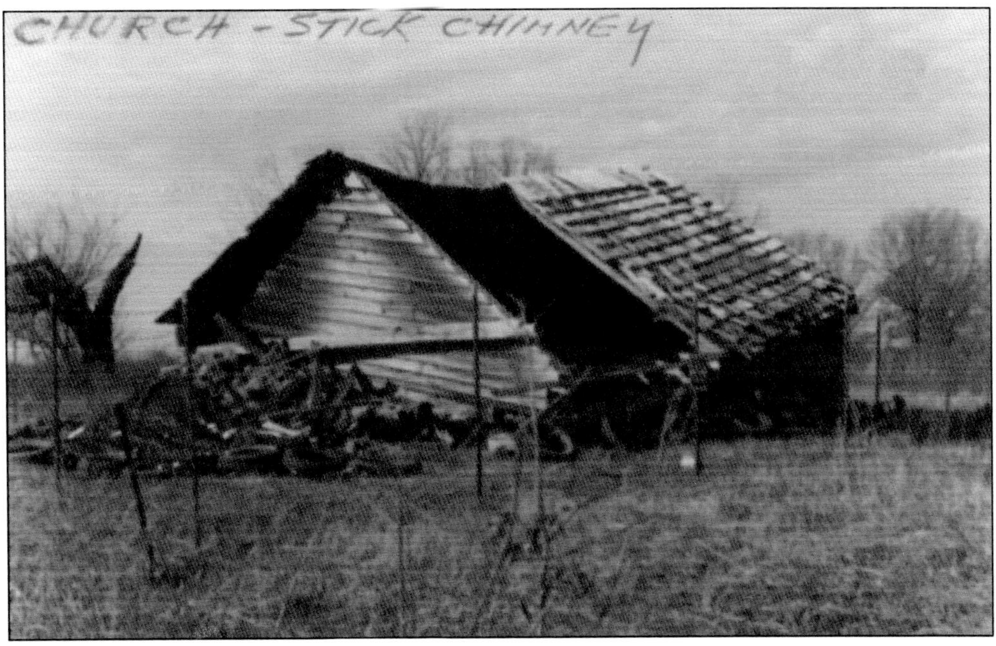

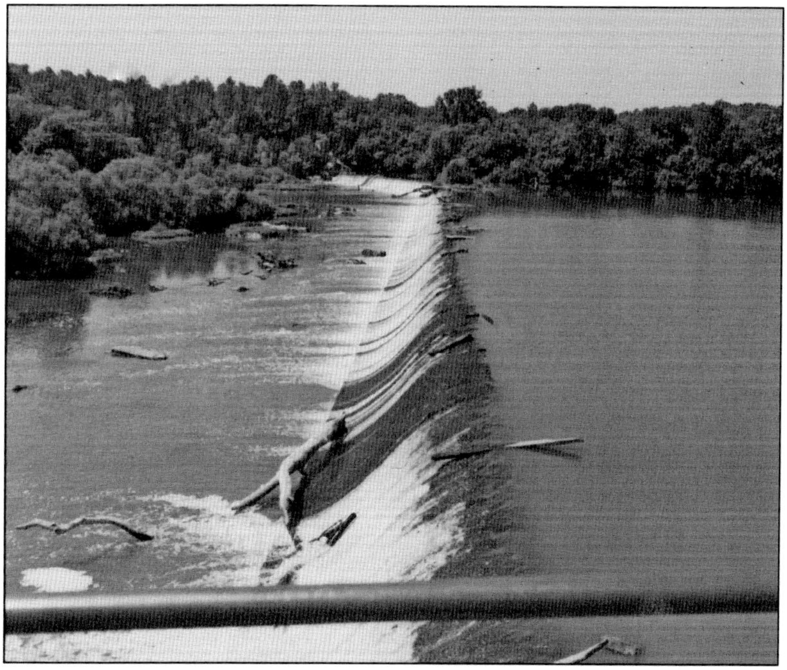

This is the view at Buckhorn Dam below Jordan Dam at Jordan Lake at 11:30 a.m. on June 16, 1981. The photograph was taken prior to the official impoundment of the dam, which took place on September 1, 1981. The Buckhorn Dam is downstream in Lee County. (Courtesy of U.S. Army Corps of Engineers.)

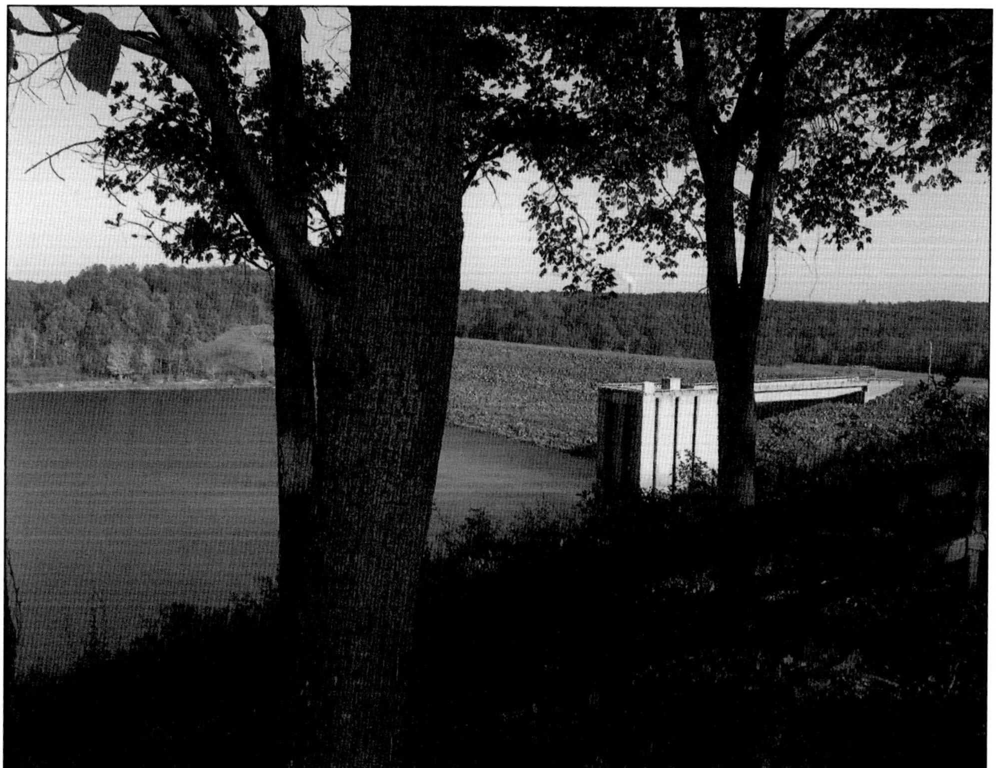

This is a close-up view of Jordan Dam in 2008. In the future, the dam may provide the opportunity for hydroelectric power to be used in the local communities. (Courtesy of U.S. Army Corps of Engineers.)

"Engineers blaze the trail for education! The engineers can place men from 18 to 40 where they can learn their trade in the Army." Pictured is an army engineer recruiting poster from 1919. (Courtesy of Library of Congress, Prints and Photographs Division, FSA/OWI Collection [reproduction number LC-USZC4-7578].)

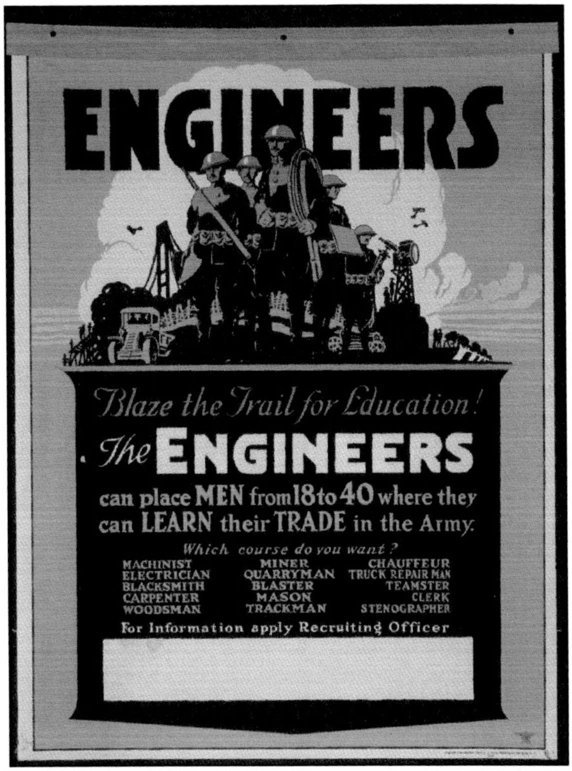

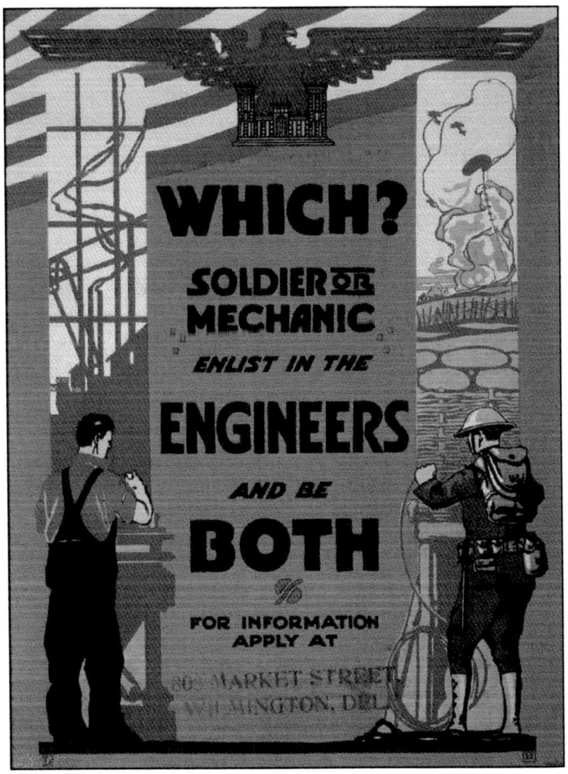

"Which? Soldier or Mechanic? Enlist in the Engineers and Be Both." A U.S. Army recruiting poster released in 1919 shows a man in both civilian and military uniform. (Courtesy of Library of Congress, Prints and Photographs Division, FSA/OWI Collection [reproduction number LC-USZC4-7544].)

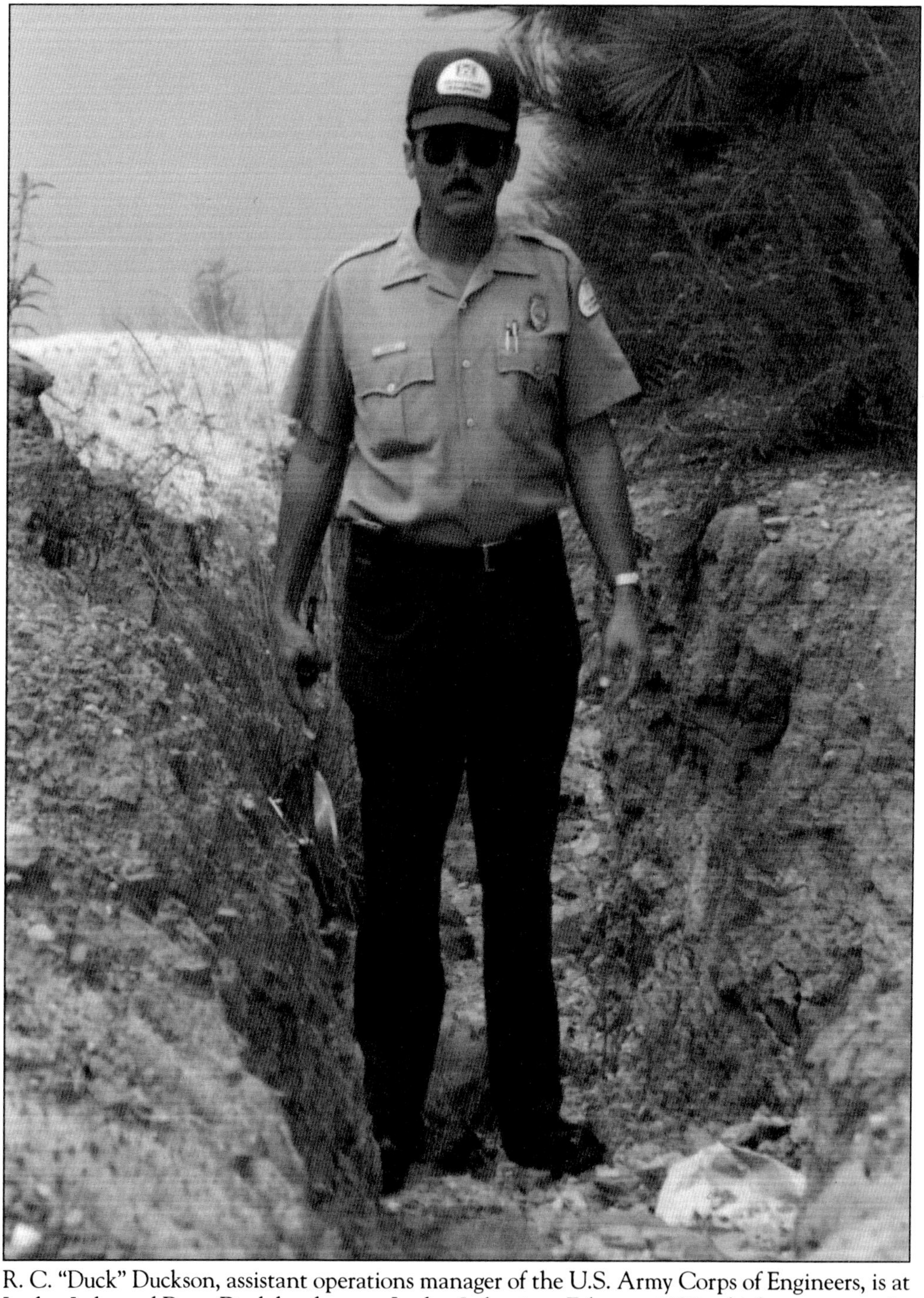

R. C. "Duck" Duckson, assistant operations manager of the U.S. Army Corps of Engineers, is at Jordan Lake and Dam. Duck has been at Jordan Lake since February 1979, which was two and a half years prior to the start of impoundment. Duck has always loved his job, and folks often ask when is he going to retire. Jordan Lake could only hope to find another member to follow in his footsteps. His dedication, experience, and knowledge have proven beneficial to such an important project as Jordan Lake and Dam. (Courtesy of U.S. Army Corps of Engineers.)

Two

Senator B. Everett Jordan

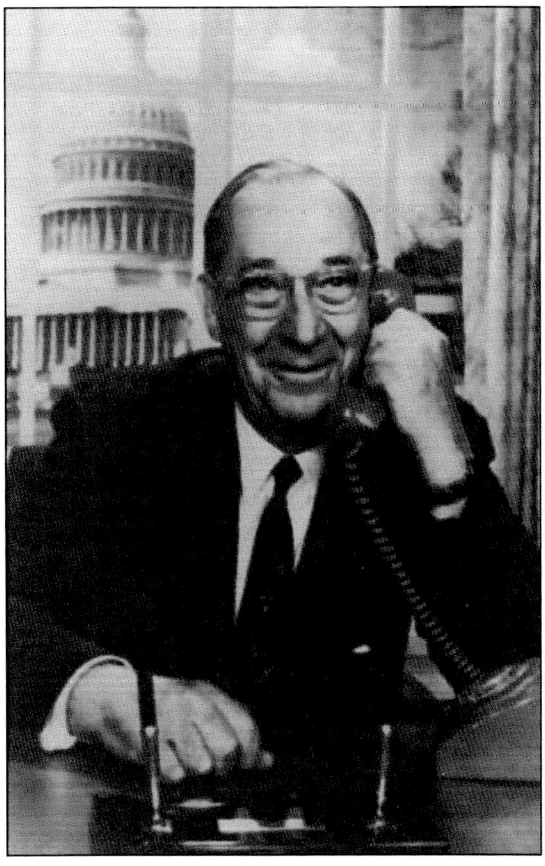

U.S. senator B. Everett Jordan served from 1958 to 1973. He was born on September 8, 1896, and called Saxapahaw his home from 1927 until his passing in 1974. He served overseas in the army during World War I. Senator Jordan often voted for what was best for his constituents and countrymen, even if it meant going against his own party's beliefs. (Author's collection.)

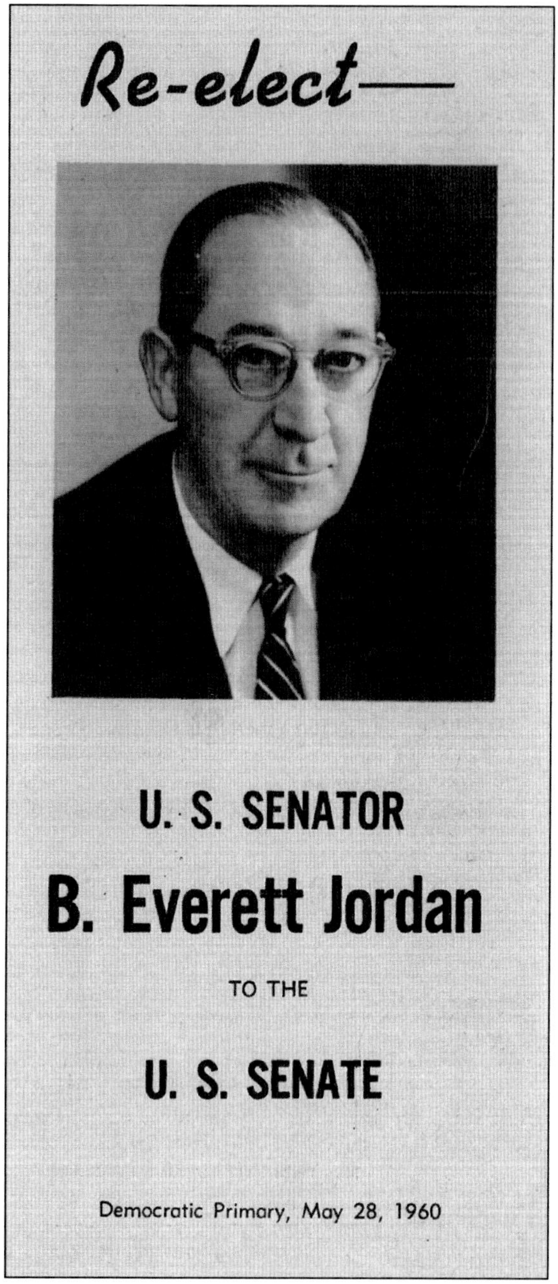

Voters reelected Senator Jordan in 1960. Per the voting brochure, Senator Jordan's stance on defense was as follows: "We must keep our military strength at such a level that no nation would dare attack the United States or any of our allies." Senator Jordan says on imports, "Imports have been increasing in recent years at a rate, which, if allowed to continue, will ruin many of our basic industries, including textiles, commercial fishing, and many others that provide jobs for a large segment of our people." Senator Jordan supported research in medical science and agriculture, industrial uses of farm products, missile development, and the mysteries of outer space. Senator Jordan was the author of the Cotton Allotment Transfer Bill, which assisted farmers with small allotments. (Courtesy of the Jordan family albums.)

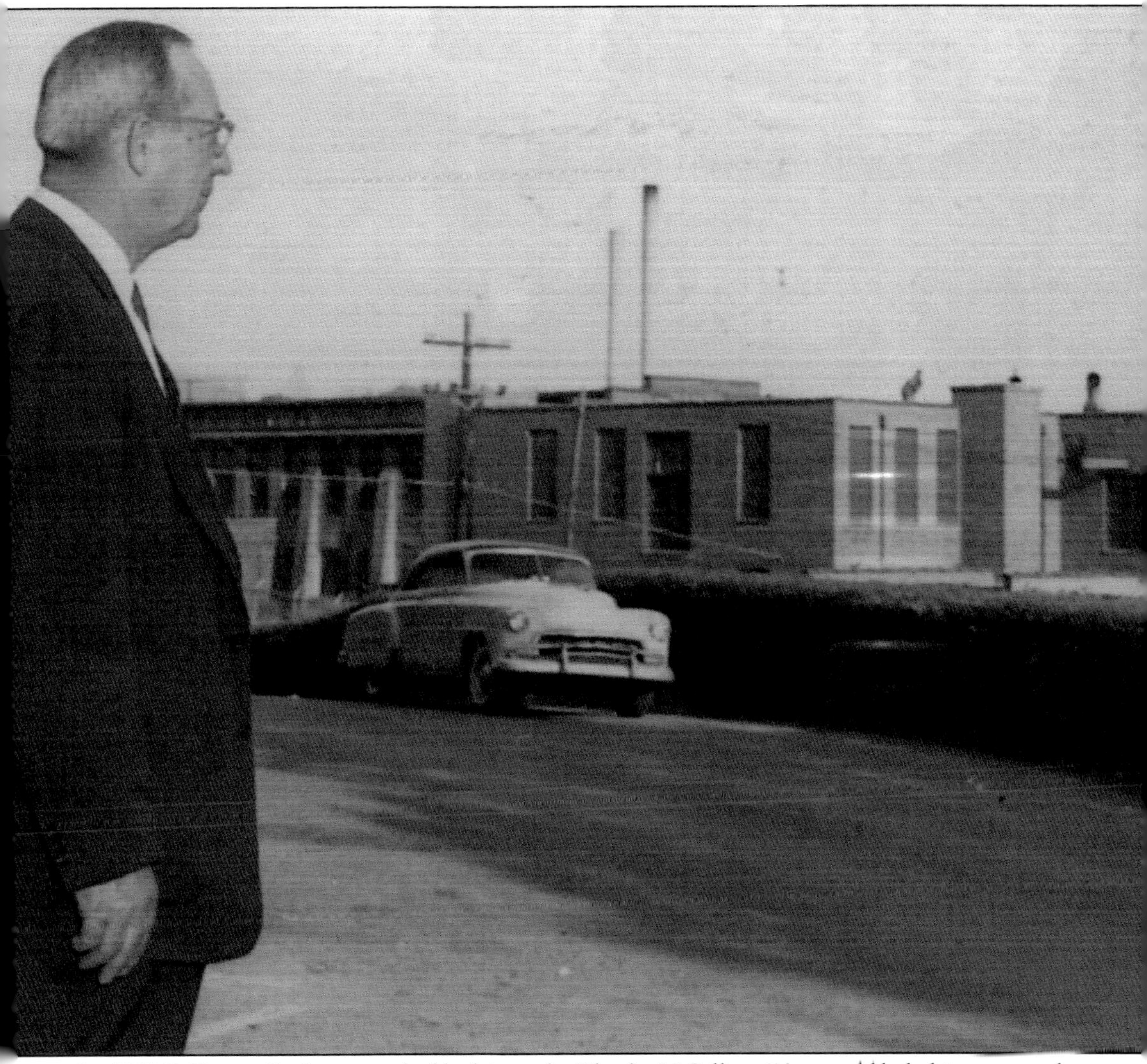

In 1927, B. Everett Jordan was asked by his uncle, Charles V. Sellars, if he would help him own and run a mill in Saxapahaw. Along with the help of his sons, Ben E. Jordan and John M. Jordan, the mill was successful for many decades. In this photograph, the senator gives a heartfelt temporary goodbye to the mill as he heads off to Washington for his role as senator. Today the mill is still within the Jordan family and has been restored and revived along with the Saxapahaw community into a sustainable green bedroom community. (Courtesy of the Saxapahaw Historical Society and Museum.)

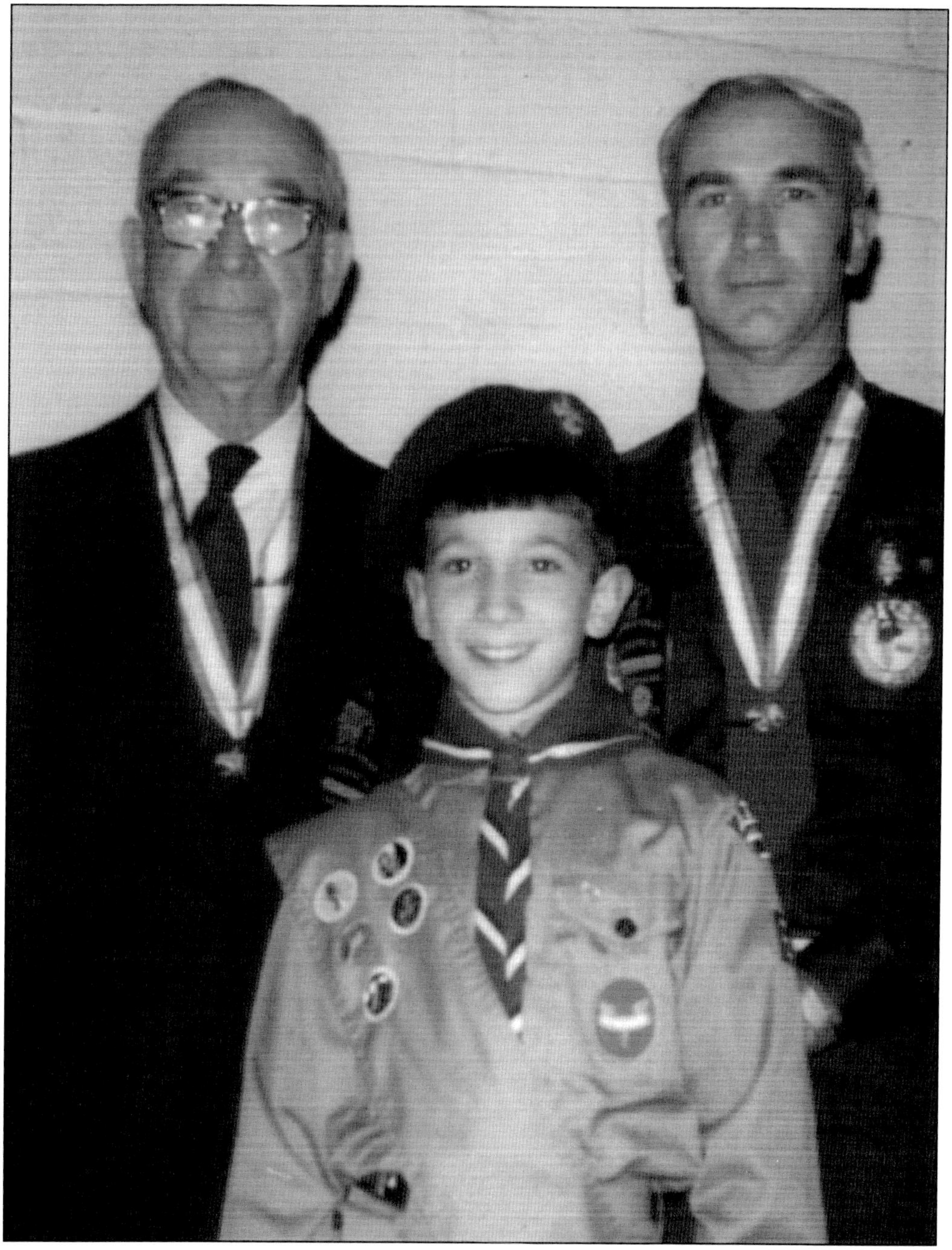

Three generations of dedicated Scouts are in this last known photograph of Senator. B. Everett Jordan (left), taken in 1973 before his illness and passing in 1974. John Jordan (right) and his father both received the Silver Beaver Award, which is the highest award one can receive in a Boy Scout council. In the center is John Jordan's son, Mac Jordan, who, along with his brother, Carter, became an Eagle Scout. This is John Jordan's favorite photograph. He wishes his father was alive today to see what a wonderful job the whole family has done with Saxapahaw's progression and keeping his father's vision alive. (Courtesy of John Jordan.)

Three

Jordan Lake Opens

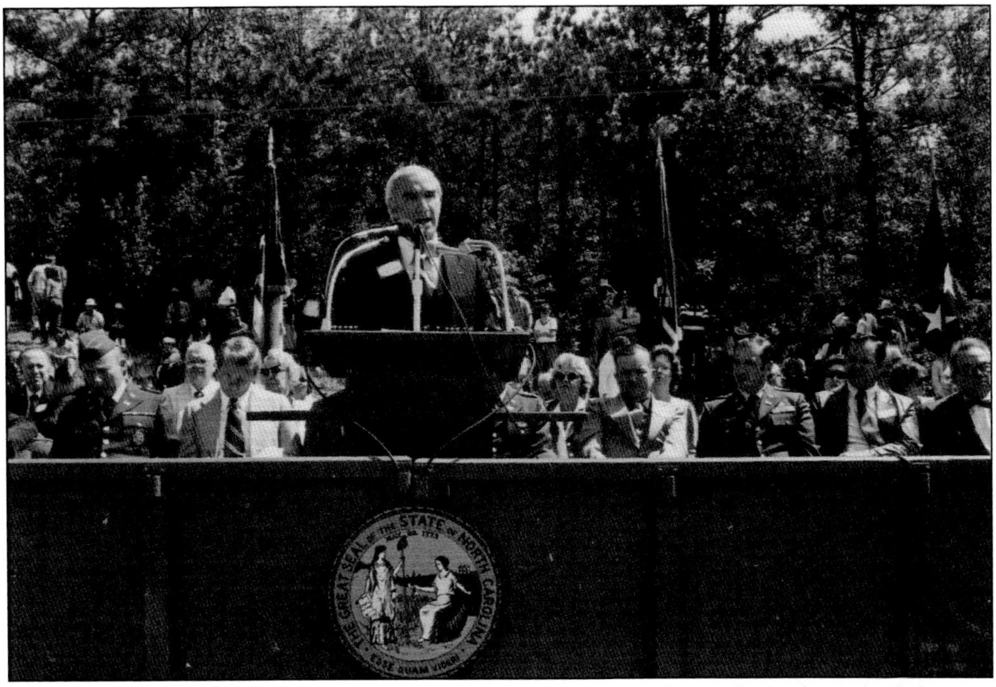

John M. Jordan, son of B. Everett Jordan, was the keynote speaker during the Jordan Lake dedication ceremony on May 1, 1982. John was elated about the lake project but saddened that his father could not be there to see the project come to fruition. The late senator B. Everett Jordan's significant contributions to society can also still be seen within Saxapahaw, North Carolina, where many of the late senator's family members still reside. (Courtesy of Jeff Starkweather.)

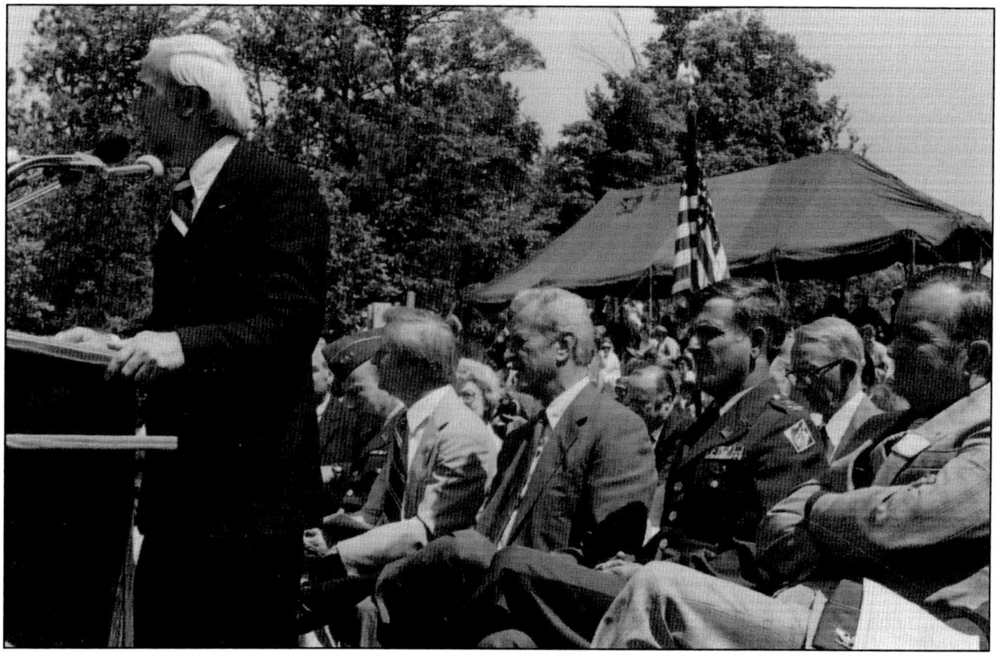

John Jordan, son of B. Everett Jordan, gives a heartfelt speech as he recalls all the years that the Jordan Lake Project was held up by environmental activists, when the lake was a huge dangerous mud puddle. Seeing the lake finally finished brought tears to John's eyes. (Courtesy of Jeff Starkweather.)

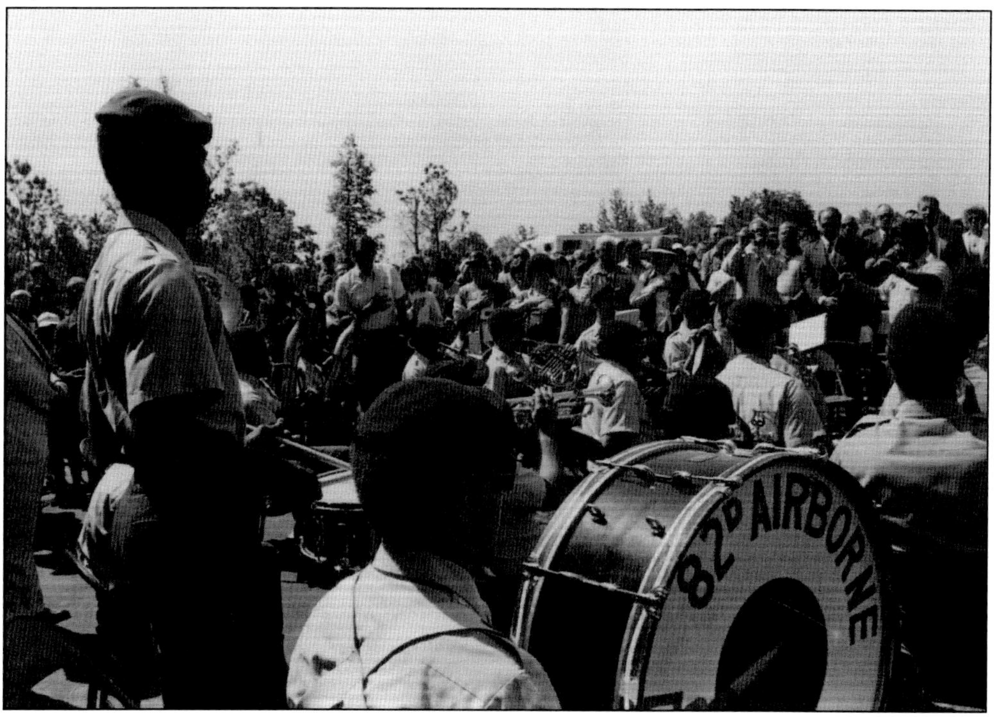

The 82nd Airborne Division Band from Fort Bragg plays for the crowds during the dedication ceremony of Jordan Lake and Dam on May 1, 1982. (Courtesy of U.S. Army Corps of Engineers.)

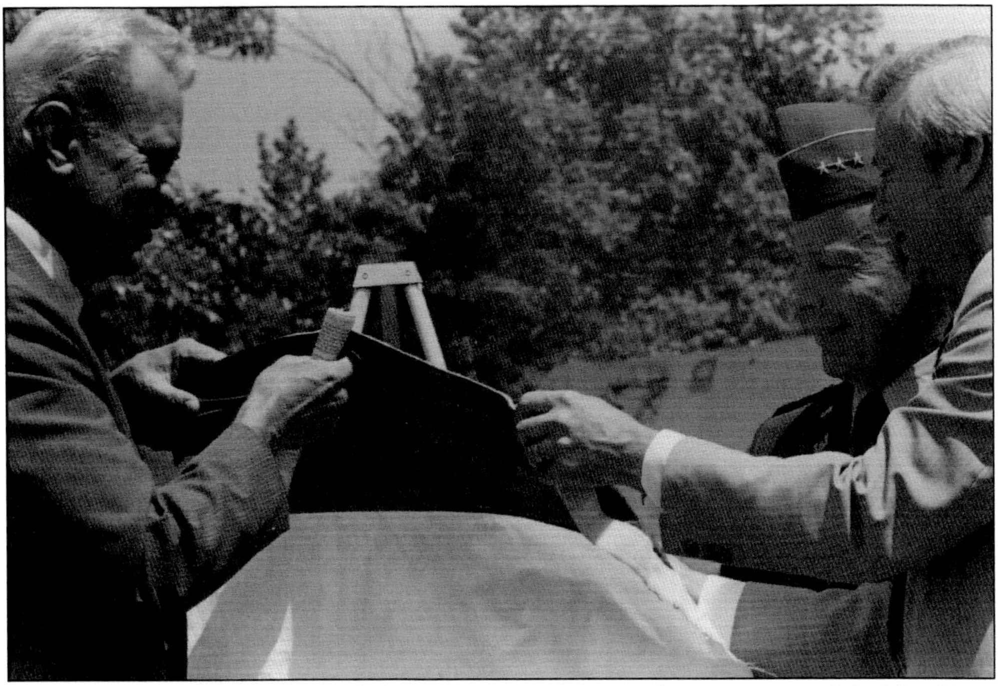

Jordan Lake was originally named the New Hope Project, as the area is part of the New Hope Valley in North Carolina. The lake was later named after supporter Senator B. Everett Jordan. These photographs were taken on May 1, 1982, during the unveiling of the dedication plaque that is now located outside of the U.S. Army Corps of Engineers Visitor Assistance Center. Pictured above are, from left to right, congressman Ike Andrews; Lt. Gen. Joseph K. Bratton, chief of engineers; and former governor James B. Hunt. Pictured below are congressman Ike Andrews (left) and Gov. James B. Hunt (right) holding the dedication plaque. The plaque records the lake's construction dates of 1967 to 1982. (Both, courtesy of Jeff Starkweather.)

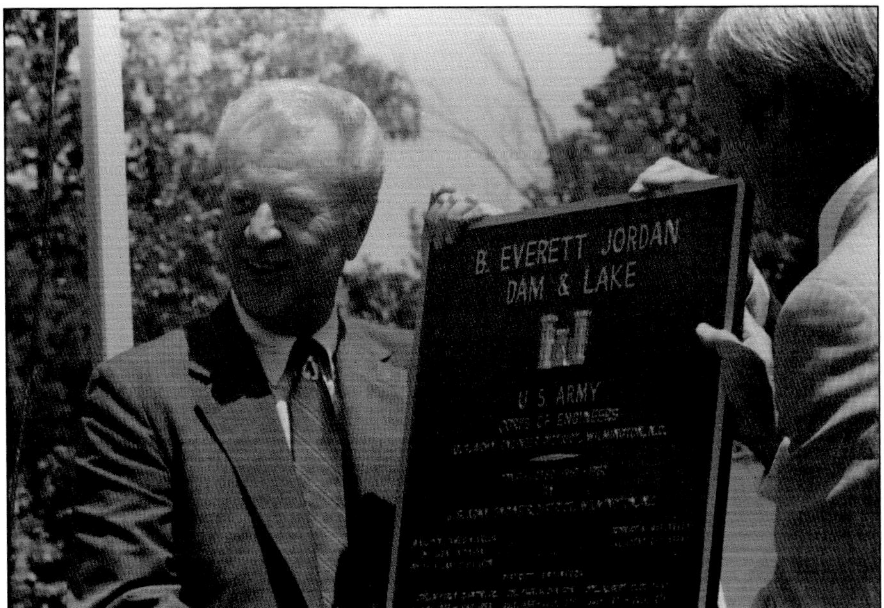

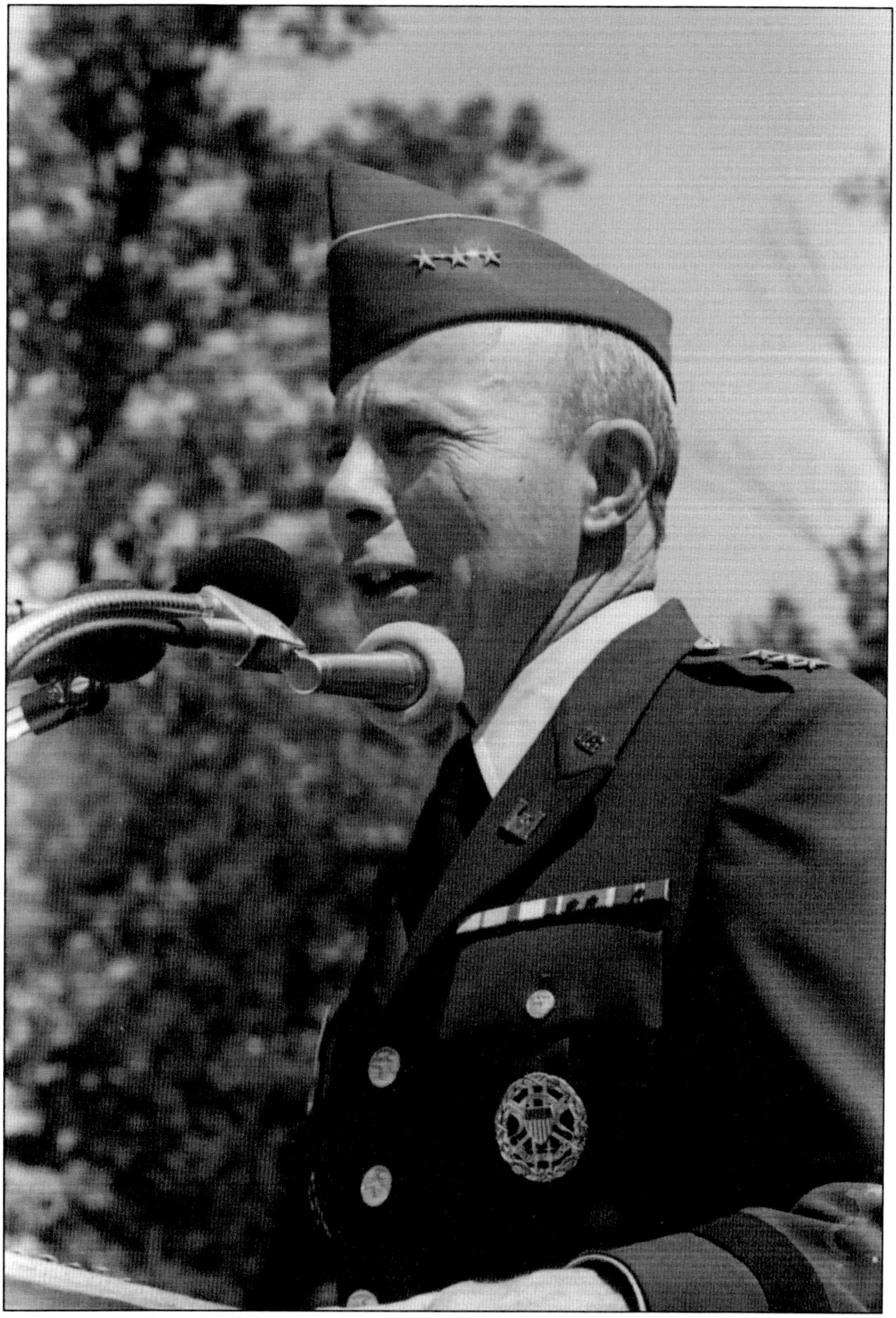

Lt. Gen. Joseph K. Bratton, chief of engineers, speaks to the crowds during the dedication ceremony of Jordan Lake and Dam on May 1, 1982. He outlined the project's benefits—downstream flood control was to be the primary purpose, and the dam's outlet structure could mix water from different levels in the lake to produce a discharge with water temperature, dissolved oxygen content, and chemical composition best suited to downstream needs. Jordan Lake may also provide local communities with up to 100 million gallons of drinking water per day. (Courtesy of Jeff Starkweather.)

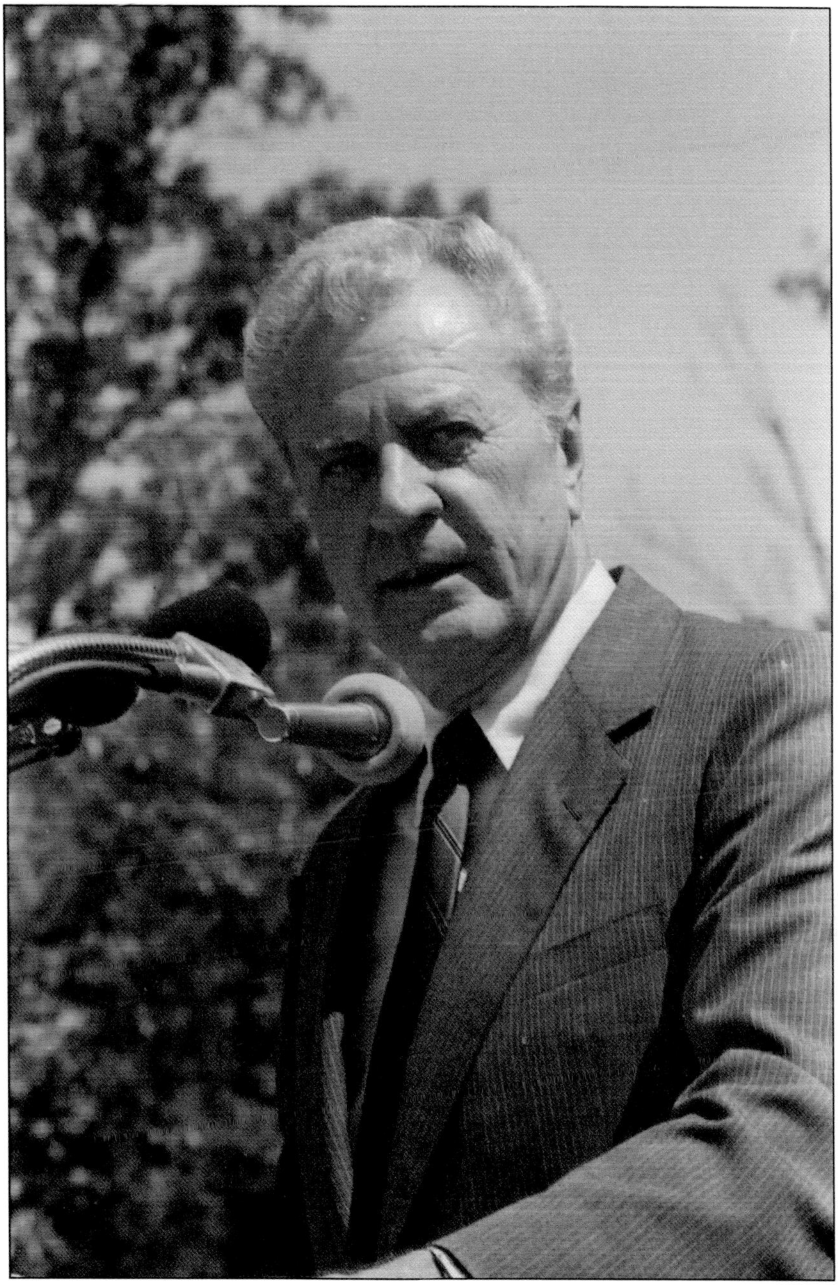

Ike Andrews gives his supportive speech during the dedication ceremony of Jordan Lake on May 1, 1982. Andrews was born in Bonlee, North Carolina, on September 2, 1925. He attended Fork Union Military Academy and served in the U.S. Army during World War II. During his tenure with the army, he received the Bronze Star and Purple Heart. Andrews earned his bachelor's degree and law degree from the University of North Carolina at Chapel Hill and practiced law in Pittsboro, North Carolina. He was elected to the North Carolina Senate in 1959 and later elected to the North Carolina House of Representatives in 1961, 1967, 1969, and 1971. Andrews served as a Democratic congressman from January 3, 1973, to January 3, 1985. (Courtesy of Jeff Starkweather.)

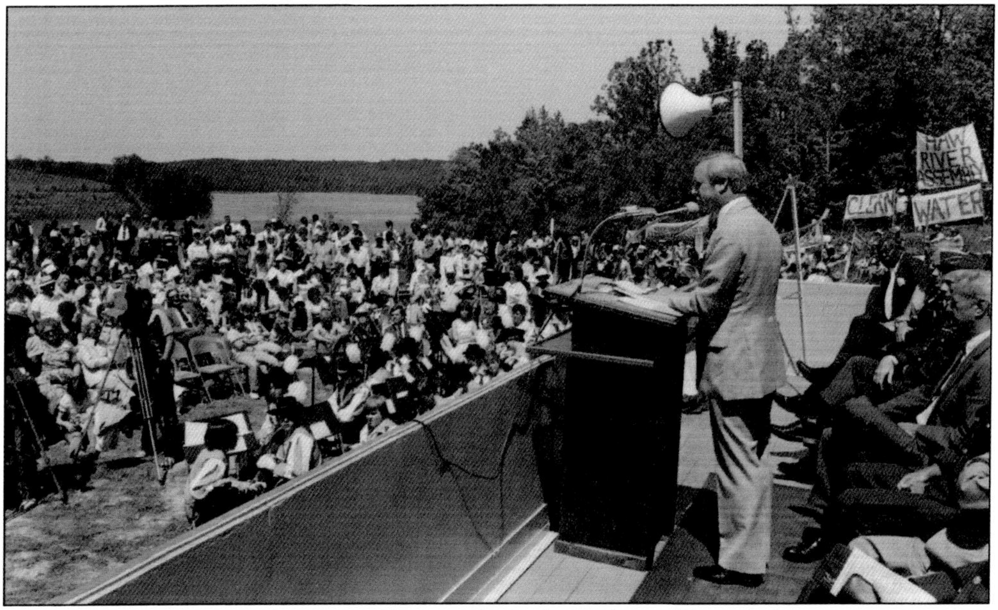

Gov. James B. Hunt gave the main address at the Jordan Lake and Dam dedication ceremony on May 1, 1982. In his speech, Hunt looked to the future of the state of North Carolina and the role Jordan Lake and Dam would play. The lake made the state better prepared to meet anticipated needs for water and flood control, outdoor recreation, and wildlife conservation. (Courtesy of Jeff Starkweather.)

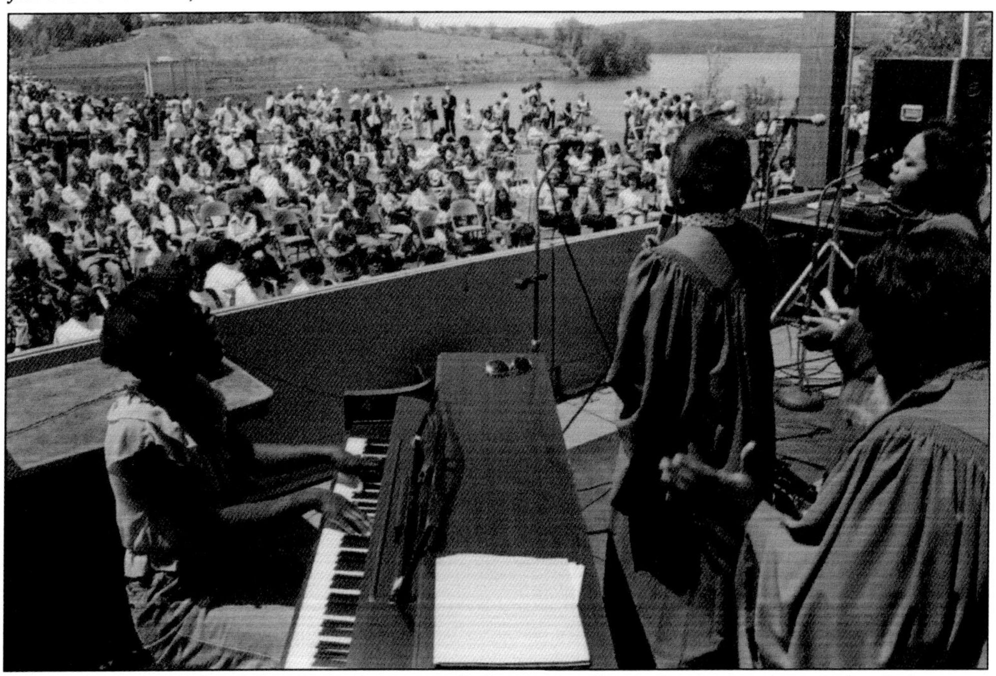

This is a photograph of the choir that provided music and a performance during the dedication of Jordan Lake on May 1, 1982. The crowds brought their own chairs and sat everywhere they could. Some even brought lawn chairs that they laid by the water's edge to be able to put their feet in the water while they watched the program. (Courtesy of Jeff Starkweather.)

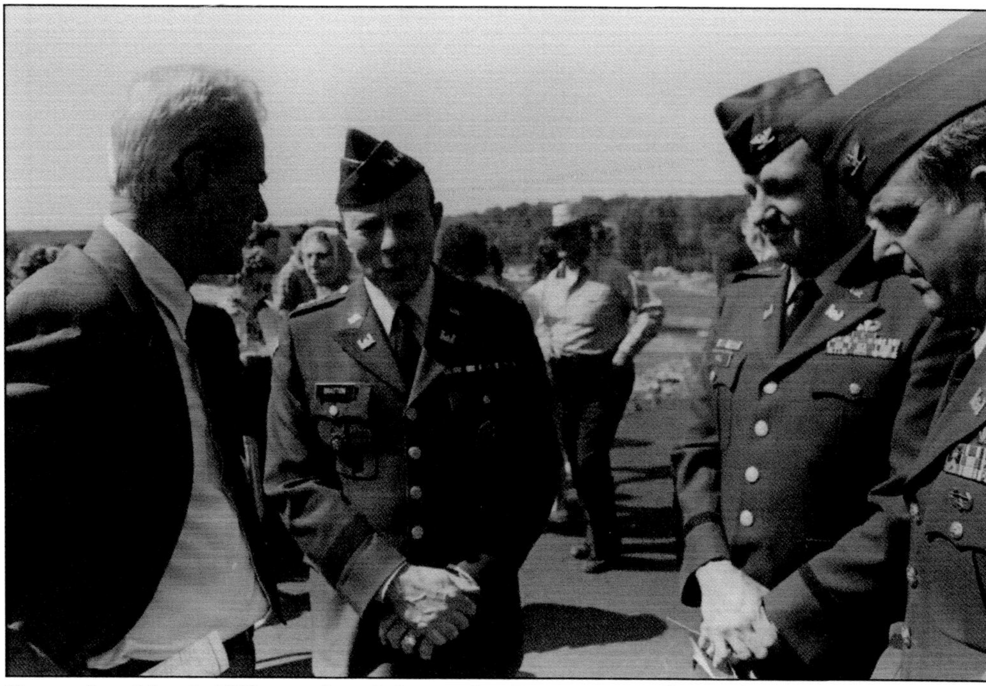

Pictured on May 1, 1982, are, from left to right, Congressman Ike Andrews, Lt. Gen. Joseph K. Bratton, and two unidentified U.S. Army Corps of Engineers officers. Lieutenant General Bratton came to Jordan Lake along with fellow officers to show their support and respect for their peers and join in with the lake celebration. Lieutenant General Bratton graduated third in his class from the U.S. Military Academy in 1948. Bratton was both a decorated army officer and nuclear engineer. He passed away in June 2007 of an aneurysm, and he was laid to rest in the Arlington National Cemetery. (Courtesy of Jeff Starkweather.)

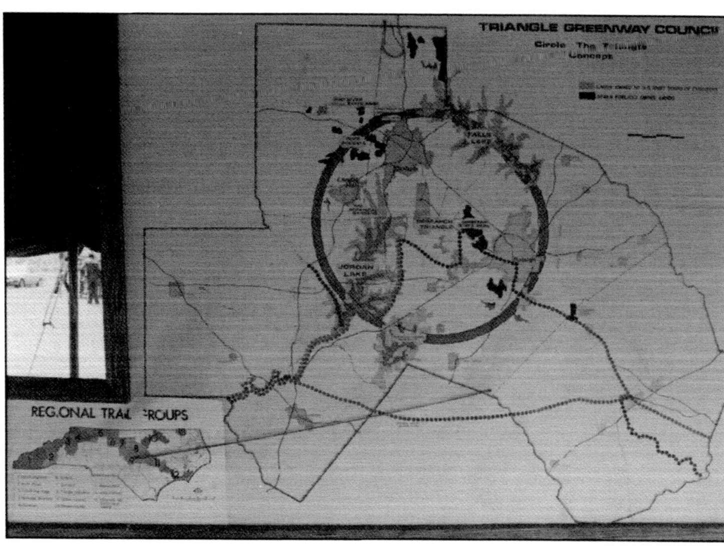

During the Jordan Lake dedication ceremony on May 1, 1982, the Triangle Greenway Council displayed several posters of current and planned trails in North Carolina's Triangle area. This poster shows region nine, which includes Jordan Lake. The council is an advocate for the creation of interconnected greenways. (Courtesy of Jeff Starkweather.)

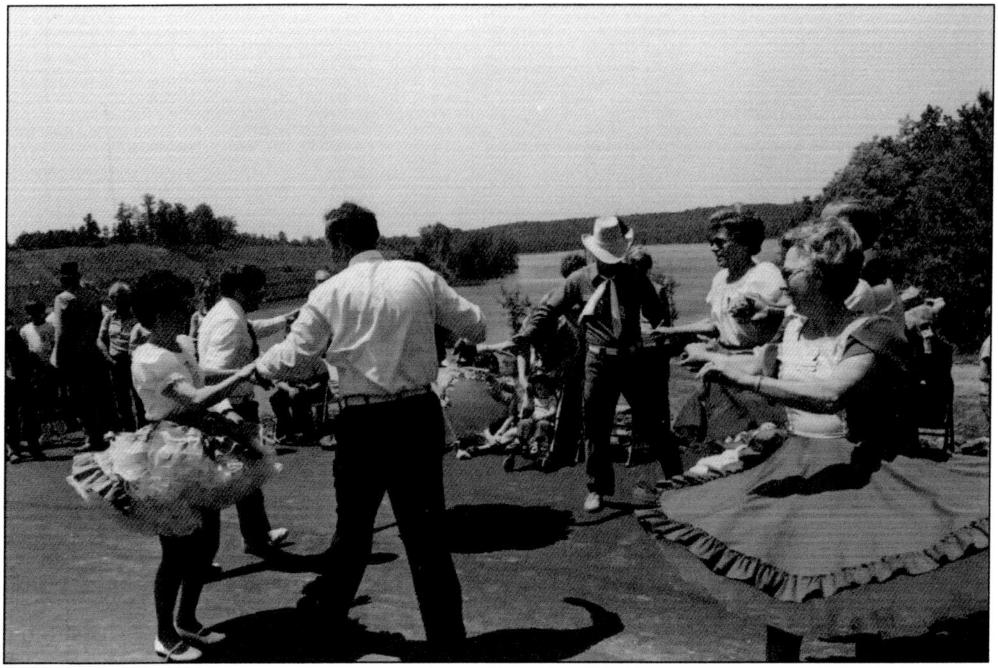

Country line dancers entertain the crowds during the Jordan Lake dedication ceremony on May 1, 1982. It was the perfect day for dancing. The lake and beautiful hillsides can be seen in the background. (Both, courtesy of Jeff Starkweather.)

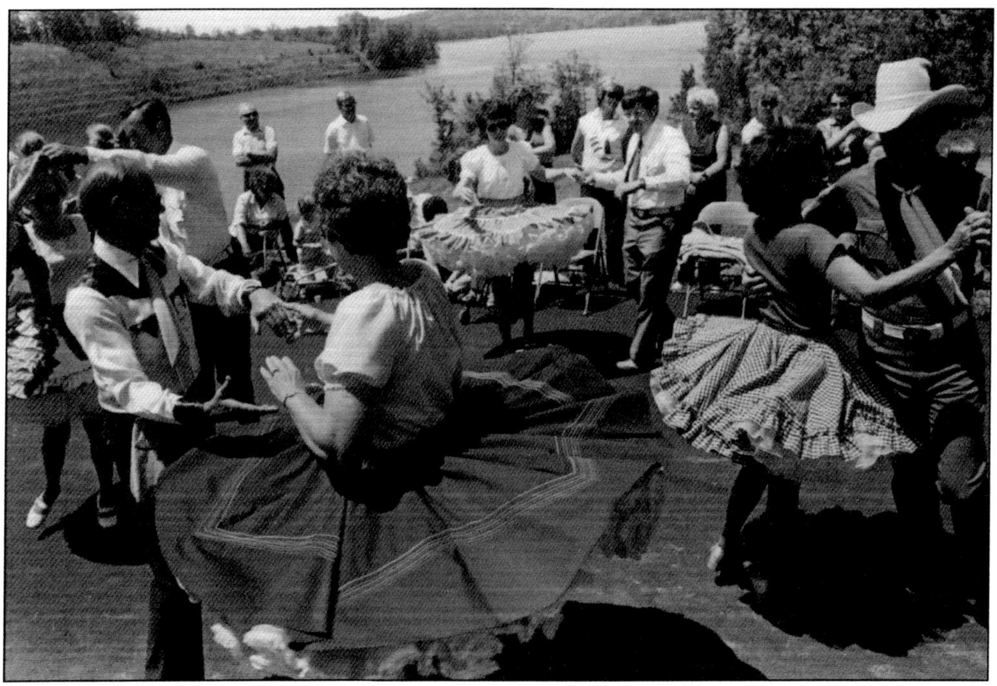

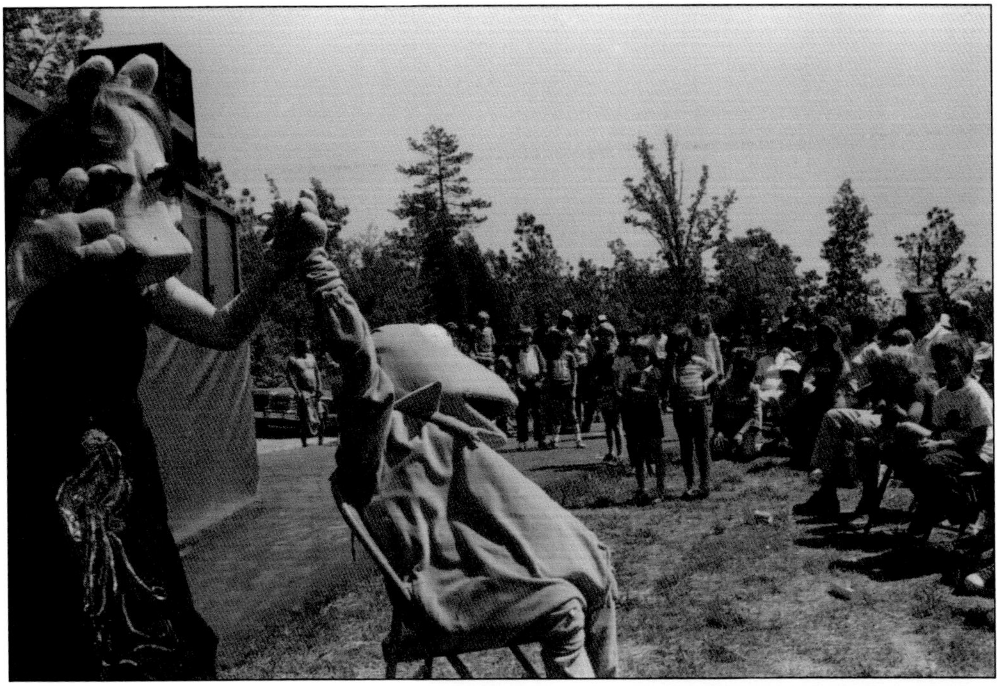

Miss Piggy and Kermit the Frog performed and entertained the children during the Jordan Lake dedication ceremony on May 1, 1982. Nobody knows who they really were. (Courtesy of Jeff Starkweather.)

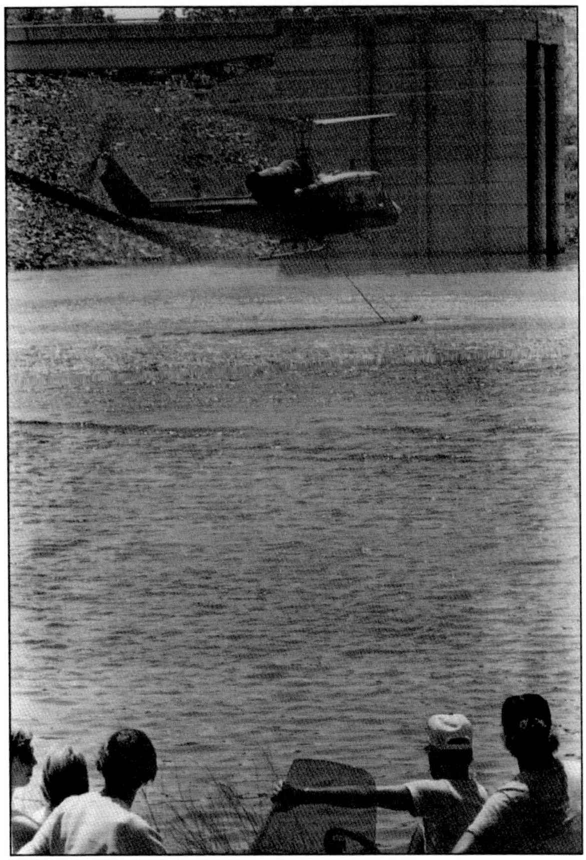

A military helicopter performed a maneuver for the audience at Jordan Lake on May 1, 1982. The large dam structure can be seen in the background. The helicopter was scooping up water from the lake into a bucket as the crowd below watched. The rumor is true that at one time there was a temporary landing strip on Jordan Lake before the lake was officially filled. (Courtesy of Jeff Starkweather.)

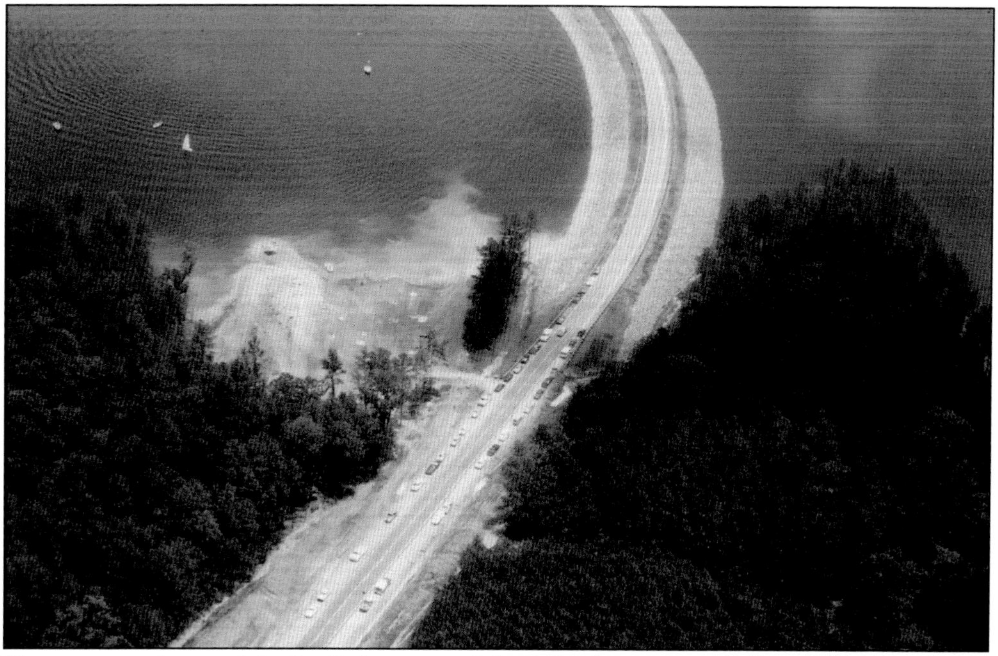

This is an aerial view of the Pea Ridge area in July 1982. This was originally called the Pea Ridge Connector road, as it connected Pea Ridge to State Road 1008. It appears the cars are on the highway, but they were actually very dangerously parked along the sides of the highway so locals could easily go for a swim and picnic on the beach. This particular area was not designated for beachgoers, who often left it dirty after partying, hence the former nickname "Glass Beach." (Courtesy of Adolph Chek.)

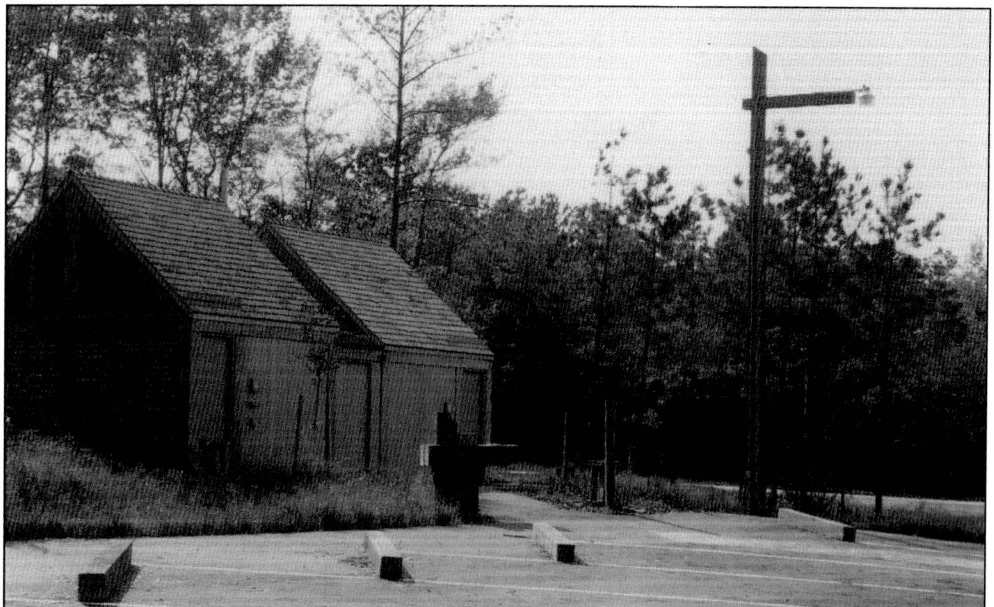

This comfort station (bathhouse) at Jordan Lake received an award for its design. The U.S. Army Corps of Engineers has placed many bathrooms and pavilions in key areas around Jordan Lake. (Courtesy of U.S. Army Corps of Engineers.)

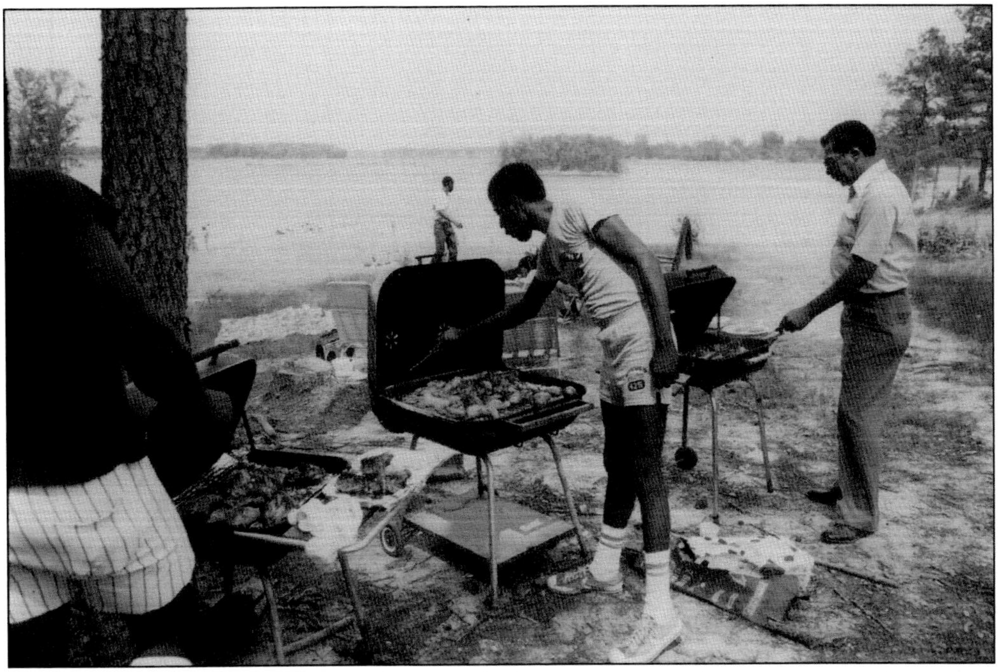

It was another perfect day for a barbecue at Jordan Lake, and this family was ready for a big day. Jordan Lake also provided picnic tables and picnic shelters. Visit the U.S. Army Corps of Engineers Visitor Assistance Center for maps and information. (Courtesy of U.S. Army Corps of Engineers.)

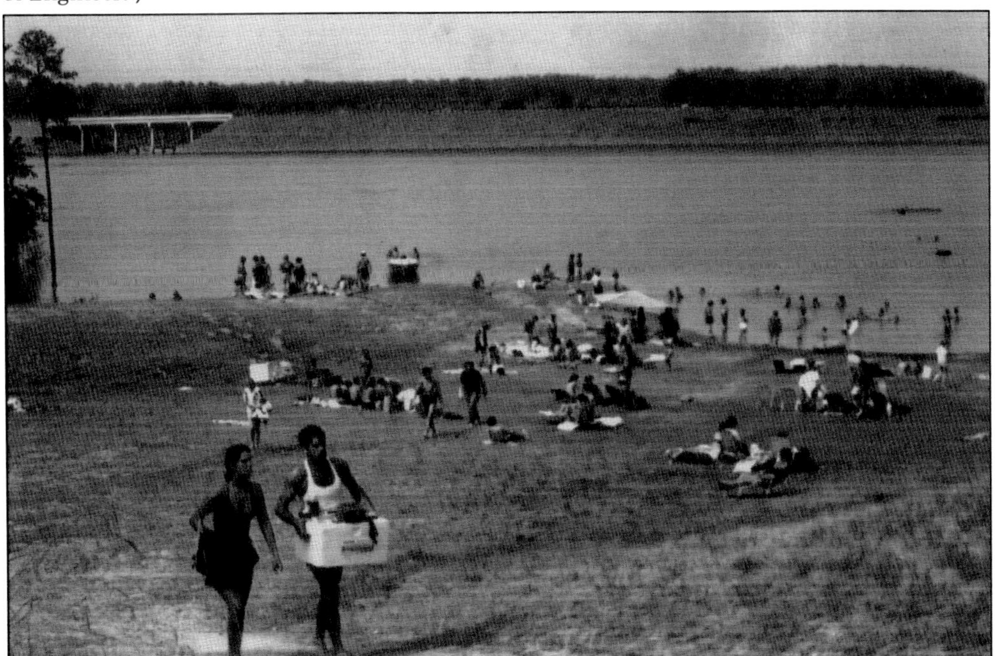

This photograph was taken during the opening summer of 1982. The U.S. Army Corps of Engineers was taking photographs documenting the amount of tourists arriving at the lake that summer. (Courtesy of U.S. Army Corps of Engineers.)

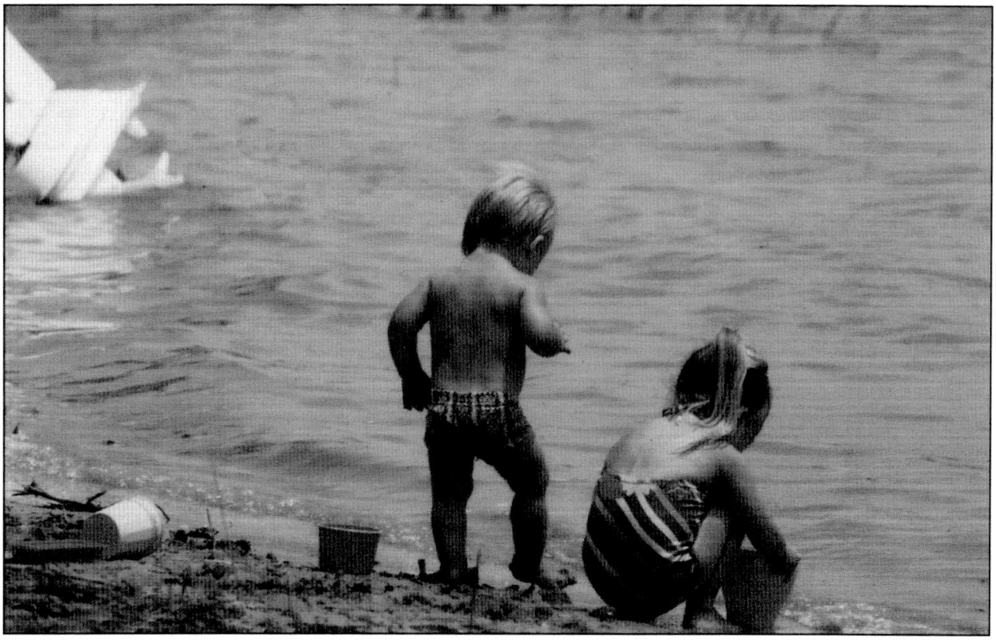

Local children are enjoying Jordan Lake in 1982 during the first summer of operation. The shallow edges of the water provide a good environment for younger swimmers. Signs in the bathhouses at the lake remind that 90 percent of all accidental drownings occur because swimmers and boaters were not wearing life jackets. (Courtesy of U.S. Army Corps of Engineers.)

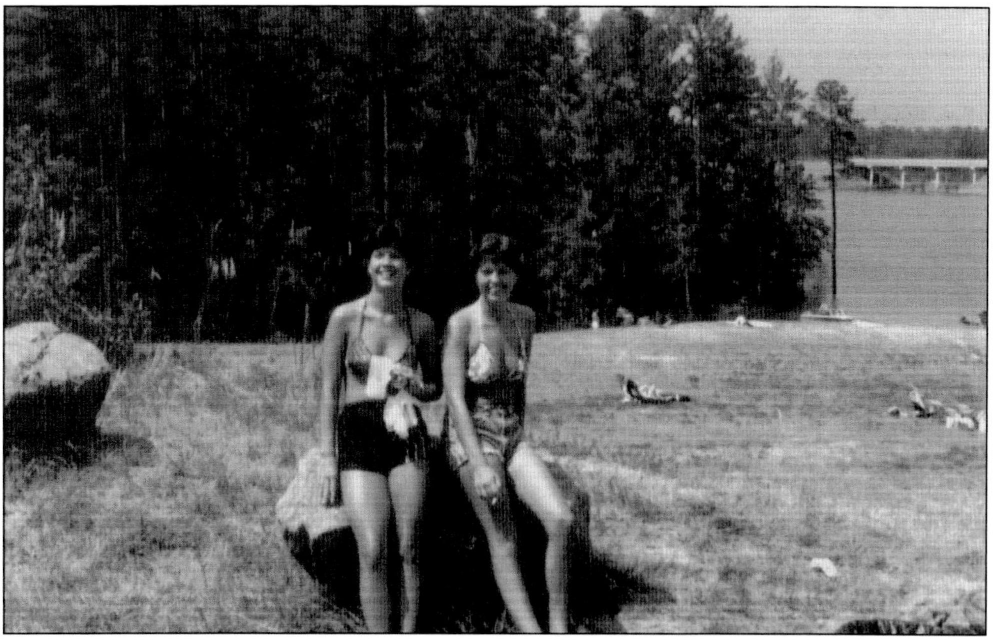

A local took this photograph during the 1982 summer, after the lake was officially opened to the public. This area was originally nicknamed "Glass Beach;" this was not a designated beach area, but locals would find it more private and tended to leave the area dirty. The cleared area was also known as "Borrow's Area," as this was one of the spots where soil was taken to create roads. This area has pretty much filled in with trees over time. (Courtesy of Vince Hoefling.)

Four

Recreation

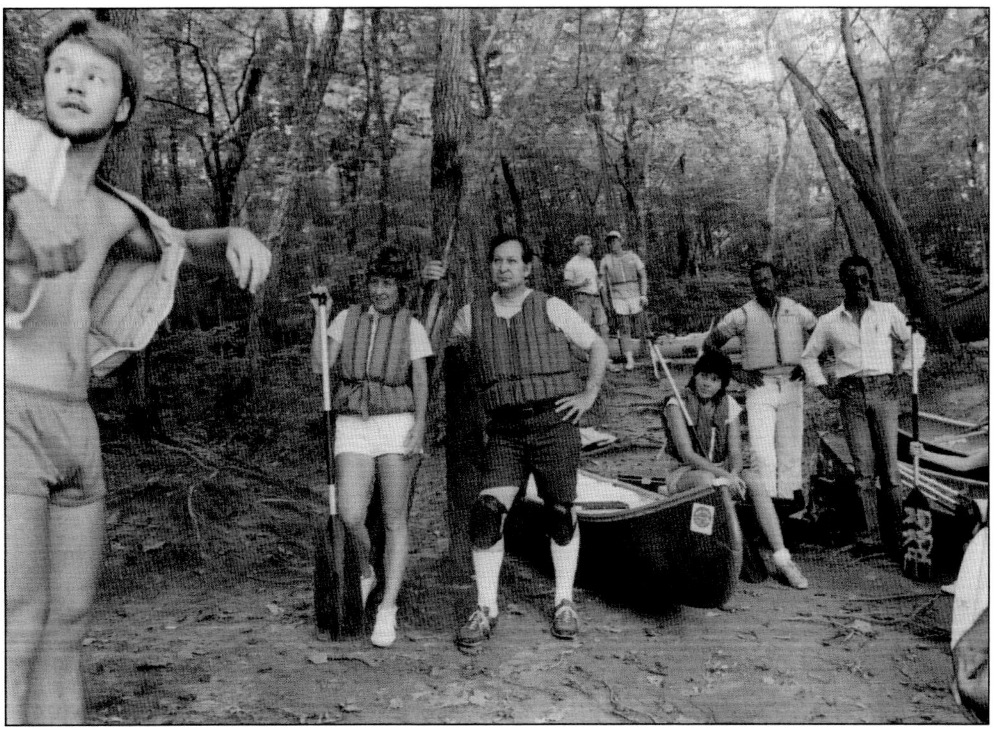

The Haw River in the New Hope Valley was known for being among the best rapids on the East Coast. *Chatham County Herald* newspaper owner Jeff Starkweather took the photograph in July 1982. (Courtesy of Jeff Starkweather.)

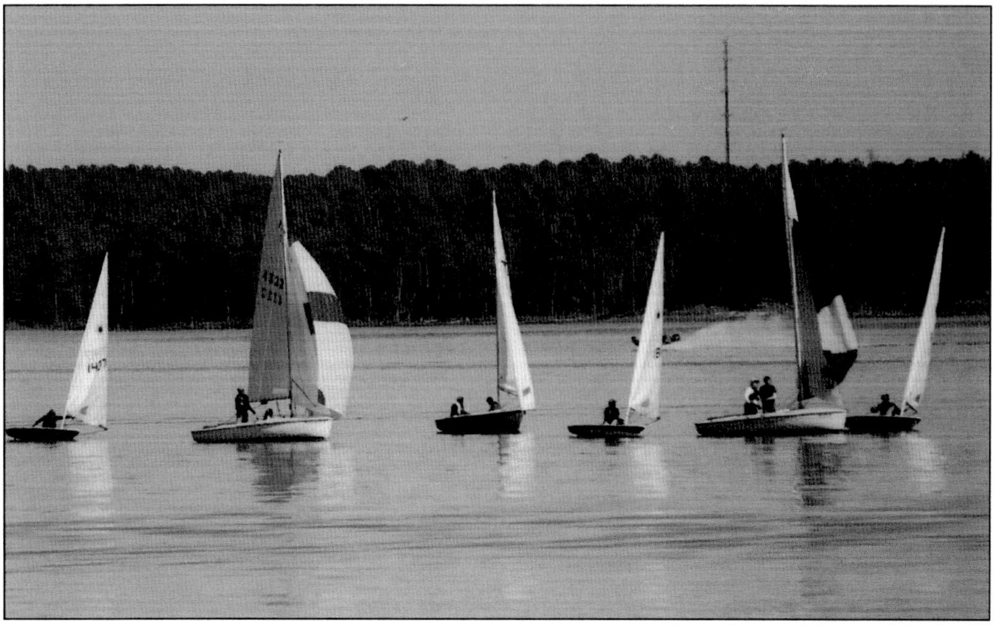

Tonya D'Angelo took this beautiful photograph of the sailboat races on Jordan Lake. Local university and high school students take sailing lessons at Jordan Lake. The Carolina Sailing Club would like to dismiss the myth that it is too cold to go sailing in the winter. They believe that in North Carolina, the weather is mild enough that winter sailing is better than sailing during the heat of the summer. (Courtesy of Tonya and Bobby D'Angelo.)

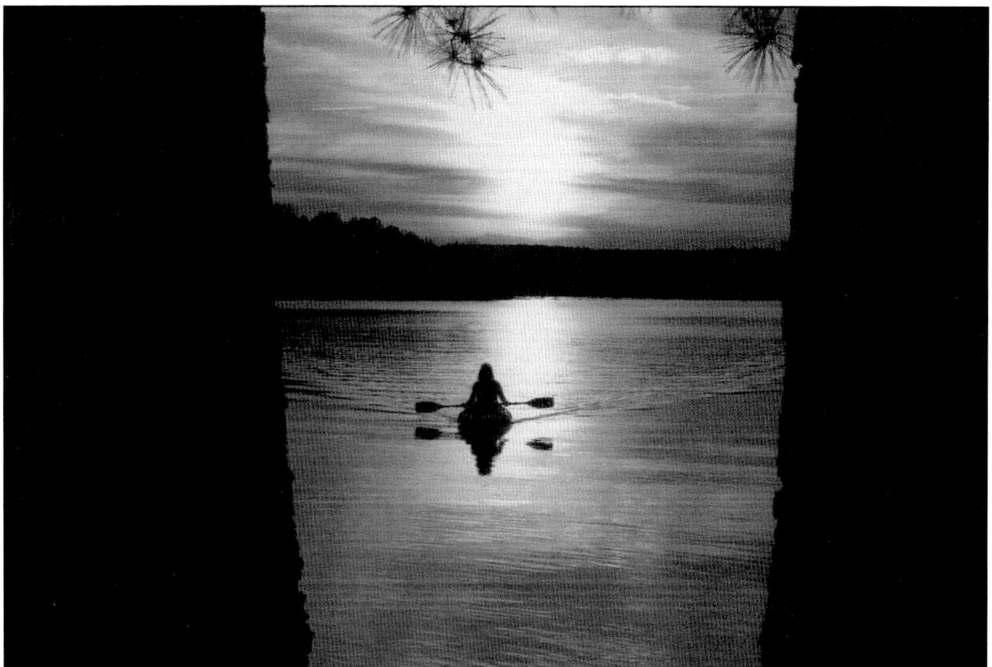

Professional photographer Stacey Smith, daughter of Teresa Smith, took this photograph. The photographer captured how placid and breathtaking Jordan Lake is at all times. Jordan Lake is a photographer's playground with its perfect scenery. (Author's collection.)

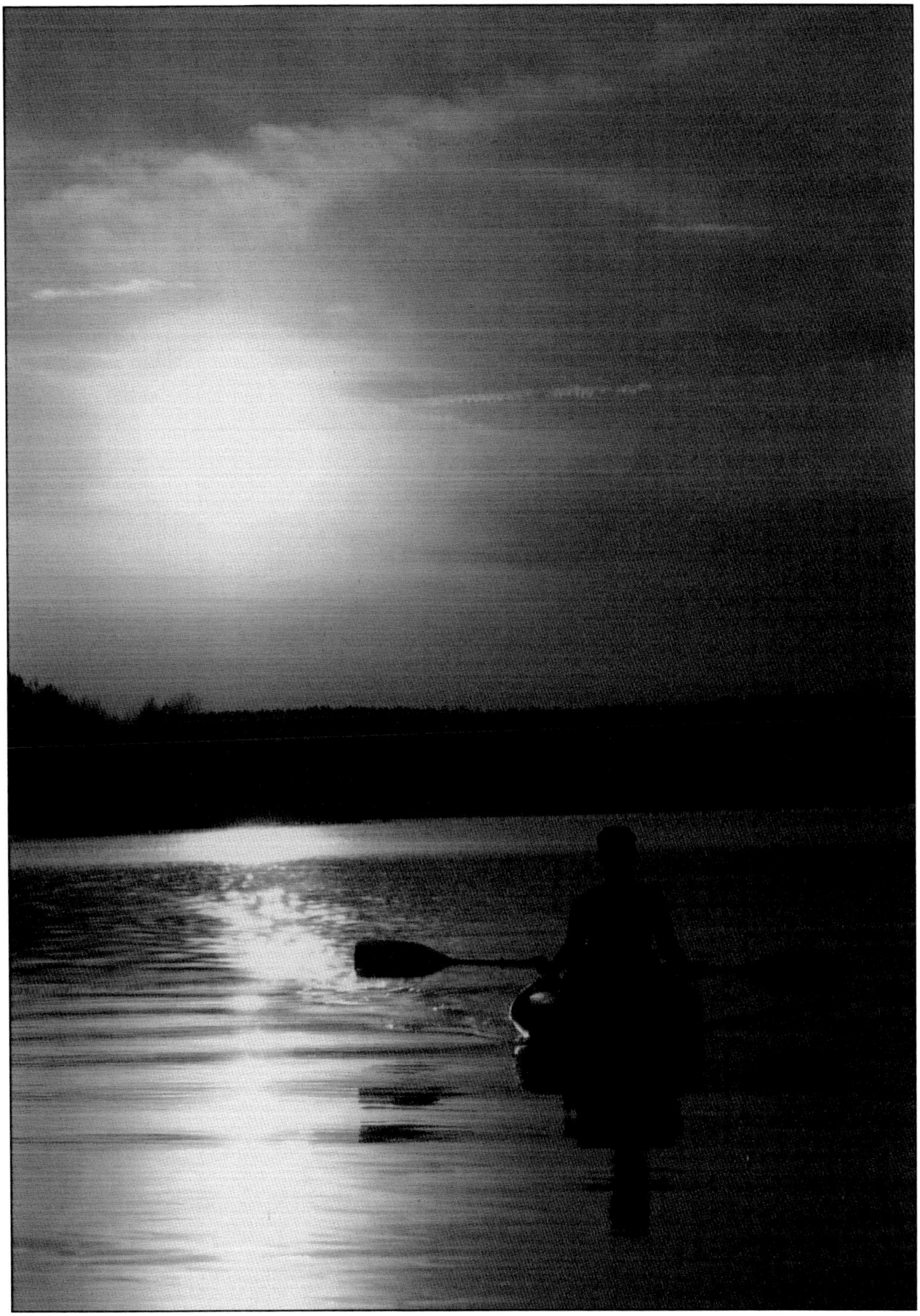

This is another award-winning photograph by Stacey Smith, daughter of Teresa Smith. Additional works by this photographer are on display at Harry's Market at Whitecross. Local artists from the Chapel Hill area are exhibited at Harry's Market, which also provides weekly entertainment and craft shows. (Courtesy of Harry's Market at White Cross.)

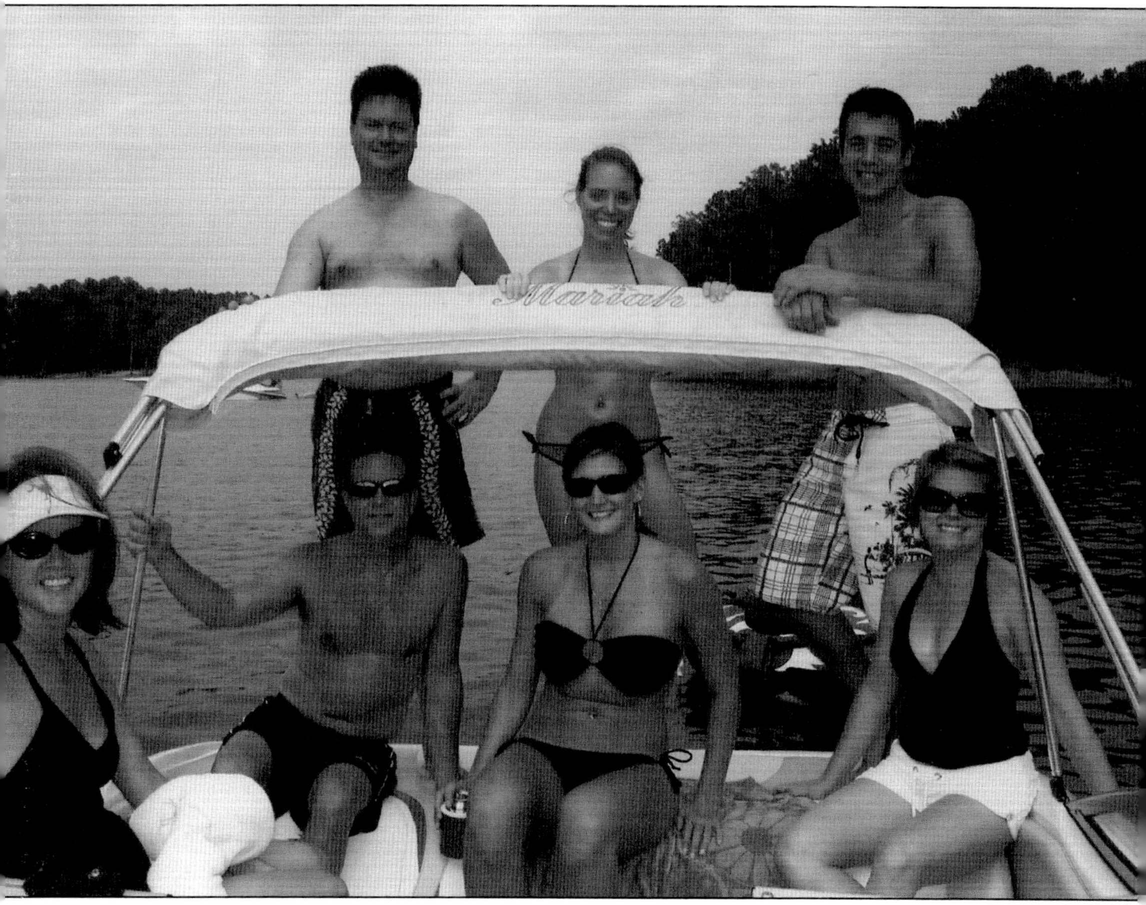

Some of the core members of the Friends of Chris Matheus (FOCM) professional networking group are on an outing at Jordan Lake. FOCM, created in Research Triangle Park near Jordan Lake, sets up social meetings and networking events for the pharmaceutical industry and other interested individuals. The group now has chapters from the East Coast to the West Coast and is growing strong. Within North Carolina, members meet at Jordan Lake a few times a week during the summer months. It is a way for those in the industry to network with fellow colleagues. Years ago, the sole way of joining the group was to personally know one person—Chris Matheus. Pictured above are, from left to right, (first row) Katherine Cloninger, Chris Matheus, Sarah Meister, and Kelly O'Brien; (second row) Vince Hoefling, Kourtney Henry, and Nicholas Macaulay. (Courtesy of Chris Matheus.)

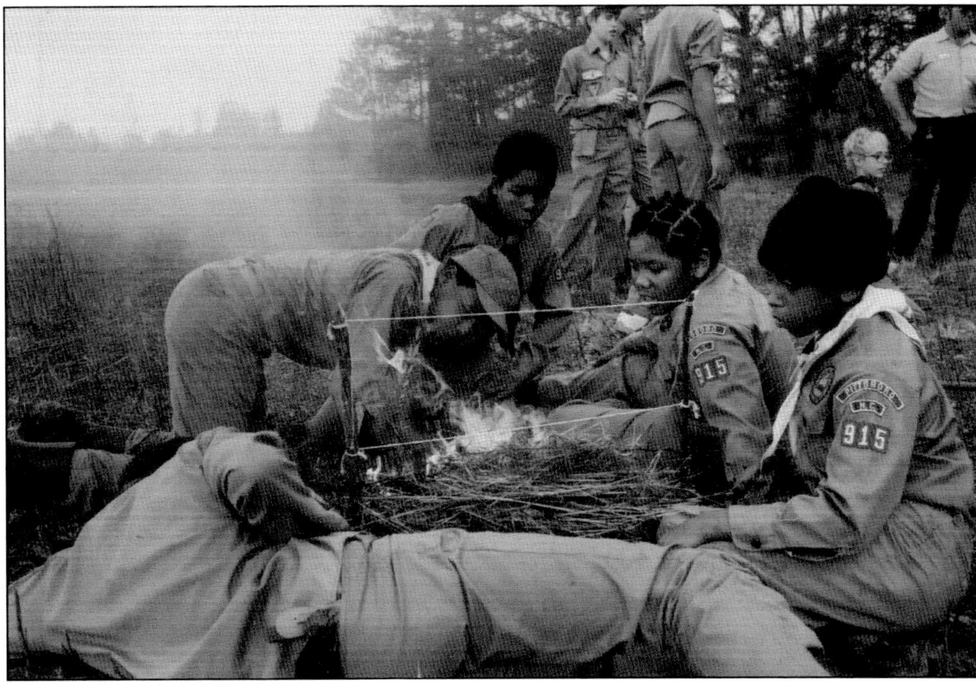

The 1977 Boy and Cub Scout Camporee was held at the Jordan Lake woods. The *Chatham County Herald* was there to take photographs of the different troops and their explorations. Several photographs were published in the November 9, 1977, edition of the newspaper. Pictured above, Pittsboro Troop 915 tests their lung power in starting a fire. Below, local Silk Hope Troop 91 has a tug-of-war match while onlookers were apparently shouting about opponent violations. Troop 91 won anyway. (Both, courtesy of Jeff Starkweather.)

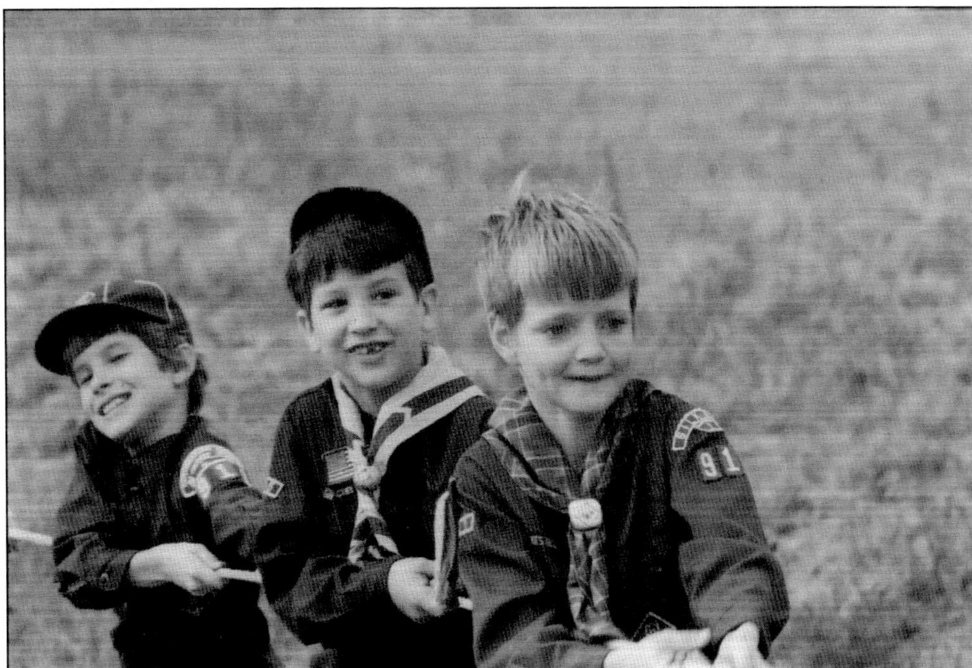

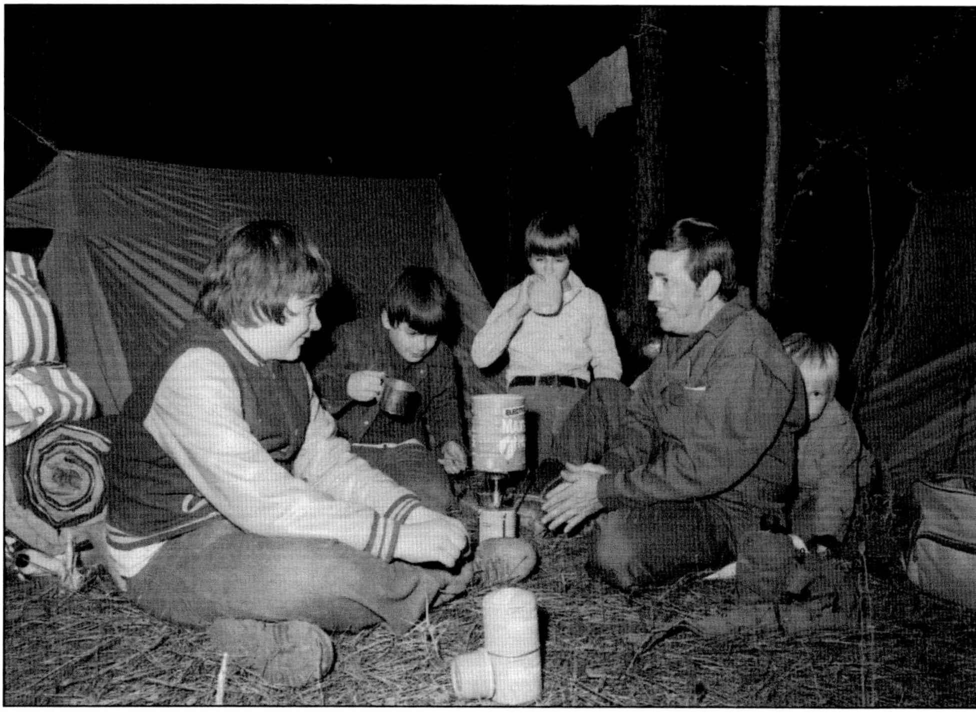

A Cub Scout troop uses a "buddy burner" to heat food during the Boy and Cub Scout Camporee at Jordan Lake in 1977, about five years before the lake was officially opened. The buddy burner is a crafty makeshift way for the boys to safely and easily heat food and drinks. Below, a Scout troop learns a new technique for cutting wood. The boys also used axes and had fun giving their loudest lumberjack hollers before commencing their chops. (Both, courtesy of Jeff Starkweather.)

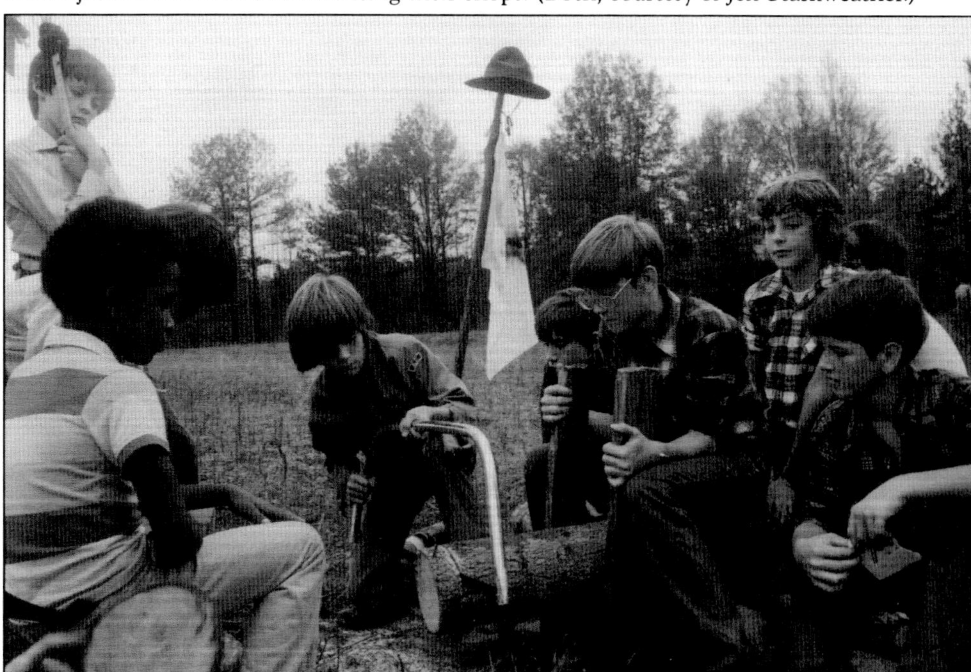

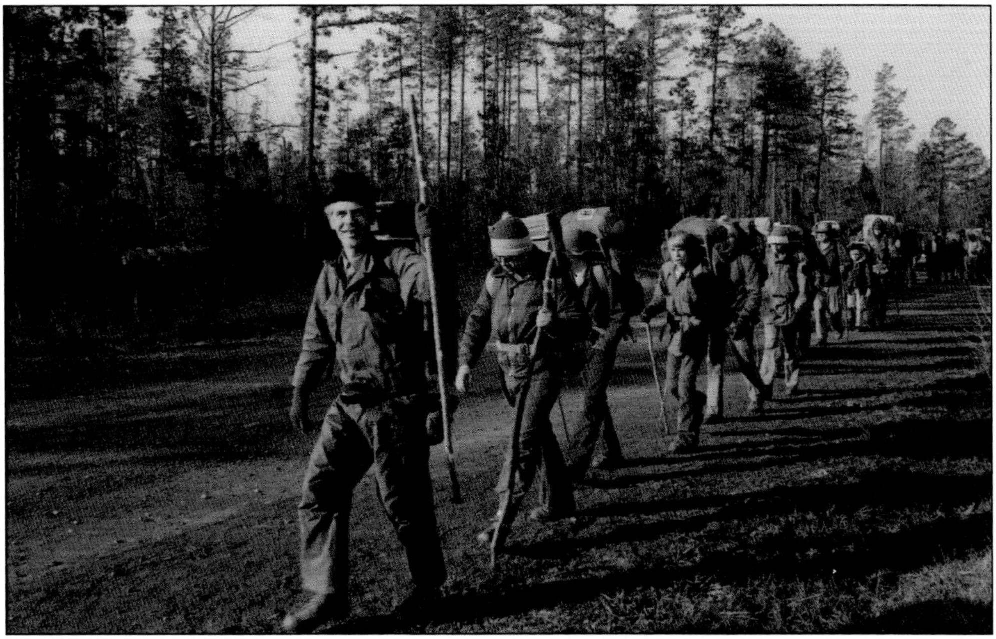

Above, the Boy Scouts are on a long hike during the November 1977 Camporee at Jordan Lake. The Jordan Lake area's previous man-made trails changed after Jordan Lake was officially flooded to capacity in 1982. However, there are two trails worth noting for significant views and exercise along Jordan Lake. The first is the Vista Point Trail, which is a 3-mile footpath that allows an easy stroll along the lake. The other is the Seaforth Recreation Area, which has a 1.4-mile footpath offering an upfront view of the lake environment. Below, the senior Scouts were well ahead of the junior Scouts and had their fire made, tents pitched, and drinks heated and were ready to share skits and stories. (Both, courtesy of Jeff Starkweather.)

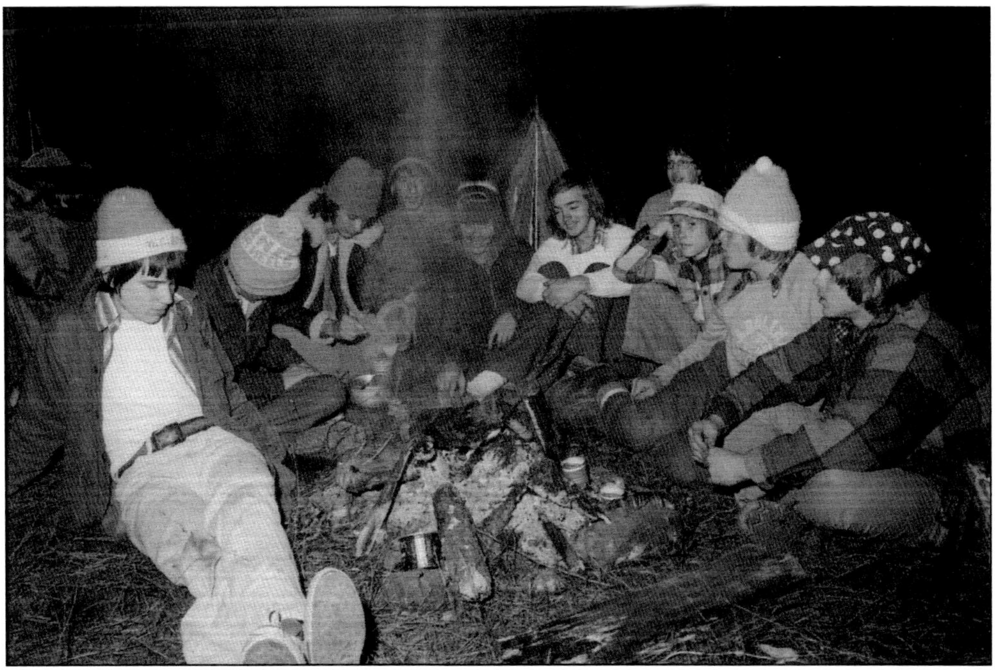

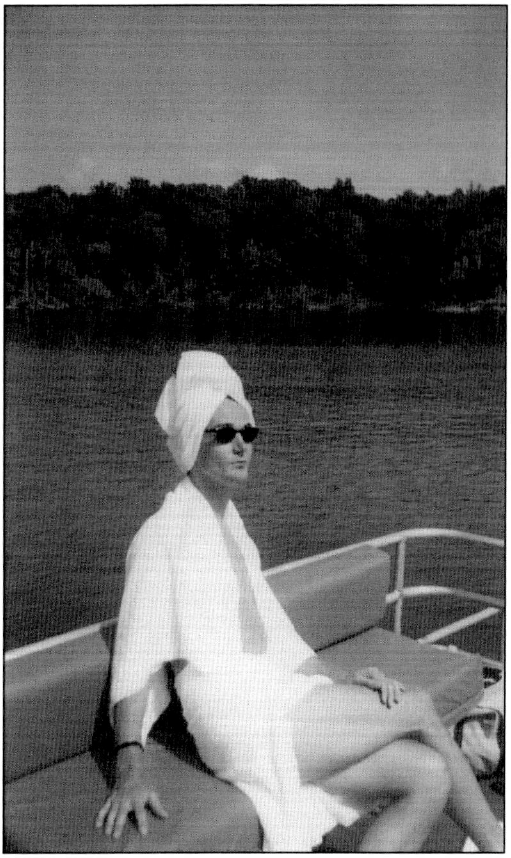

Pictured at left, Frankie Hayes, a former model and musician, playfully enjoys his first moments on Jordan Lake in 1982. Below, artist Johnny Hayes (left) and his brother Frankie Hayes (right) spent a weekend camping and boating on Jordan Lake in the summer of 1982. This is a tradition that Frankie Hayes has kept up every year since Jordan Lake first opened. The photograph below was taken on the last day of their trip. (Both, courtesy of Frankie Hayes.)

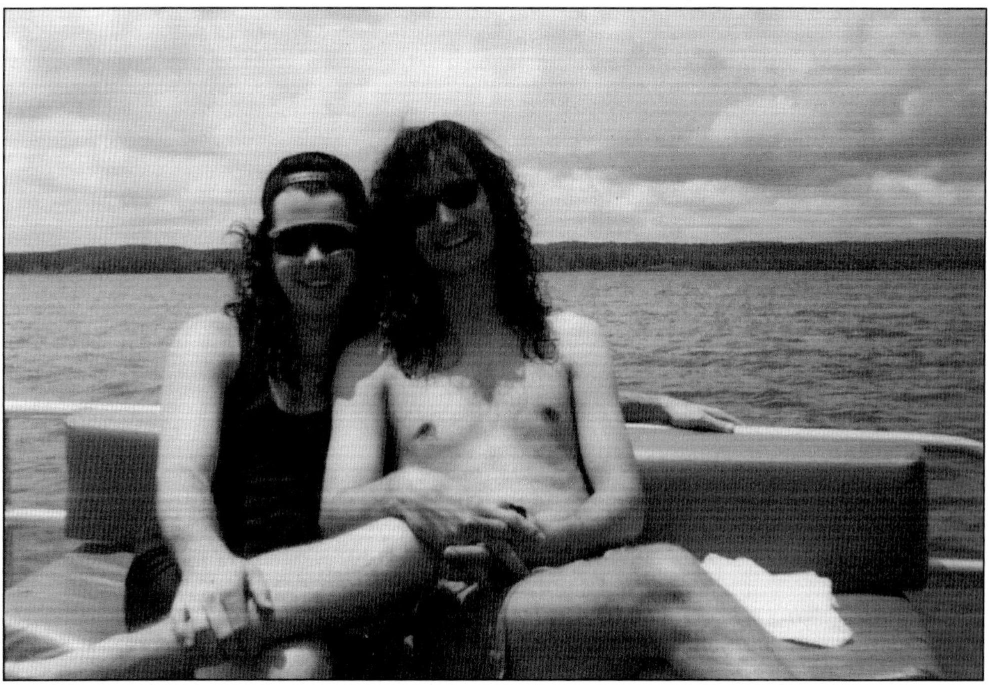

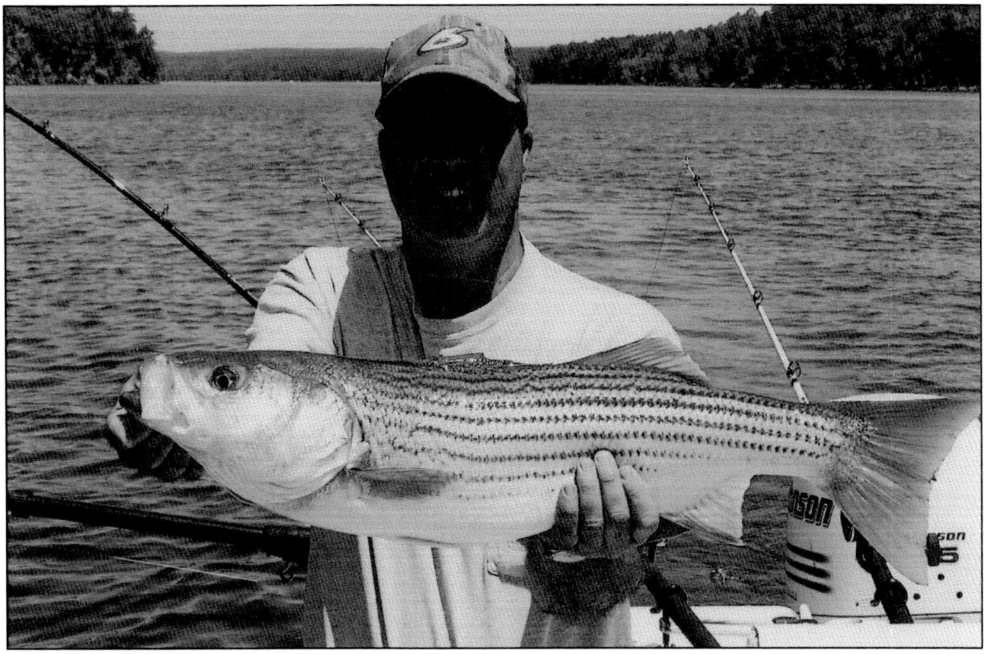

Mike Keen holds a 12-pound striper, a personal best for his fishing trips. A state biologist told Mike that the largest striper caught at Jordan Lake was 16 pounds. (Courtesy of Dwayne Duquette.)

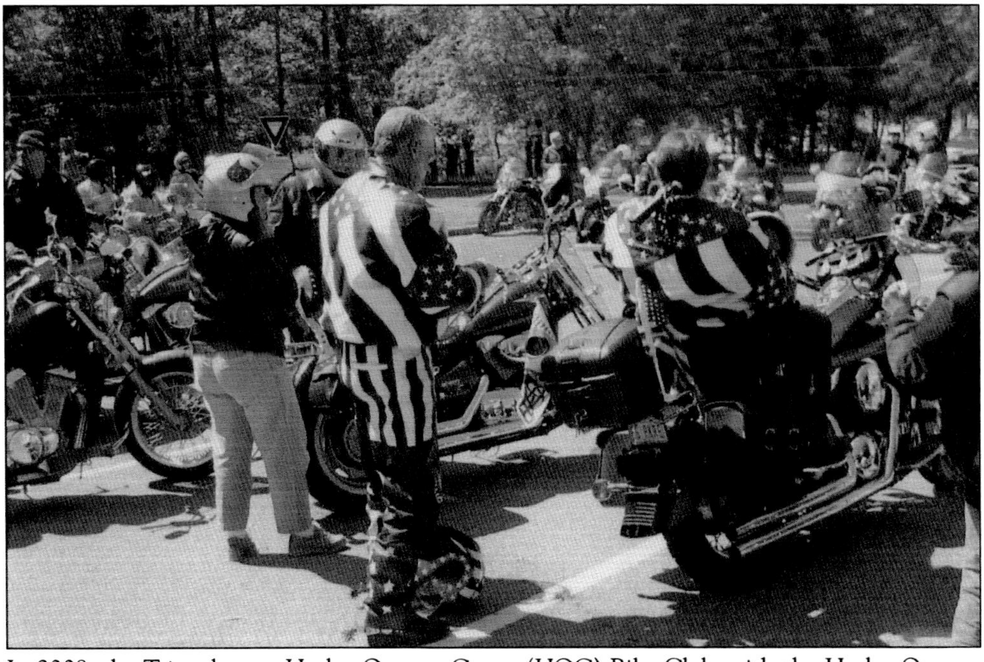

In 2008, the Triangle-area Harley Owners Group (HOG) Bike Club, with the Harley Owners Group national organization, raised almost $34,000 for the Pediatric Brain Tumor Foundation. The foundation considers the club to be one of the nation's top 20 performers. This photograph was taken at one of the yearly fund-raiser rides that begins at Jordan Lake. More than 300 people attended this ride. The local police often give them escorts and block roads during major fund-raisers. (Courtesy of John Covert.)

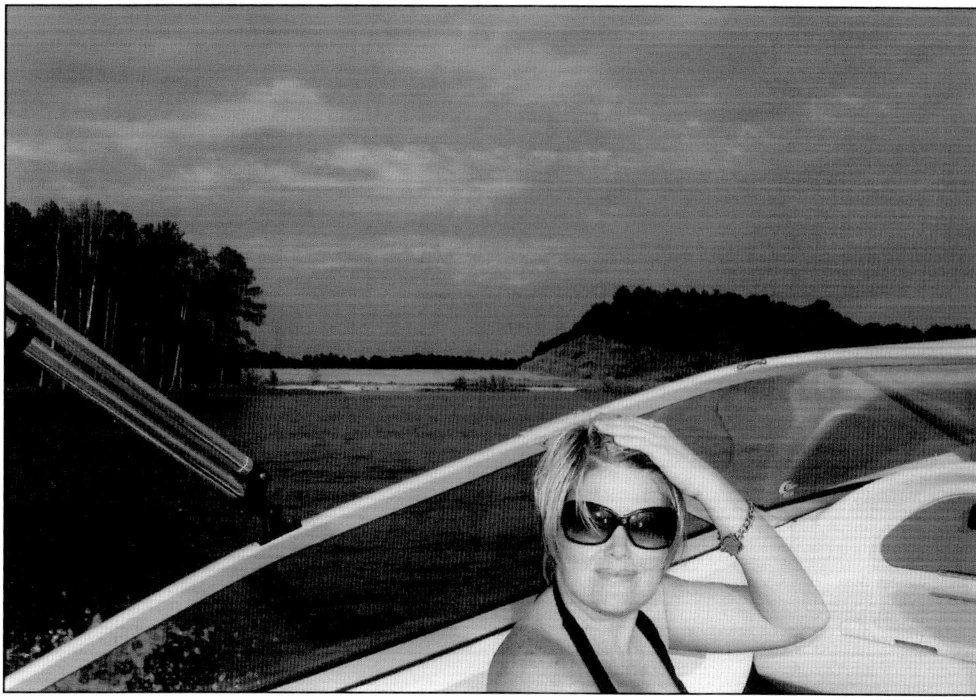

The classy Kelly O'Brien enjoys another beautiful sunset at Jordan Lake. Kelly O'Brien says, "If everyone spent time in the sun and water, the world would be a better place, where birds sing and dogs dance." (Courtesy of Kelly O'Brien.)

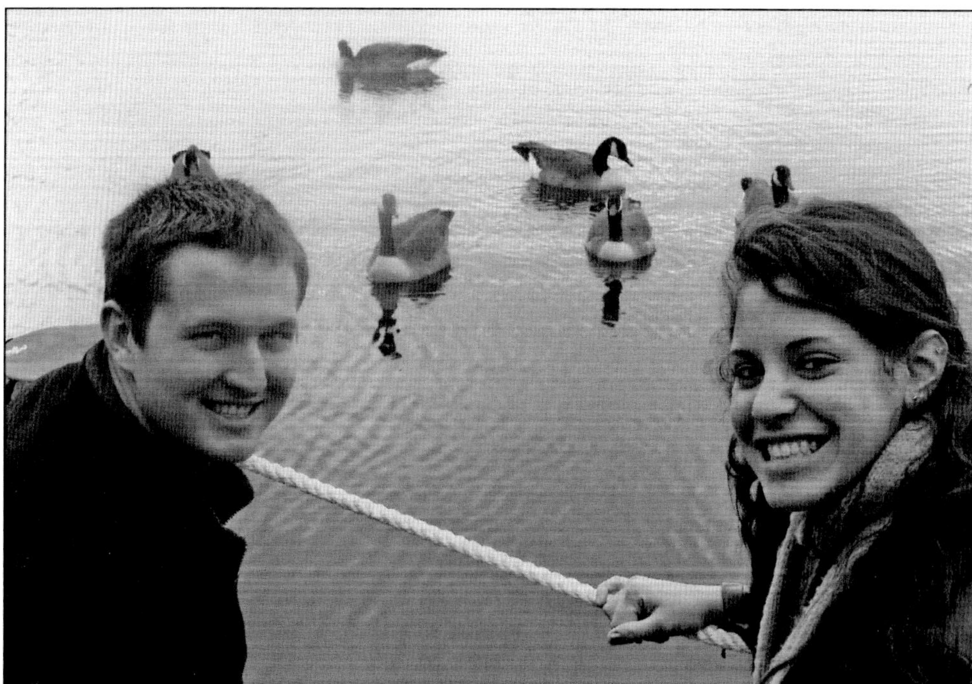

Keith Kosman (left) and Aerial Ward (right) enjoy wildlife adventures. (Courtesy of Daniemarie Jimenez Mars.)

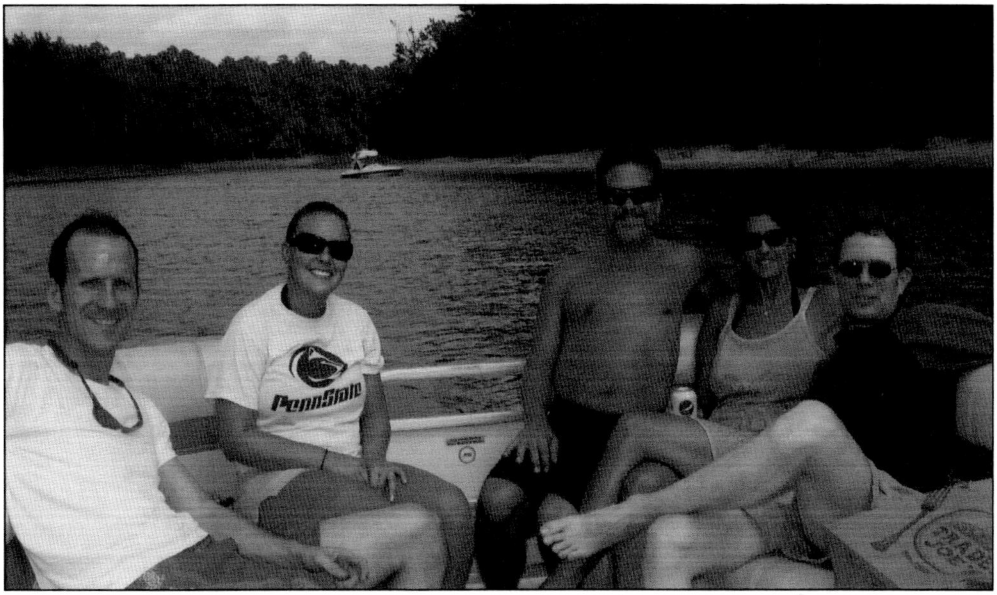

Party cove at Jordan Lake was not seeing much action on this particular day. It must have been the middle of the work day! Pictured here are, from left to right, Mike Wheeler, Nikki Jendrasek, Chris Matheus, Deb Jendrasek, and Mike Burrows. Deb's daughter, Nikki, came down from Penn State University to spend the weekend swimming and boating on Jordan Lake. Chris Matheus becomes so elated when he is out on Jordan Lake that he wishes he could buy the world a carbonated beverage and a smile of sunset happiness. (Courtesy of Chris Matheus.)

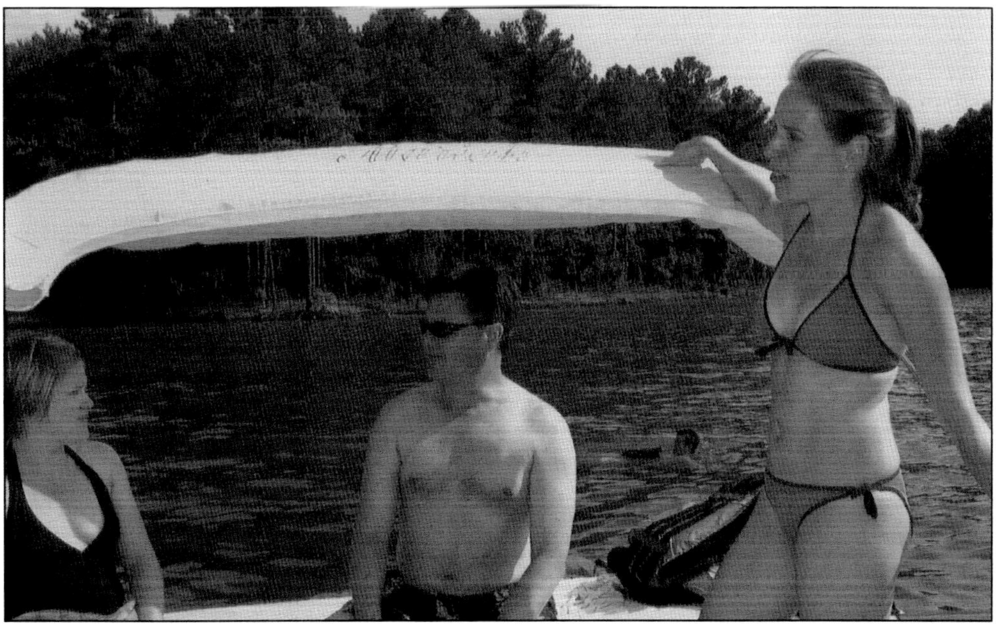

Kelly O'Brien (left), Vince Hoefling, and Kourtney Henry, pictured during an FOCM event, discuss going tubing, having another beer, water skiing, buying a bigger boat, the depth of the water, where does the sun go when the sun goes down, why they are so lucky there are no alligators or sharks at Jordan Lake, and how did Nicholas Macaulay just do that back flip off the boat into the water behind them? (Courtesy of Chris Matheus.)

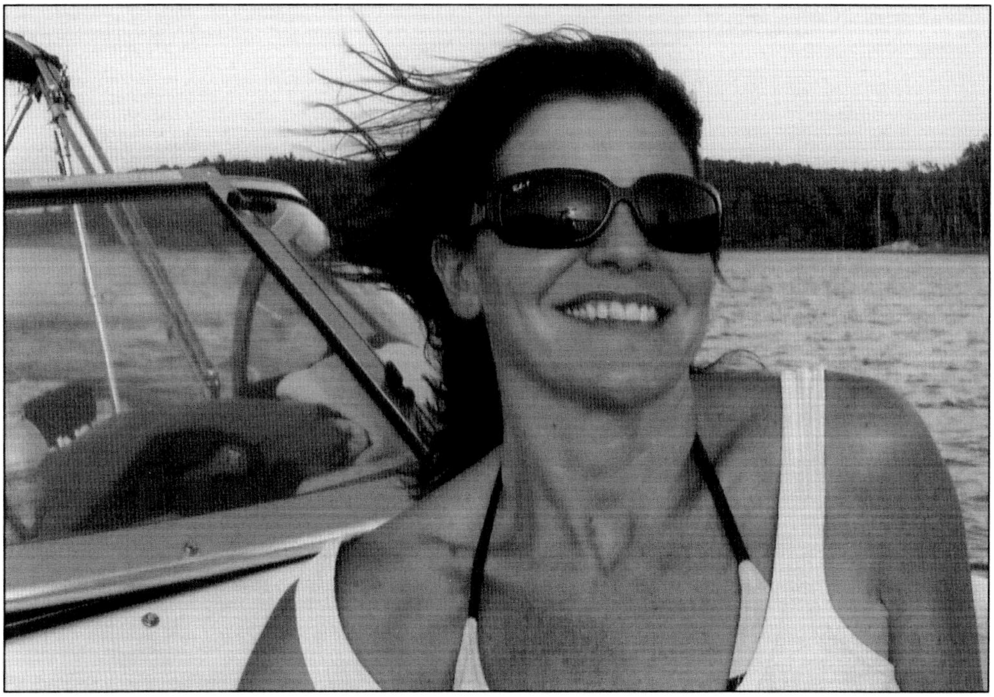

The beautiful Lisa Monette contemplates her next exotic vacation while enjoying a day of boating and sunshine on Jordan Lake. Lisa is a business development executive for a company in Research Triangle Park. (Courtesy of Lisa Monette.)

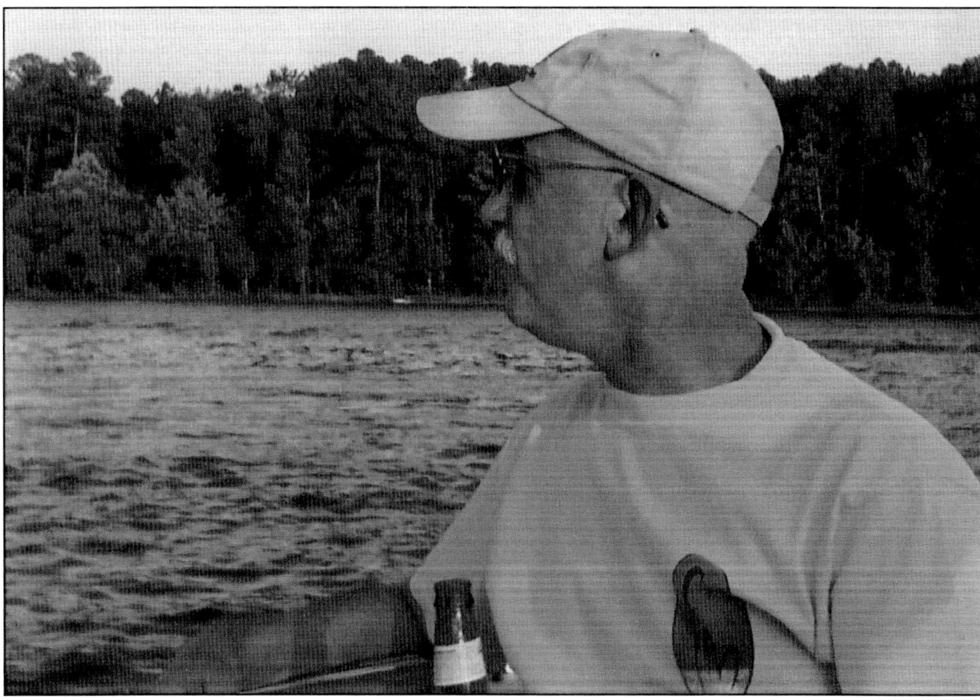

Phil Keicher is an executive within the pharmaceutical industry and often unwinds on a boat at Jordan Lake. (Courtesy of Phil Keicher.)

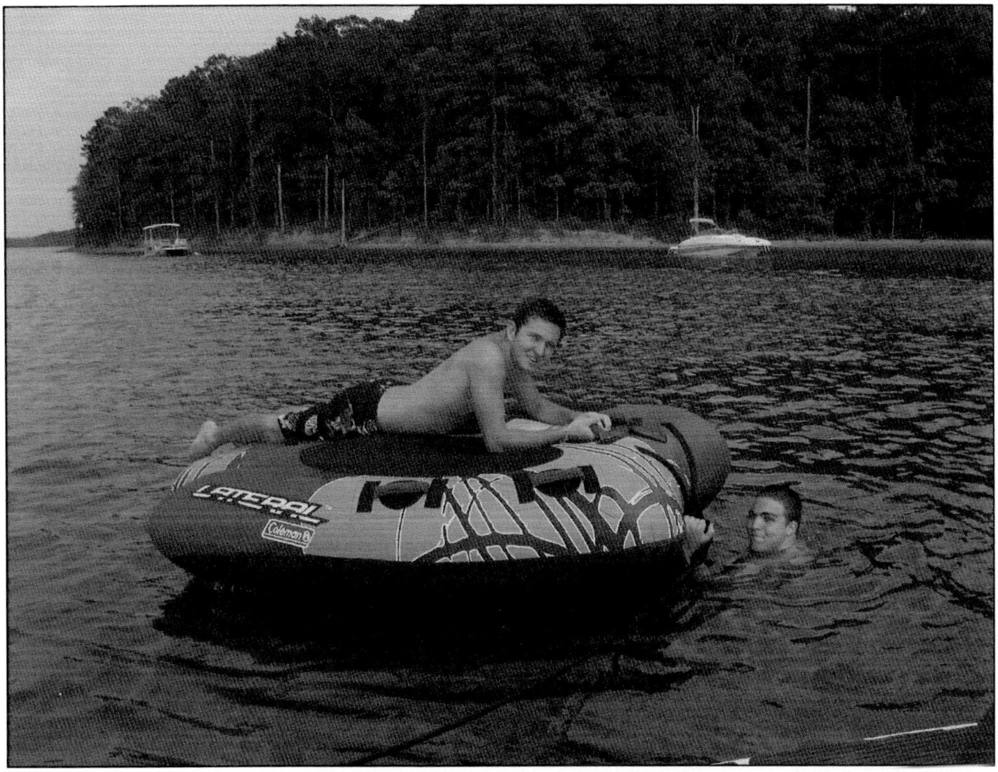

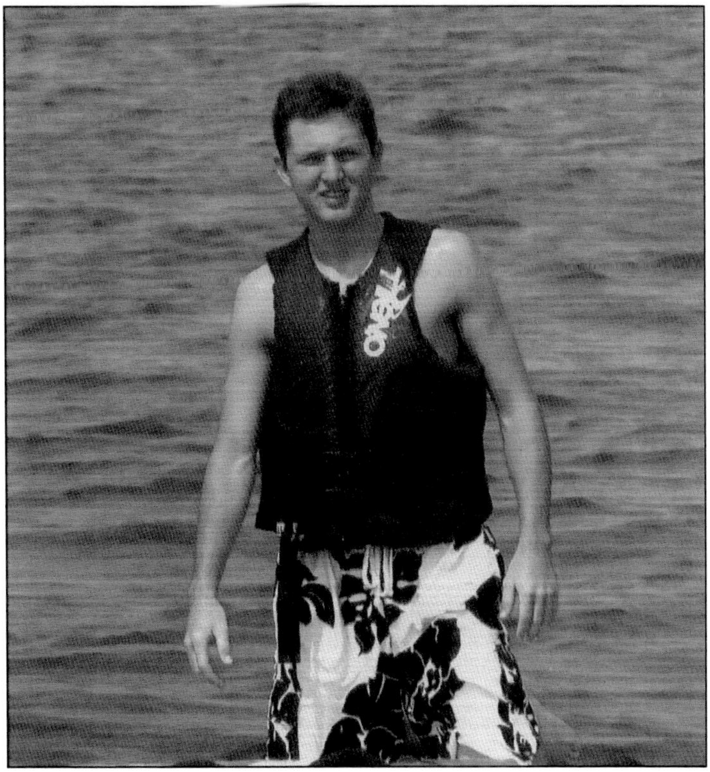

College students from the University of Florida and the Kappa Alpha fraternity visit Jordan Lake during summer break. Pictured above are, from left to right, Keith Kosman and Joshua Caleb Bradley. At right, Keith Kosman is on his knees after tubing, wondering why the boat captain goes so slowly and why his mother keeps yelling at the boat captain to slow down. Jordan Lake has been Keith's favorite place in North Carolina. Whenever Keith gets upset he loves to say, "go to the beach." (Both, courtesy of Chris Matheus.)

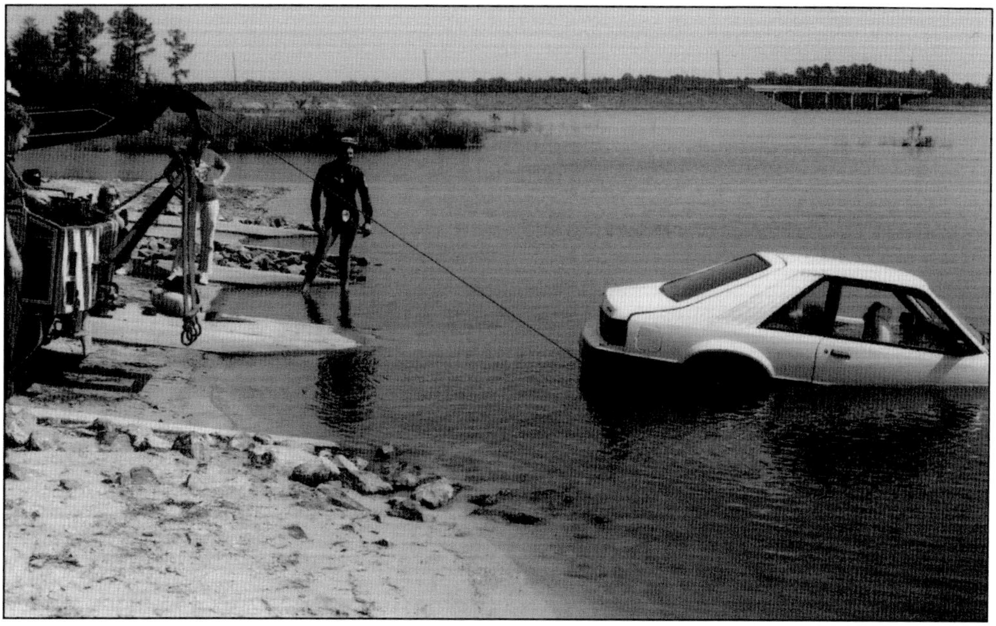

This car sat in the water overnight after a local man went to the edge of Jordan Lake and got out of his car to go to the bathroom. He did not realize that he left the car running, and it drove itself into the lake. The man was lucky, since he was apparently so inebriated that when he did call the authorities the following day to inform them his car was in the lake, he could not remember where it was. The car was completely submerged, and divers spent most of the morning looking for it. (Courtesy of U.S. Army Corps of Engineers.)

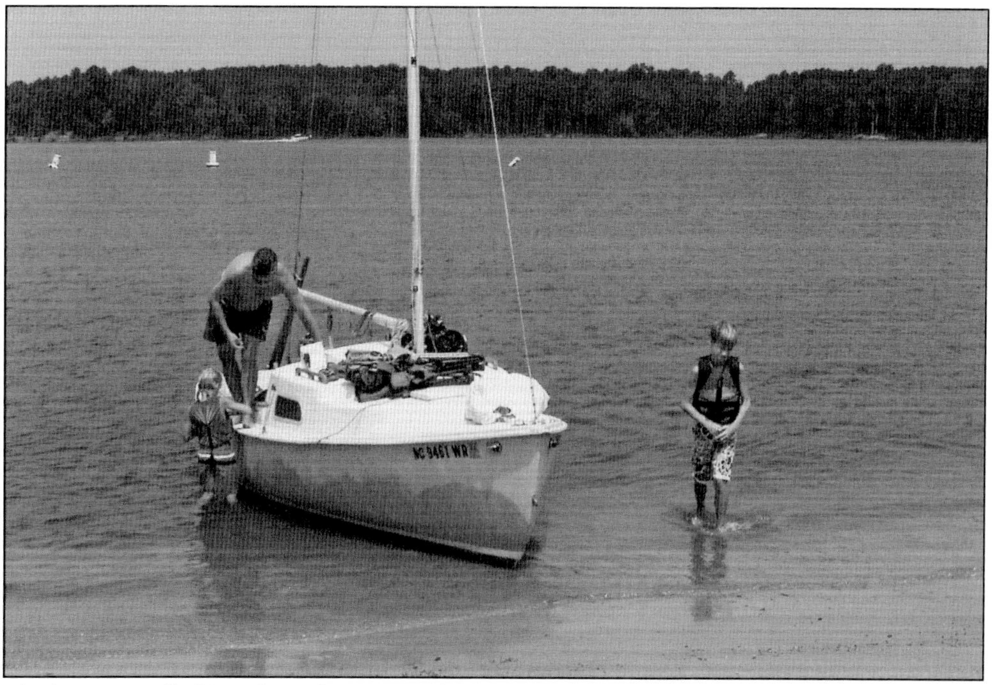

The boat was called *Dumbo* and was named by the boat owner's grandchildren because when the boat's flaps are open, the boat appears to look like Dumbo. (Courtesy of John Shillito.)

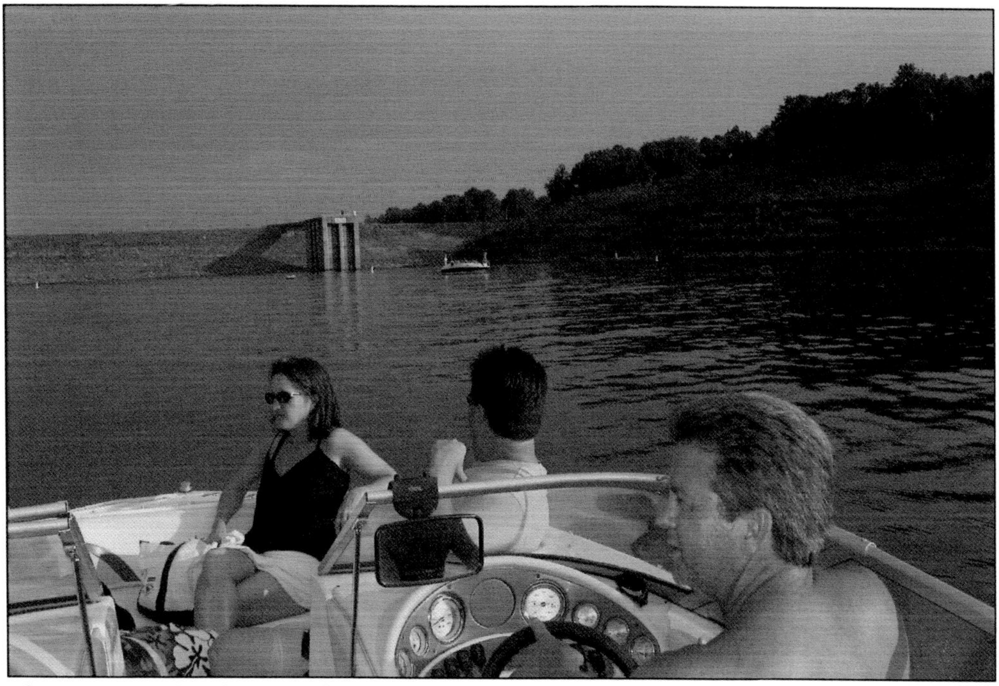

This is a view of Jordan Dam from a boat. The captain driving the boat is Chris Matheus, with Vince Hoefling in the middle and Katherine Cloninger in background. The Jordan Dam is a must-see. While facing the dam in the water, the U.S. Army Corps of Engineers Visitor Assistance Center can barely be seen during the summer months, because it is behind the beautiful tall trees on the hill to the right. Locals volunteer to help keep the shoreline of Jordan Lake looking so clean. (Courtesy of Chris Matheus.)

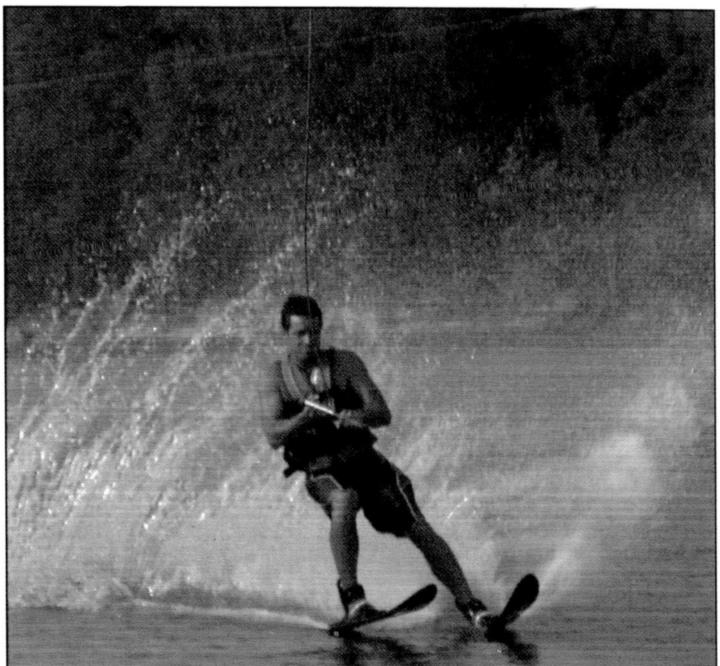

Nicholas Macaulay's background as a competitive snow skier and cyclist has allowed him the ability to stay up on water skis for a really long time. When this photograph was taken, the driver of the boat was trying his very best to take every sharp curve to try and throw Nicholas off of his skis. (Courtesy of Ron Macaulay.)

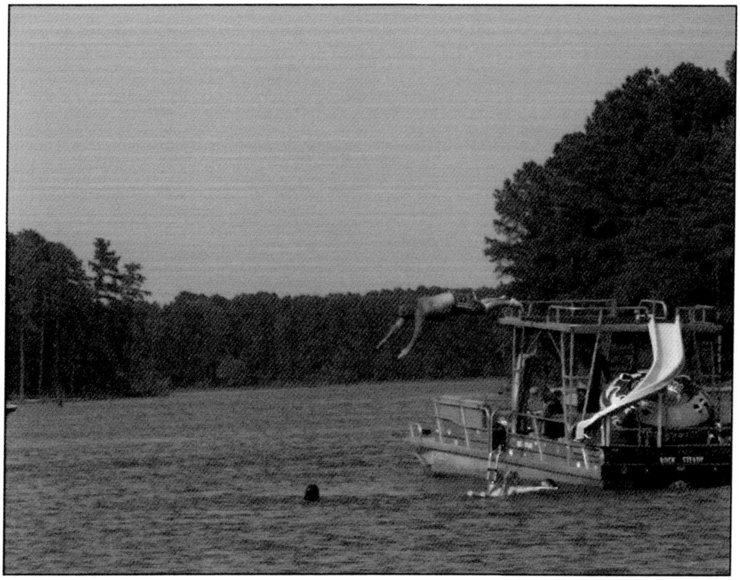

A man performs a dangerous activity by diving off the top of the boat. Fatalities have occurred when others have dived off their boats into shallow water, and authorities discourage this activity. The boat is called *Rock Steady*. It is often seen at Jordan Lake with a beautiful family who allow people to dock next to them to enjoy the slide and boat rooftop. (Author's collection.)

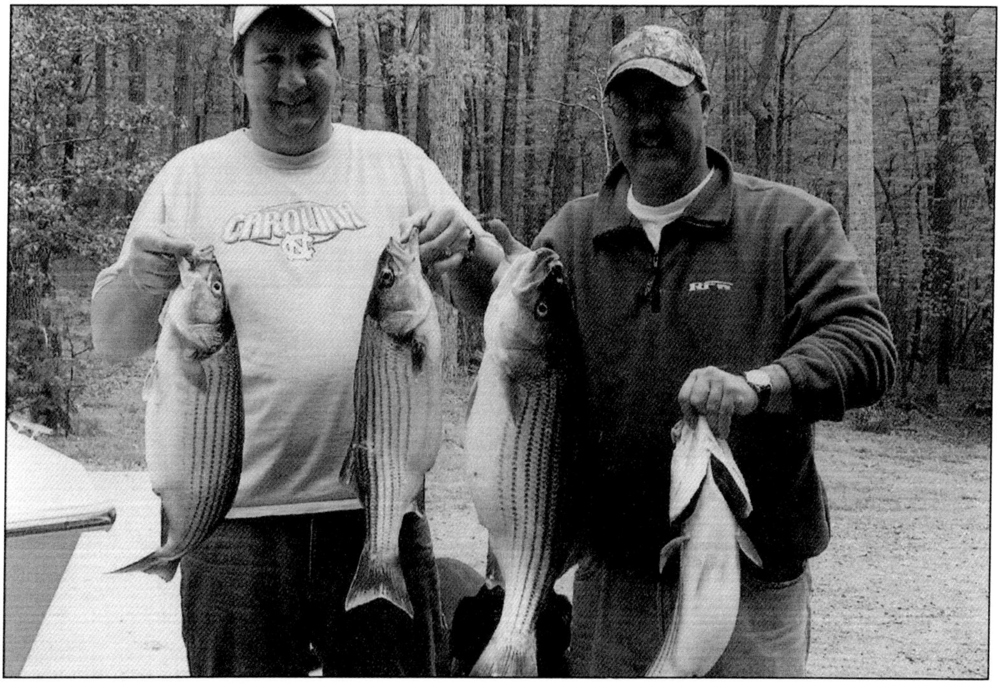

Dwayne Duquette (left) and Mike Keen (right) have been best friends since grade school. This was their first striper fishing trip to Jordan Lake, and Mike is holding a 10-pound striper. The two had been going to the Roanoke River for years for the annual striper run, but that trip began getting old when the river started to become overwhelmed with boats and fishermen. When they heard about stripers at Jordan Lake, they hired a guide (Mark Edmunds) to not only fish with but to also learn how to fish for stripers in the lake so they could start fishing for them on their own. (Courtesy of Dwayne Duquette.)

Five

WILDLIFE

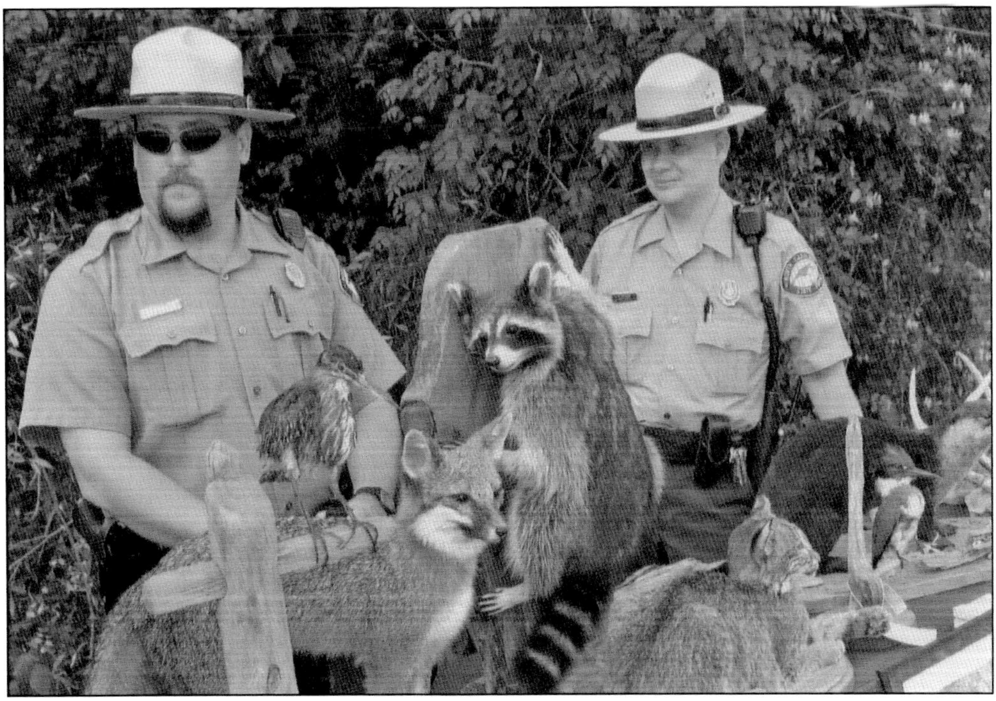

Paul Kalish (left) and Fred Watkins, with the North Carolina State Parks division, give an educational lesson about local wildlife to children at a festival. The animals in the photograph are very lifelike and do not appear stuffed at first glance. (Courtesy of John Shillito.)

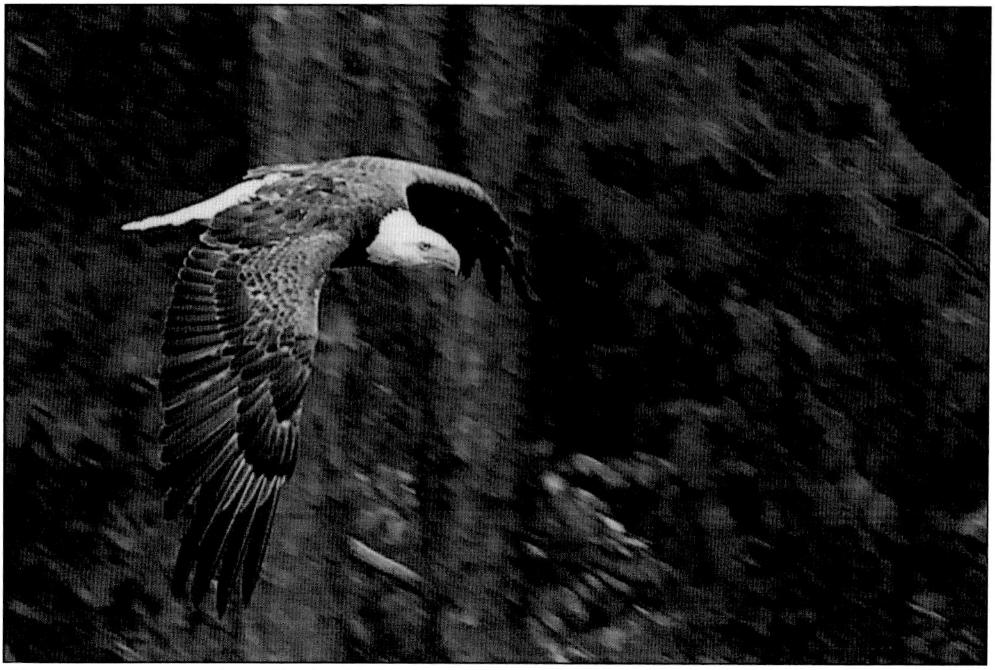

This is a mature eagle in flight. Jordan Lake has a dedicated reserve that attracts one of the largest concentrations of bald eagles in the Southeast. The locale provides mature trees and large undisturbed private areas. (Courtesy of Doug Wakeman.)

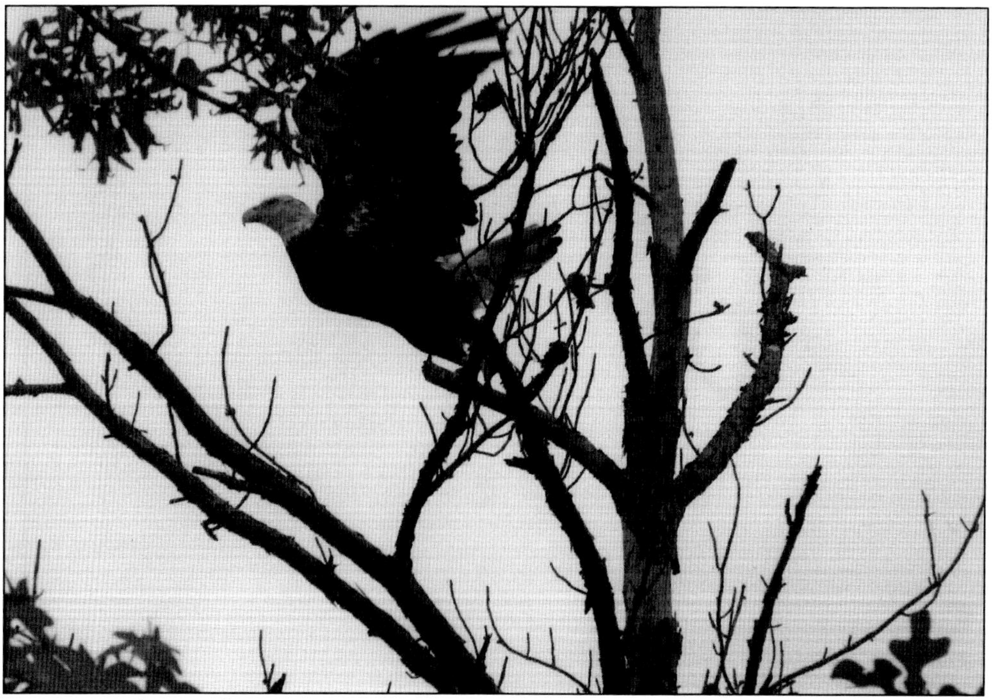

A mature eagle spreads its wings getting ready for flight. The location of the bald eagles' nests at Jordan Lake is protected. Paul Kalish took this photograph while working at the lake. (Courtesy of Paul Kalish.)

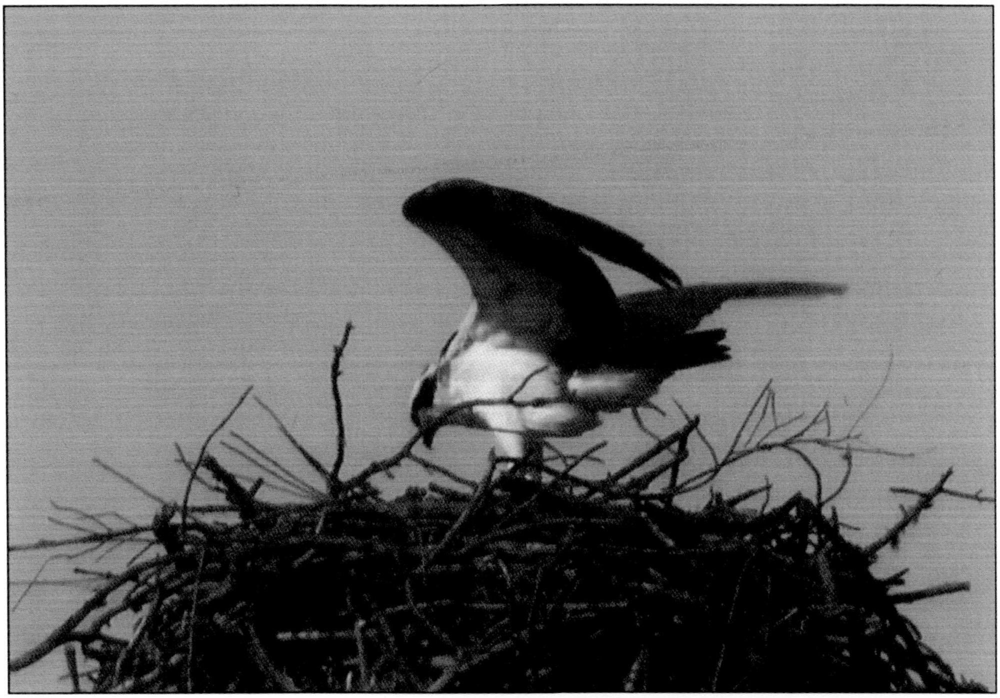

An adult osprey is nesting at Jordan Lake. The osprey is a raptor that reaches 24 inches in length with a 6-foot wingspan. The osprey's diet is exclusively fish. Its talons are rounded rather than grooved. The osprey is the only raptor whose outer toe is reversible, allowing it to grasp its prey with two toes in front and two toes from behind. (Courtesy of Paul Kalish.)

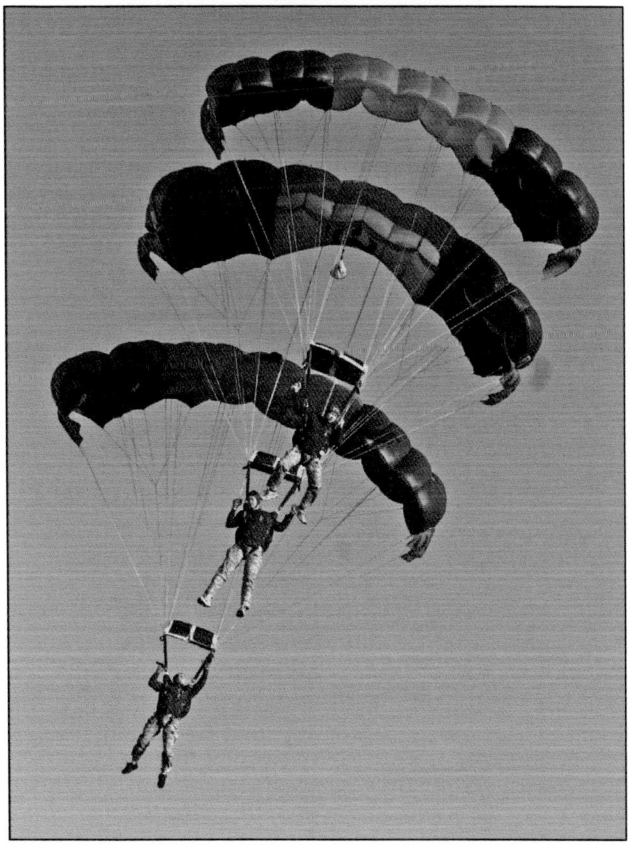

From top to bottom, S.Sgt. Dewey Vinaya, SFC David Rose, and Sgt. Anthony Galusha from the U.S. Army Special Operations Command Black Daggers parachute demonstration team complete a complex three-stack canopy formation and are breaking free for a water landing on Jordan Lake as part of the Fourth Annual Warriors on the Water military appreciation event held at the New Hope Ramp at Jordan Lake. (Courtesy of Kim Ringeisen.)

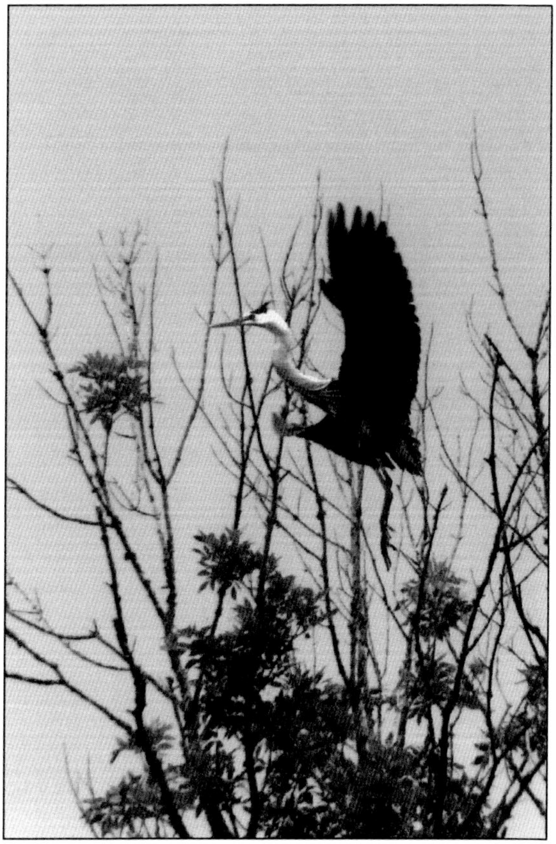

This is a photograph of a heron as it is landing at the heron rookery at Jordan Lake near Bush Creek. (Courtesy of Elaine Chiosso.)

Paul Kalish took this ironic photograph of turkey vultures sitting on a sign at Jordan Lake that reads, "Caution, unprotected area. No lifeguard on duty." It appears only the vultures get to enjoy this nice beautiful beach today. (Courtesy of Paul Kalish.)

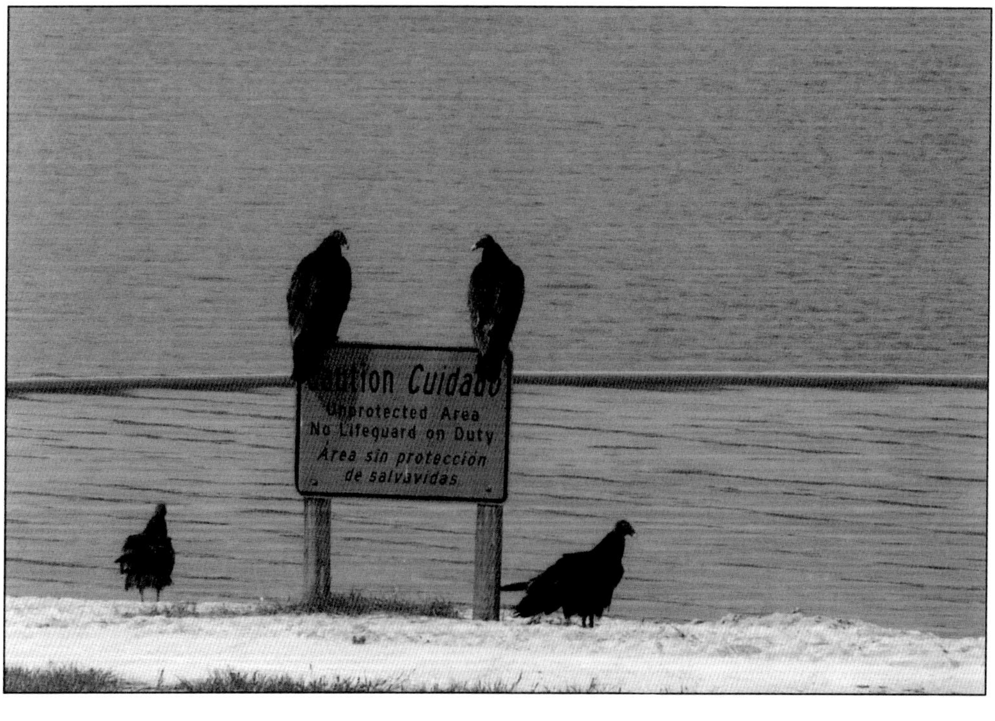

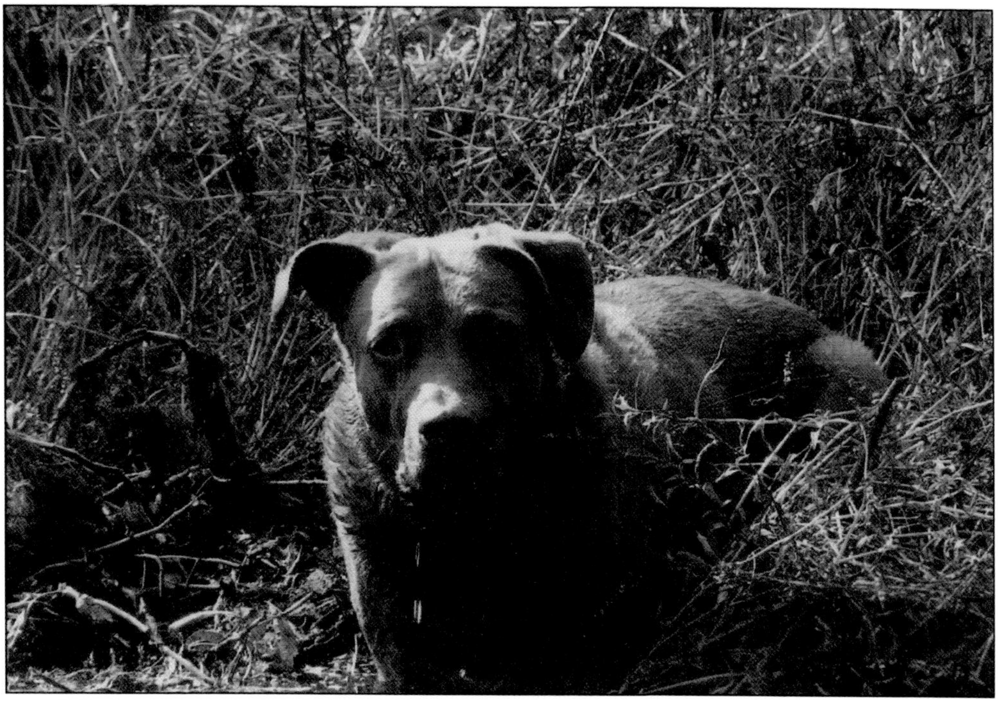

Even dogs get to enjoy Jordan Lake, and some even make it out onto the boats to go for a swim! The handsome dog above belongs to Paul Kalish. Below is a postcard that is free to the public as a reminder to clean up after pets. The ability to take a dog to Jordan Lake while camping is not a privilege anyone wants to lose. (Above, courtesy of Paul Kalish; below, courtesy of U.S. Army Corps of Engineers.)

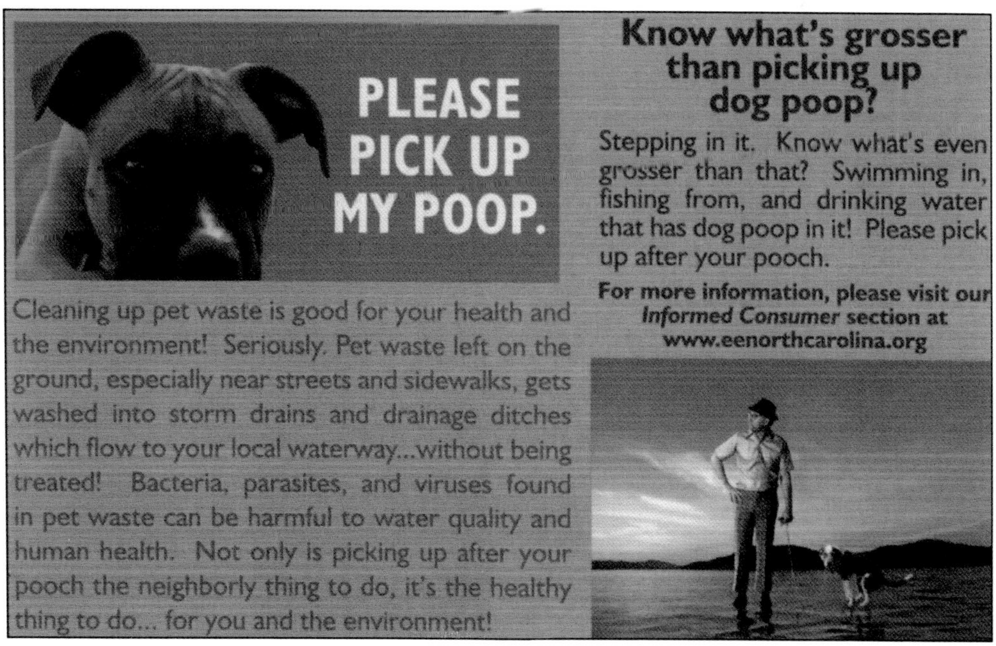

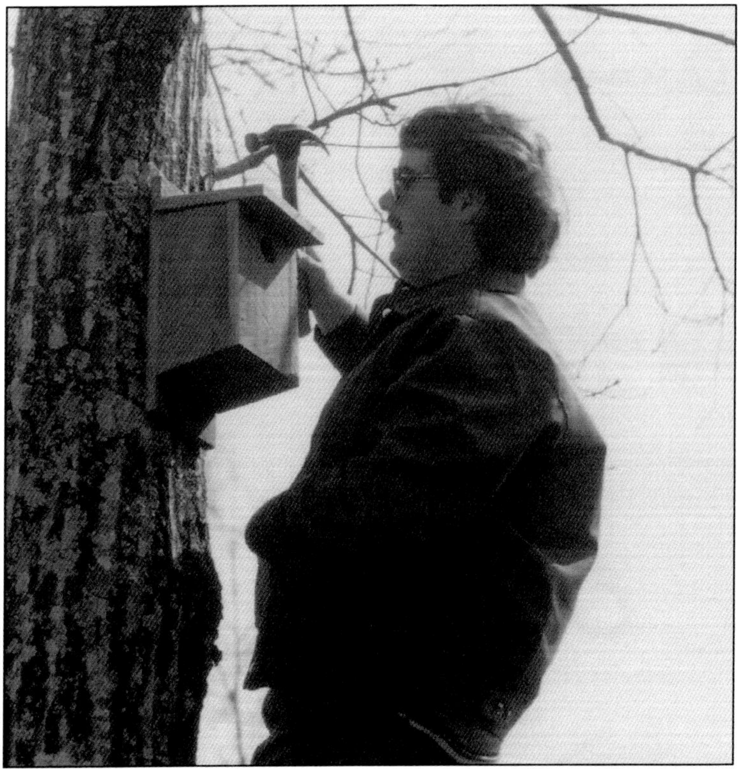

A ranger with the U.S. Army Corps of Engineers in 1981 is hanging a bluebird box. Many bird boxes were hung for habitat around the lake. Staff members and co-op students still check the boxes. They keep records and statistics of the number of chicks and types of birds for their success rates. The rates have significantly increased each year. (Courtesy of U.S. Army Corps of Engineers.)

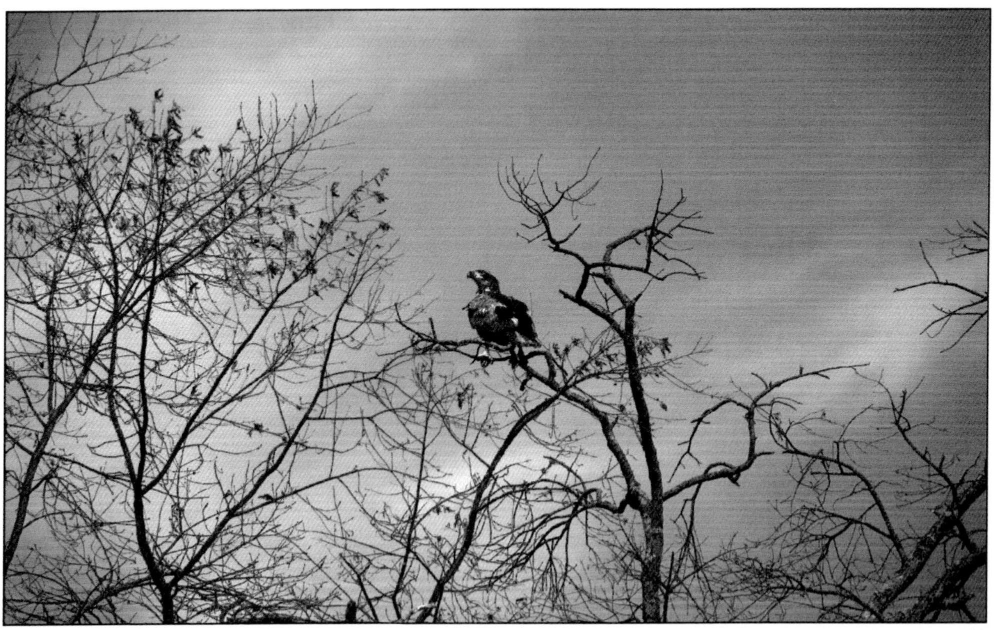

An immature bald eagle is sunning in a tree at the Jordan Lake State Recreational Park Bald Eagle Preserve. For protection reasons, the location of the bald eagle's nests is not publicized. It takes a lot of energy for a bald eagle to fly, and with so many tourists trying to get a closer look, the bald eagle is compromised to fly, quite often resulting in a shorted lifespan. (Courtesy of Paul Kalish.)

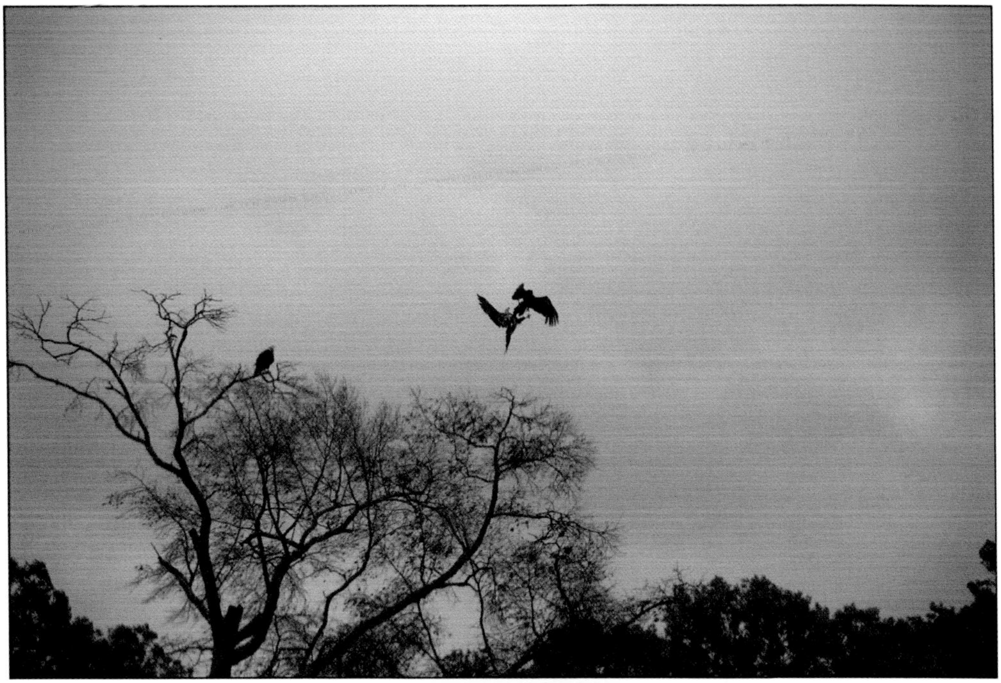

This is another photograph taken by Paul Kalish during his lunch break at work on Jordan Lake. Two immature eagles are fighting while the adult eagle in the tree watches. (Courtesy of Paul Kalish.)

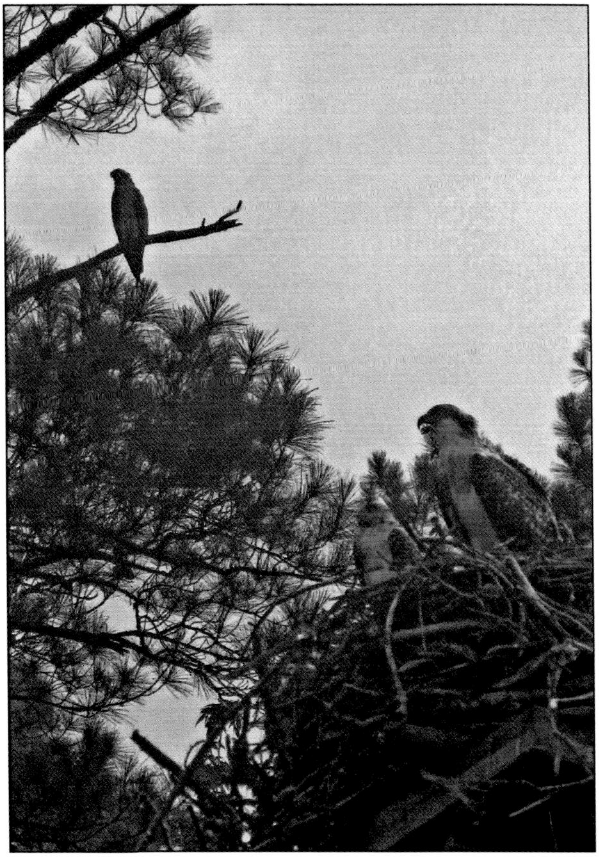

An osprey parent is seated with two immature ospreys. An osprey sighting is almost guaranteed on every trip to Jordan Lake. (Courtesy of John Shillito.)

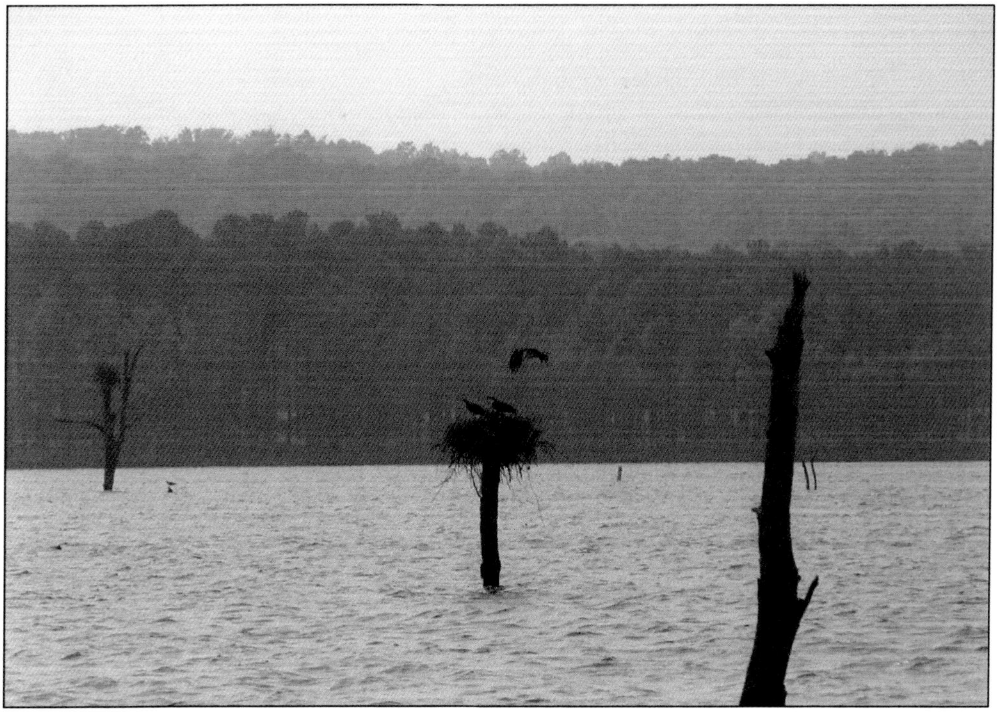

The osprey nests are on stumps at Jordan Lake. The stumps that are left behind provide a natural habitat for wildlife. (Courtesy of John Shillito.)

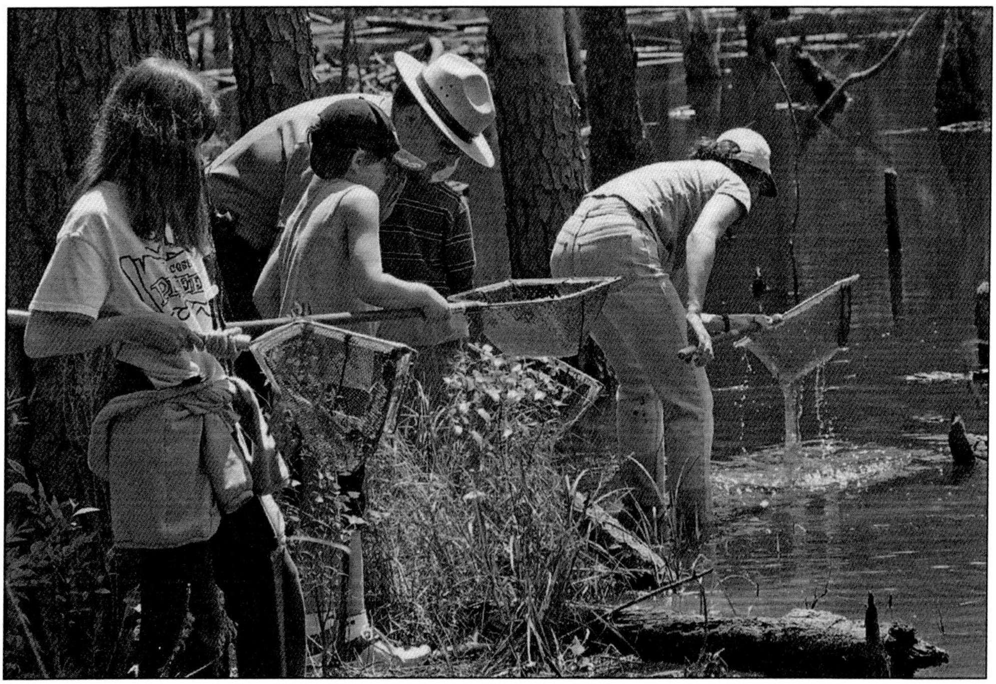

This is swamp netting at Jordan Lake. Forest rangers and certified environmental educators, Paul Kalish and Fred Watkins Jr. are giving a swamp netting environmental educational class to children at a yearly festival. (Courtesy of Paul Kalish.)

Six

Environment

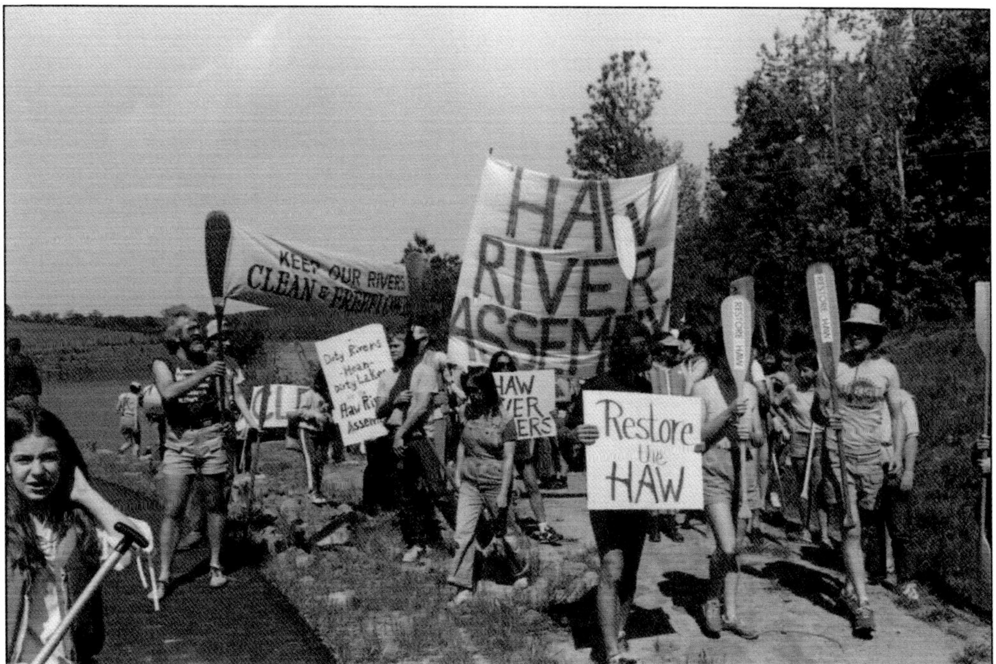

This is the Haw River Assembly on May 1, 1982. HRA director Chuck Brady said in June 1982, "A lot of us had heard good-natured kidding that the 'Haw River Assembly' sounded like a church name. After 12 days in the forest, swamp, and some of the most beautiful rivers imaginable, I got to thinking about that. The overwhelming feeling I had on the river was one of awe, reverence, and respect for what we have been given. In knee-deep water in the middle of a beaver pond, surrounded by deer and lush vegetation, it is not difficult to remember that we are stewards of God's world. I believe that with people like you, we are not going to let Him down." (Courtesy of Jeff Starkweather.)

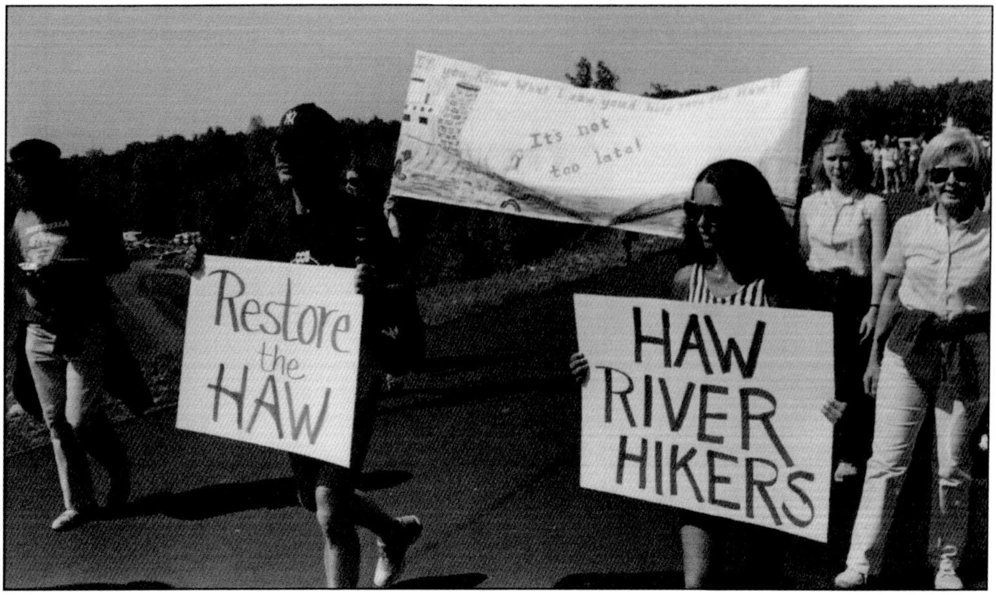

The Haw River Assembly and the Haw River Hikers are marching on May 1, 1982. In the April 2007 HRA newsletter, HRA director Elaine Chiosso says, "Twenty five years later, we share Chuck Brady's feelings of awe and reverence as we watch the herons fishing along the Haw's whitewaters, as we marvel at the eagles and ospreys soaring over Jordan Lake, or as we paddle down a lazy stretch of river under the arching sycamore trees. We pledge to carry on as stewards of the Haw." (Courtesy of Jeff Starkweather.)

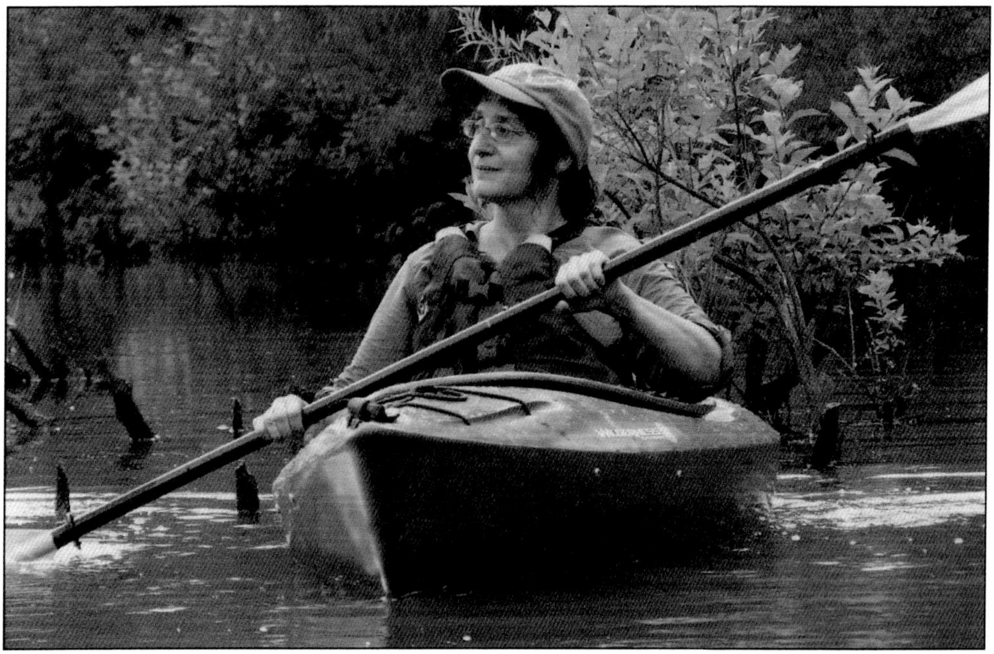

Haw River keeper Elaine Chiosso is kayaking on Jordan Lake in May 2009. Since its founding in 1982, the Haw River Assembly has a solid record of efforts to achieve its mission: to protect and restore the Haw River, its tributaries, and Jordan Lake and to build a community that supports this vision. (Courtesy of Haw River Assembly; photograph by Suzanne Gomolski.)

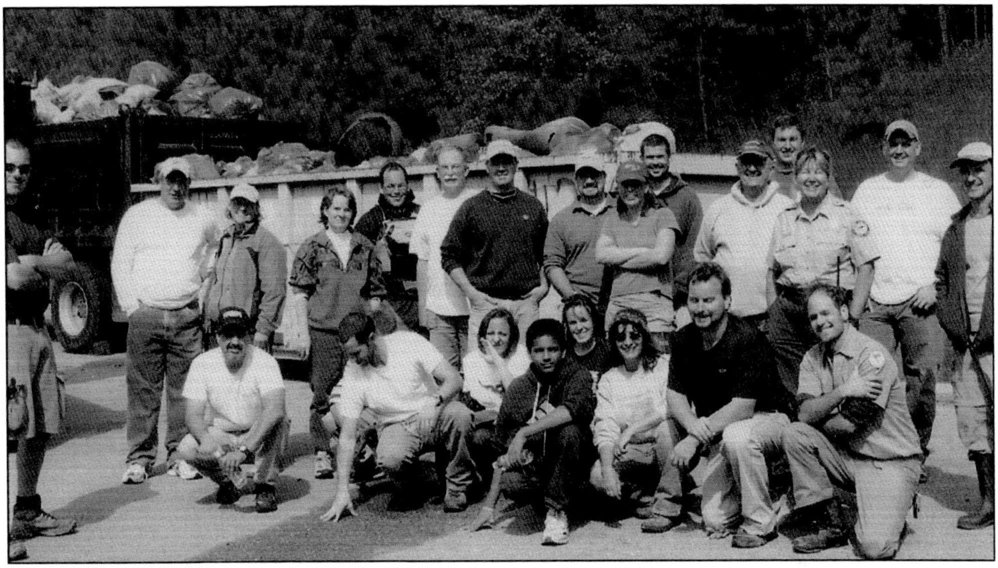

About 70 volunteers picked up 3,500 bags of trash—about 14 tons—from a remote cove on the eastern side of the Haw River arm of Jordan Lake on October 18, 2008. The lead organizer was Tom Colson, an amazing volunteer. The trash filled a dumpster and two dump trucks at the boat docks. The HRA thanked Chatham County and North Carolina State Parks for helping with staff, equipment, and trash removal and Big Sweep for partnering with bags and gloves. Many members from the HRA and local paddling clubs also took part. (Courtesy of Haw River Assembly.)

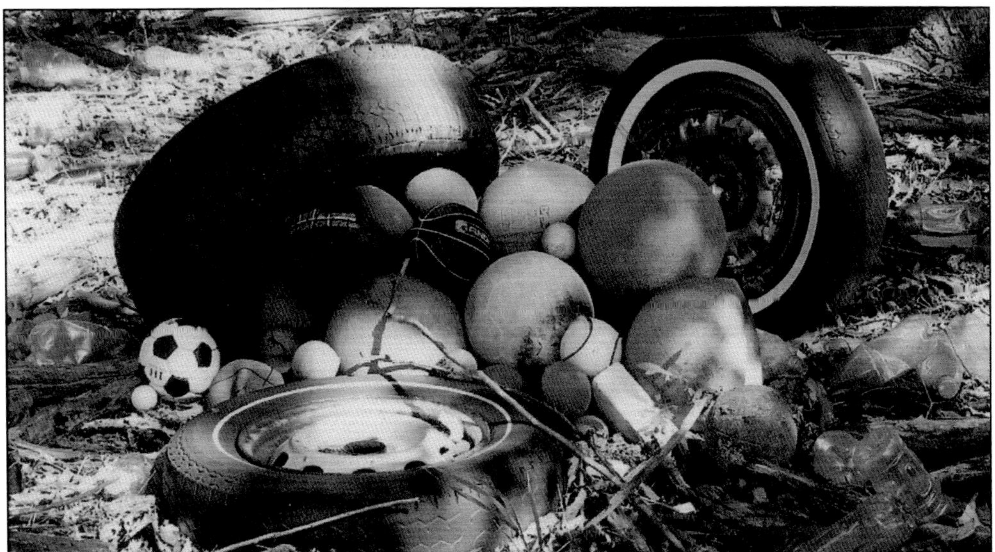

The trash has been coming down the Haw River with storm water since the lake was built from as far away as Greensboro and Burlington. Prevailing winds push the trash into Jordan's coves and deposit it up the hillsides during high waters. A high percentage of the trash is various kinds of soda bottles and cans—a good case for pushing for a "bottle bill" in North Carolina. The Haw River Assembly has been doing clean-ups along the Haw River and Jordan Lake for almost 20 years. It plans to continue this current partnership with Tom Colson, Chatham County, and state and federal agencies to complete the job of removing the terrible amount of trash that is fouling Jordan Lake. (Courtesy of Haw River Assembly.)

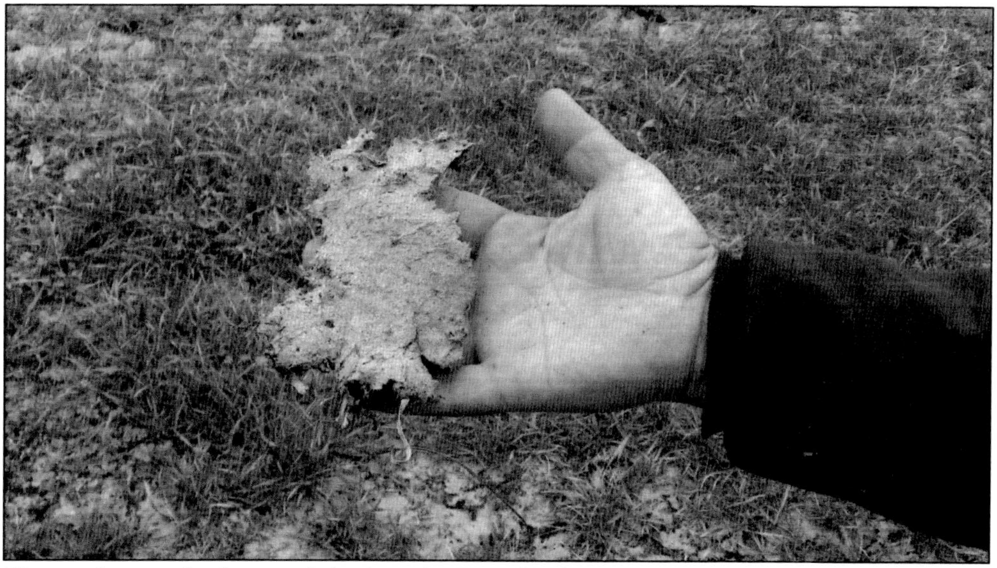

This is a photograph of sewage sludge from the City of Burlington's wastewater treatment plant sprayed onto a farmer's field. Sewage sludge contains thousands of unregulated and untested pollutants not removed in the wastewater treatment process. In addition to posing a risk to food crops and public health, sludge runoff contaminates surface waters used for drinking. The Blue Ridge Environmental Defense League (BREDL) works to educate farmers and consumers about the risks of using sewage sludge as a fertilizer and advocates for stricter regulations concerning the application of sewage sludge as a fertilizer on farmlands. (Courtesy of Sue Dayton, BREDL.)

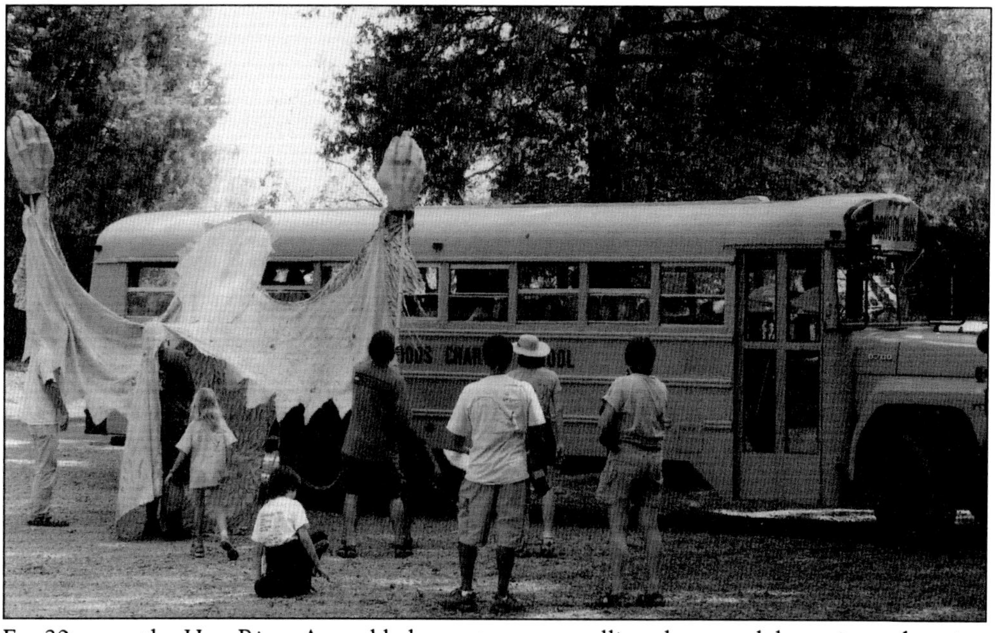

For 20 years, the Haw River Assembly has put on a travelling three-week-long river education program called the Haw River Learning Celebration to help fourth graders learn about their own watershed. These photographs are from the Bynum site with kids from Chatham and Orange County schools. Over 37,000 fourth graders have now taken part in the program with hundreds of volunteers who make it possible. (Courtesy of Elaine Chiosso, Haw River Assembly.)

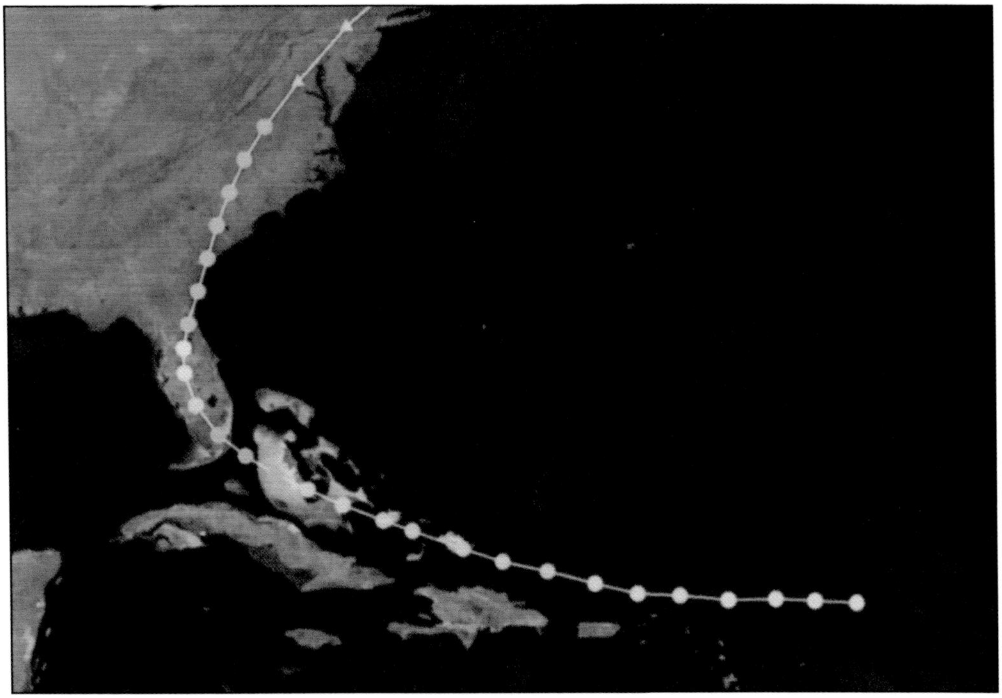

Hurricane No. 9 left a path of destruction. In 1945, the devastating hurricane rocked the Carolinas and hovered over the New Hope River Valley, severely flooding and incapacitating the area. This storm was one of the last to hit the region before hurricanes were properly named in the 1950s. The impact of Hurricane No. 9 had significantly increased government interest in protecting the area, and Congress directed the U.S. Army Corps of Engineers to undertake a comprehensive study of water resource needs. (Author's collection.)

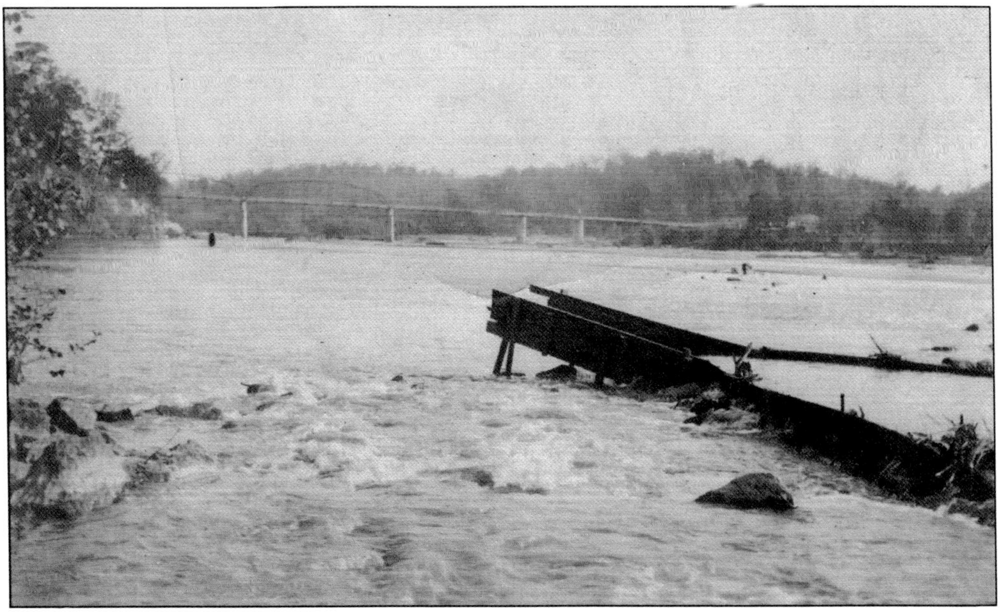

This is a photograph taken in the New Hope River Valley by the Jones family in 1945 of the flood caused by remnants of Hurricane No. 9. (Courtesy of Joyce Jones Cotten.)

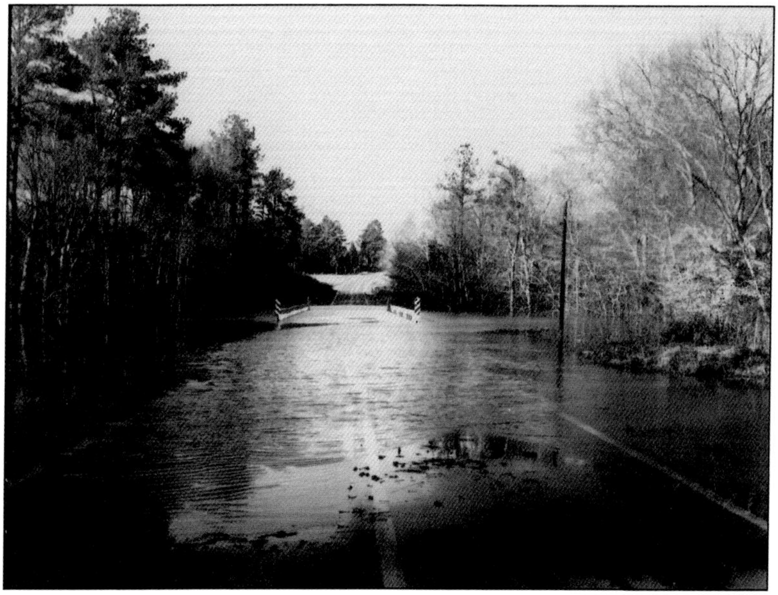

This is a typical flooding scenario after normal rainfalls in the New Hope Valley area. This photograph was taken at the intersection of SR 1008 and White Oak Creek on December 17, 1972. (Courtesy of U.S. Army Corps of Engineers.)

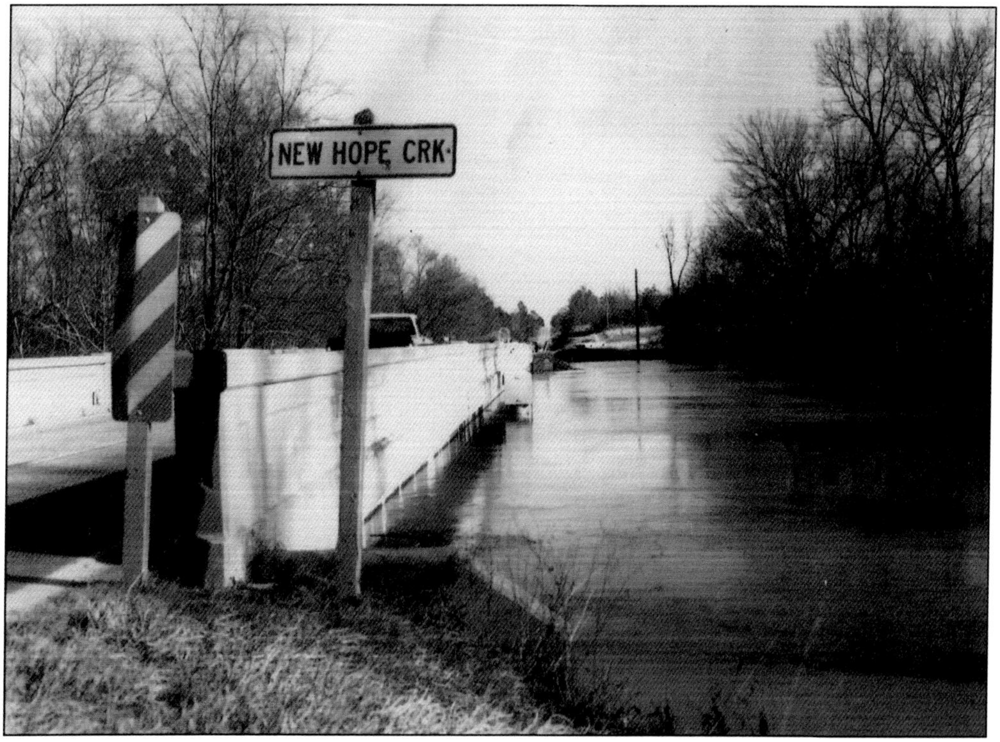

The New Hope Creek rises to flood levels after a storm on December 17, 1972. This photograph was taken looking east at Highway 64. The highway was relocated during the Jordan Lake Project. (Courtesy of U.S. Army Corps of Engineers.)

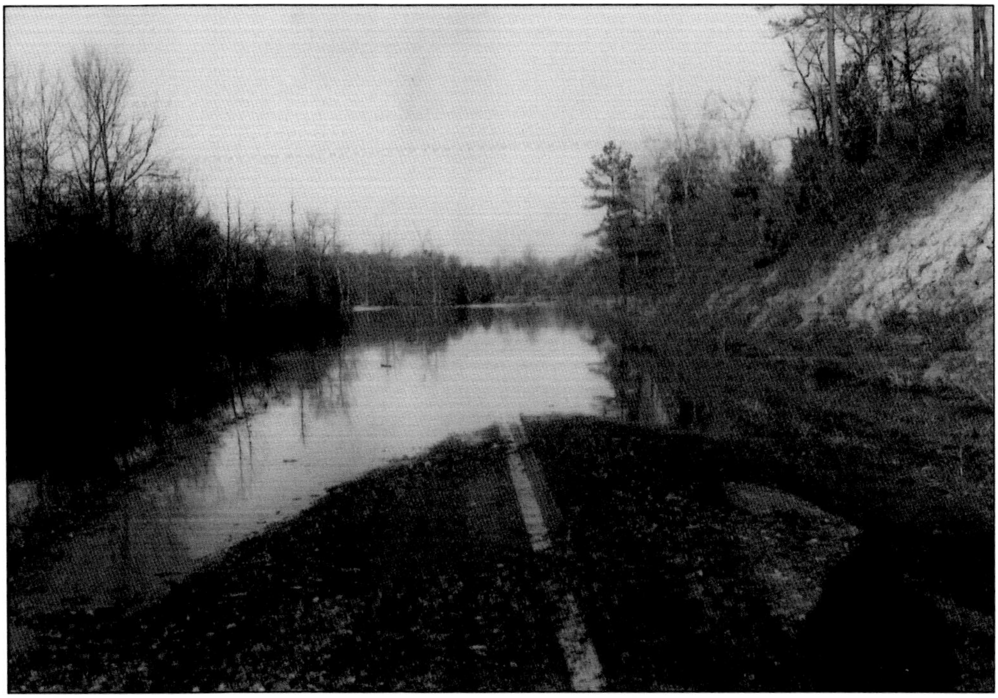

Providence Church Road is flooded after a storm on December 17, 1972. This is just another photograph of many showing how easily this area in Chatham County, North Carolina, would flood after normal storms. Flood prevention is one of the main goals of the Jordan Dam. (Courtesy of U.S. Army Corps of Engineers.)

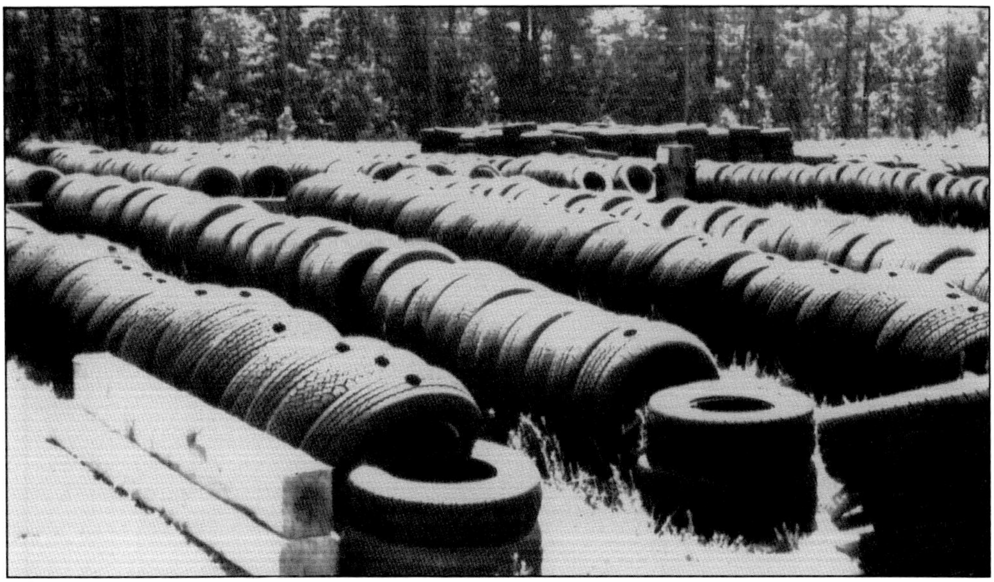

The U.S. Army Corps of Engineers drilled holes into hundreds of tires and anchored them to the bottom of Jordan Lake to benefit natural habitat. Many have tried to claim that tires found at Jordan Lake were those from this effort, but the tires that floated down the river or were illegally dumped had rims in them and did not have the punched hole markings for the habitat. Not a single tire from this effort has ever surfaced at the lake. (Courtesy of U.S. Army Corps of Engineers.)

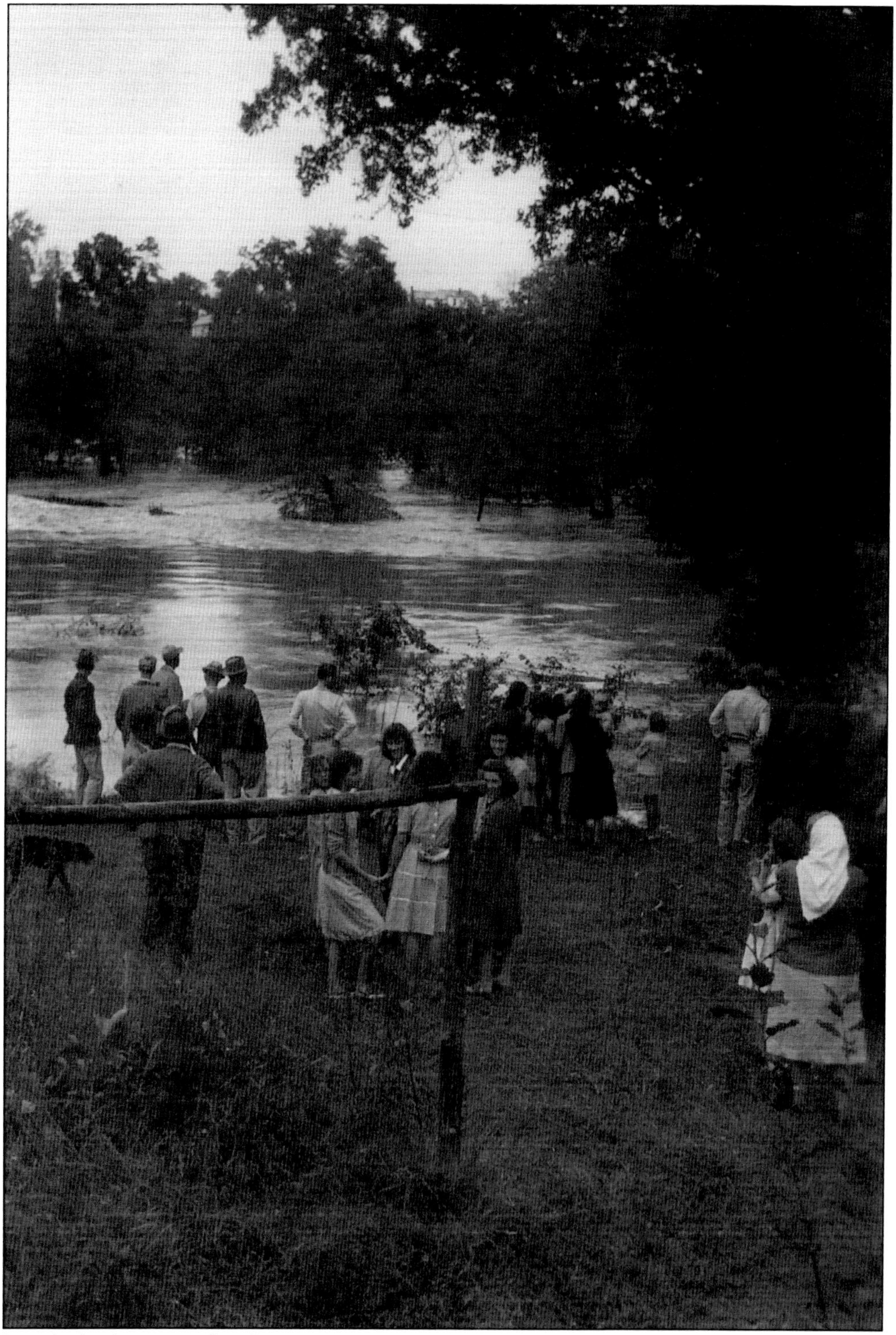

Locals look on as floodwaters rise in September 1945. (Courtesy of Crayton and Frances Hardin.)

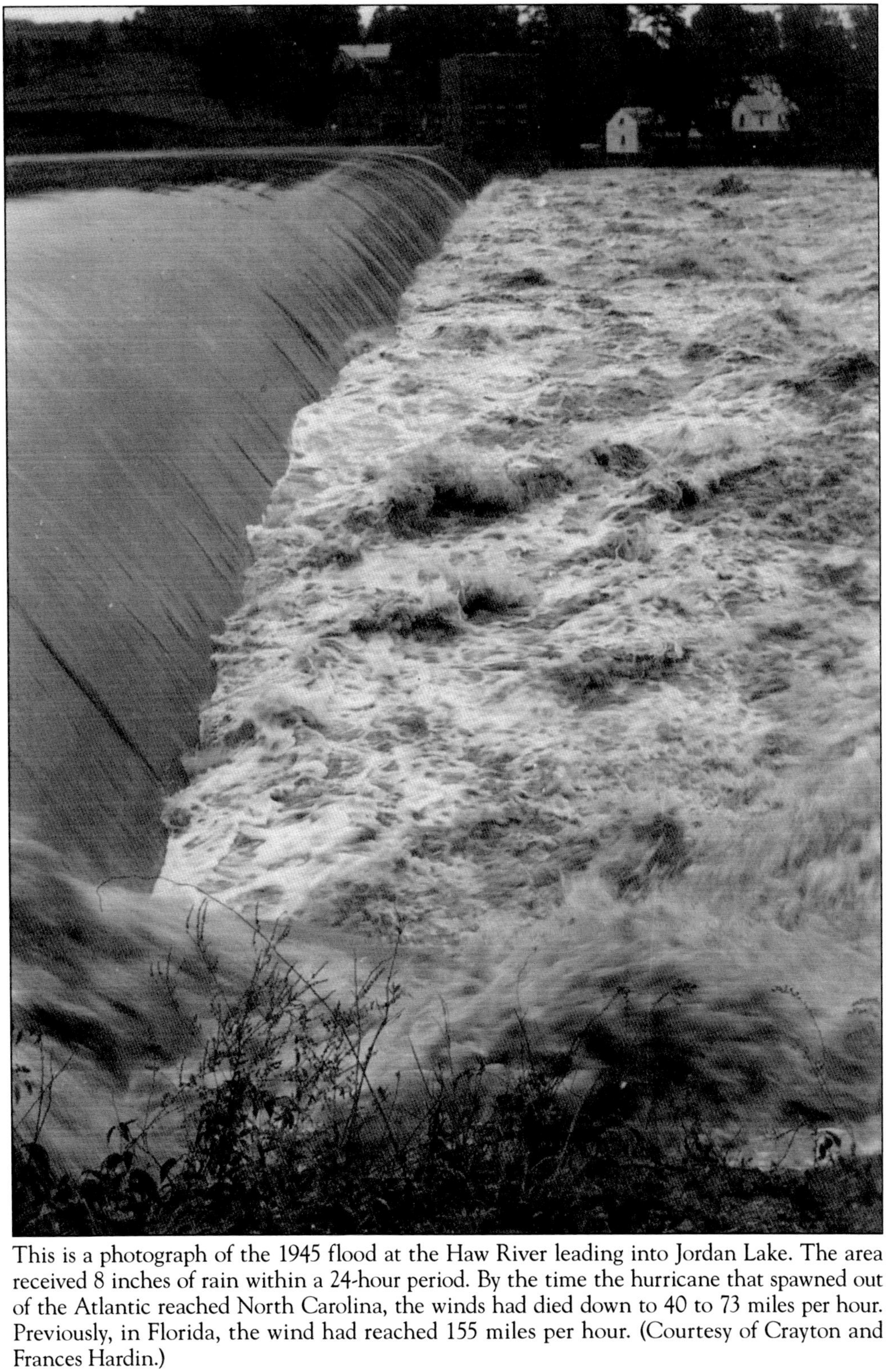

This is a photograph of the 1945 flood at the Haw River leading into Jordan Lake. The area received 8 inches of rain within a 24-hour period. By the time the hurricane that spawned out of the Atlantic reached North Carolina, the winds had died down to 40 to 73 miles per hour. Previously, in Florida, the wind had reached 155 miles per hour. (Courtesy of Crayton and Frances Hardin.)

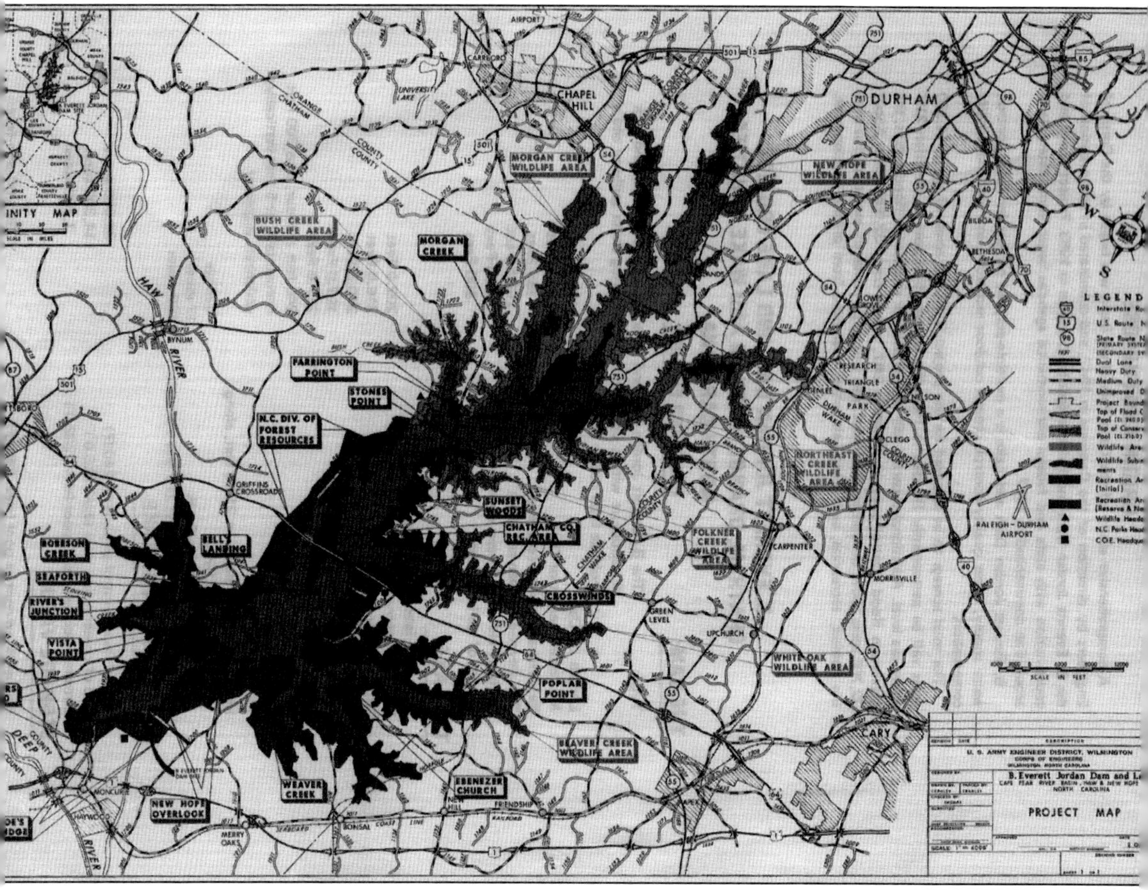

This map of Jordan Lake from 1978, a few years before the lake was open to the public, shows the recreation areas planned for the future at Jordan Lake. (Courtesy of U.S. Army Corps of Engineers.)

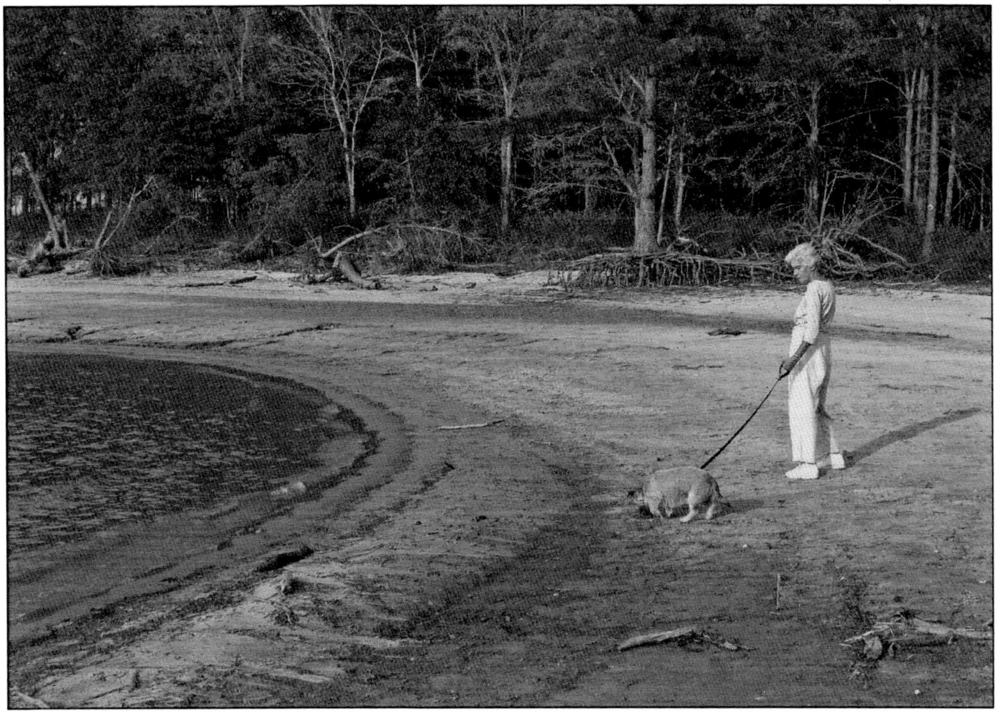

Bunny Shillito and her dog, Cricket, are on a beach at Jordan Lake during the 2006 drought. The drought was so severe that water restrictions in some areas lasted more than a year. The photographer is retired neurosurgeon Dr. John Shillito, who now photographs stories for the local Chatham County newspaper. (Courtesy of John and Bunny Shillito.)

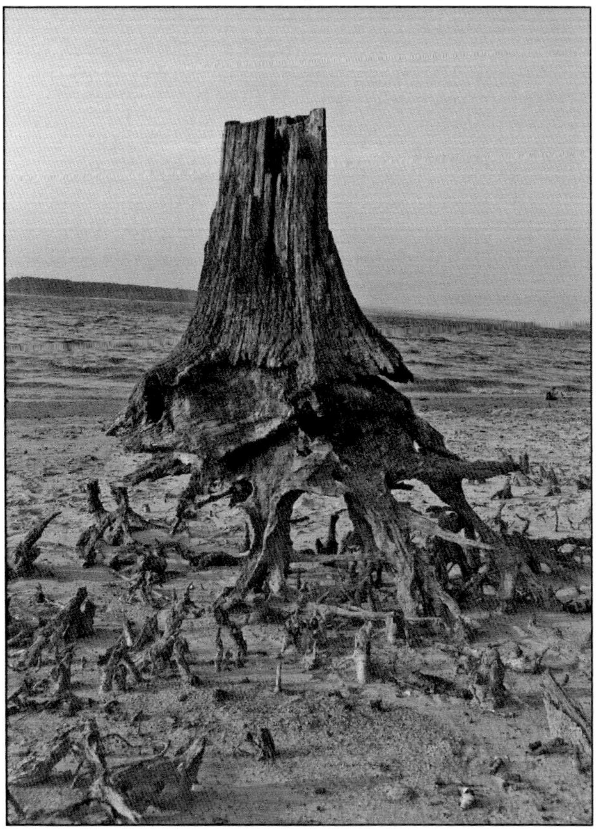

This photograph was taken during the 2006–2007 drought at Jordan Lake. Normally this tree stump and its roots would be completely covered by water. (Courtesy of John and Bunny Shillito.)

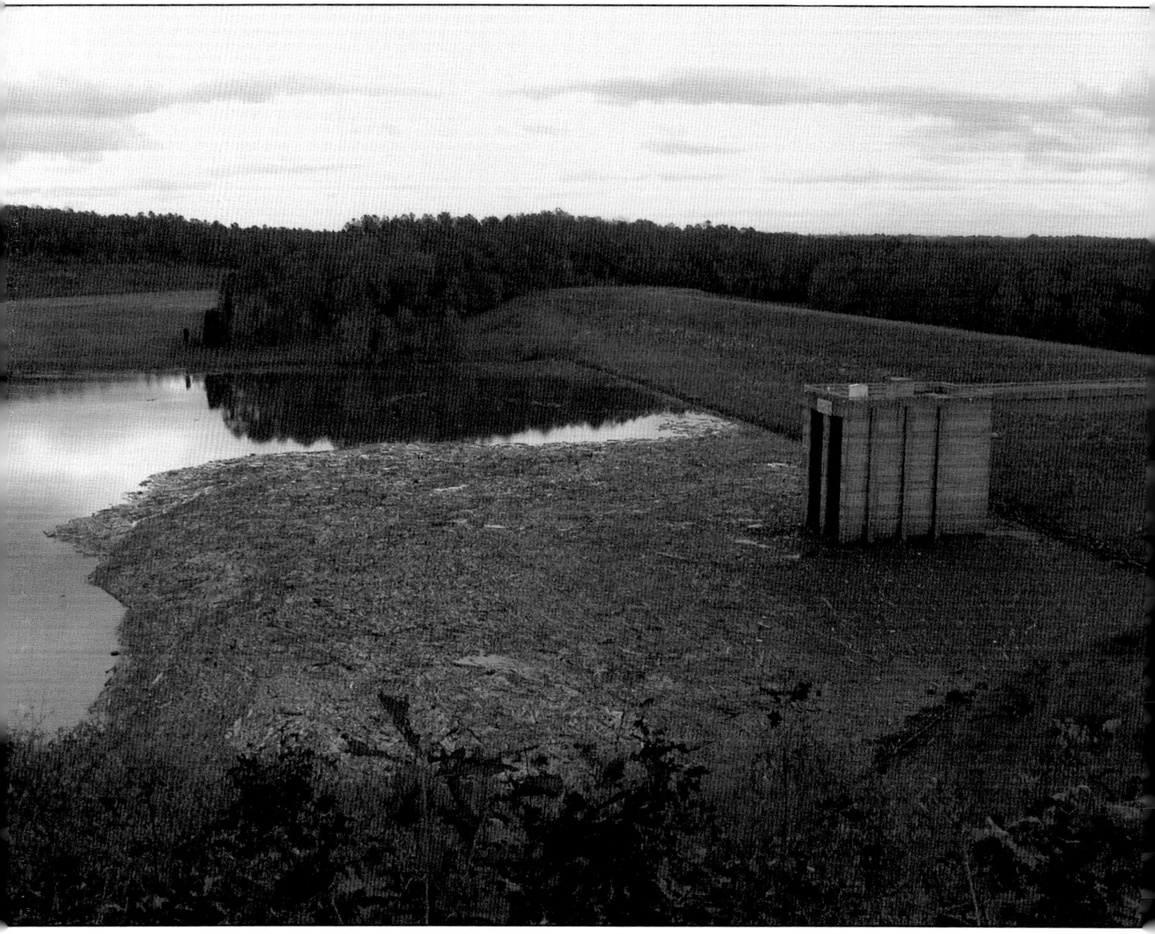

Remnants of Hurricane Ida in November 2009 caused severe amounts of debris to float downstream and in front of the Jordan Lake Dam. Some of the debris included footballs, basketballs, volleyballs, and even a rain barrel! It is very dangerous to go speedboating after a significant storm. As the debris breaks away from the tower and floats back into the lake, area boaters need to take extra care to watch for the unexpected in the water. Eventually this debris will make its way to the shores of the lake, and future cleanup efforts will be underway. Volunteers are always welcome. Please contact the U.S. Army Corps of Engineers Visitor Assistance Center for volunteer information. (Author's collection.)

Seven

The Story of Lost Pea Ridge

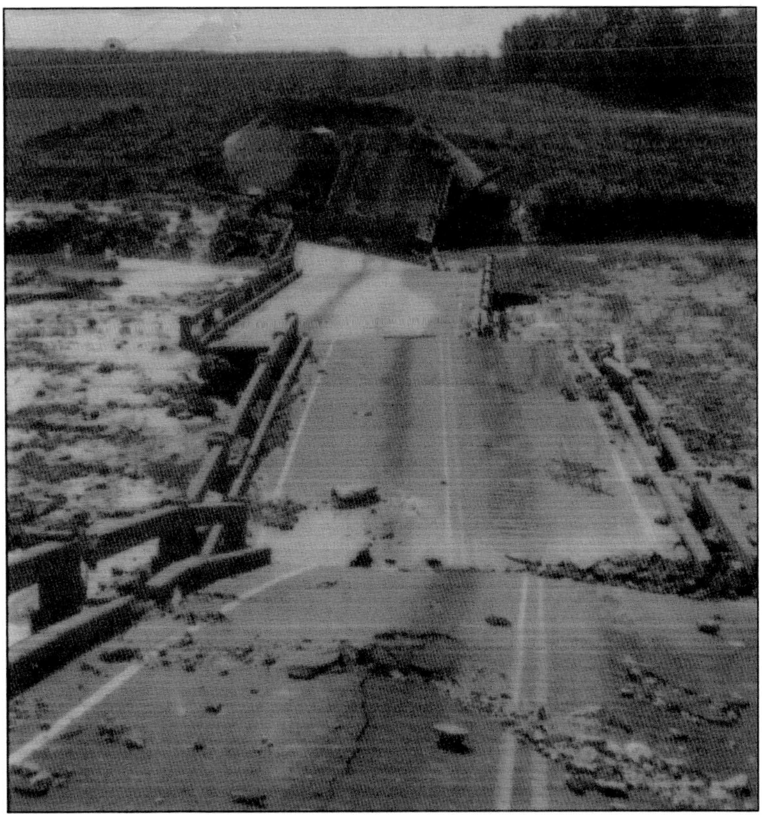

This photograph was taken on October 9, 1979, showing the end result of the demolition of the Pea Ridge concrete bridge. (Courtesy of U.S. Army Corps of Engineers.)

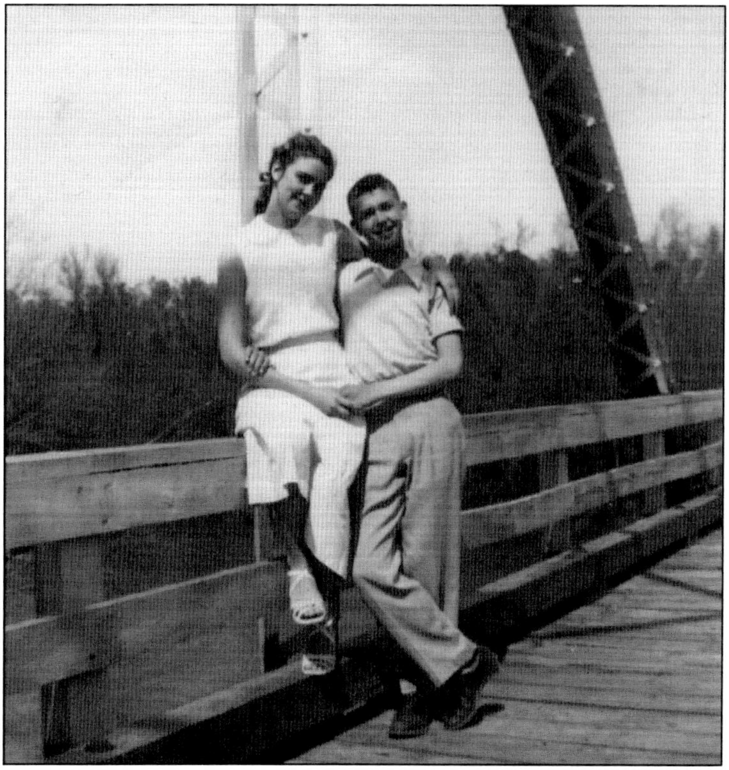

Pictured here are Patsy Jones (Reynolds) and her cousin John Lewis on the Haw River Bridge in 1951. (Courtesy of Joyce Jones Cotten.)

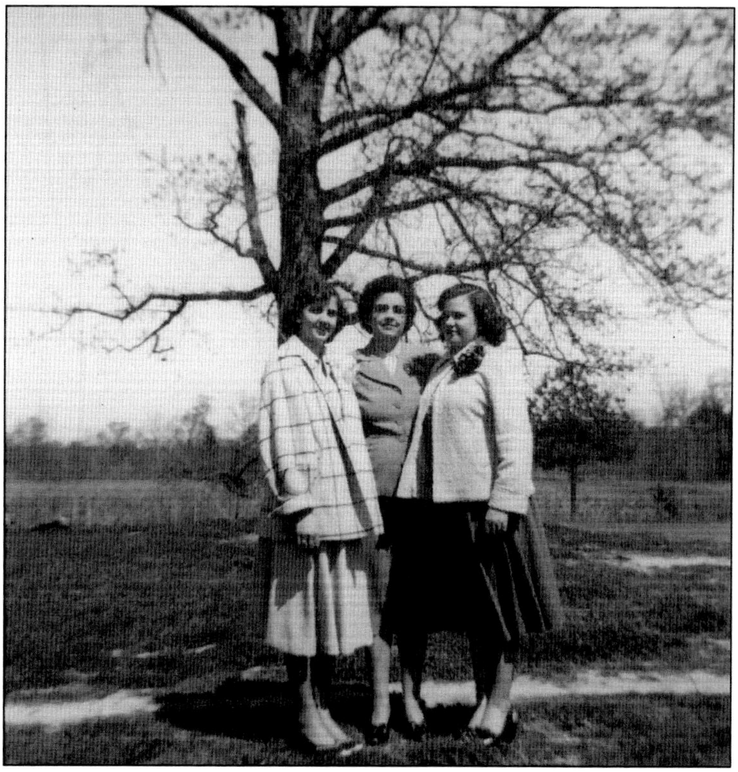

Pictures were a rarity and were only taken when people were dressed in their Sunday best. This photograph was taken on Easter Sunday; the women are all wearing corsages, which was typical for that time. Pictured here are, from left to right, Patsy Jones (Reynolds), Pansy Jones, and Marie Jones (Stone) in the front yard at the Jones homestead in 1952. (Courtesy of Joyce Jones Cotten.)

Pictured are Betty Jones (Livingston) and Marvin Hearn at New Hope Bridge. This bridge was demolished and the road was relocated about a quarter-mile south around 1950. The New Hope Bridge was about 35 feet above the New Hope Creek. After a big rain, the water would rise to the bridge level. (Courtesy of Joyce Jones Cotten.)

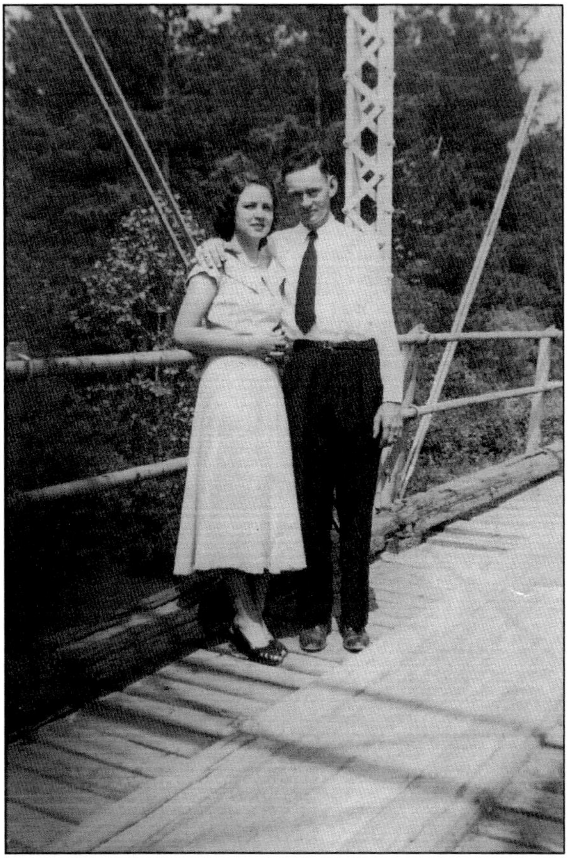

The Jones family had many cousins. Patsy and Sam had 18 siblings between them. Pictured here are, from left to right, (first row) Betty Jones (Livingston) and Joyce Jones (Cotten); (second row) cousin Patricia Yates (Tunstall), Marie Jones (Stone), Patsy Jones (Reynolds), and cousin Jo Ann Cass (Dixon) on the Jones farm in 1948. (Courtesy of Joyce Jones Cotten.)

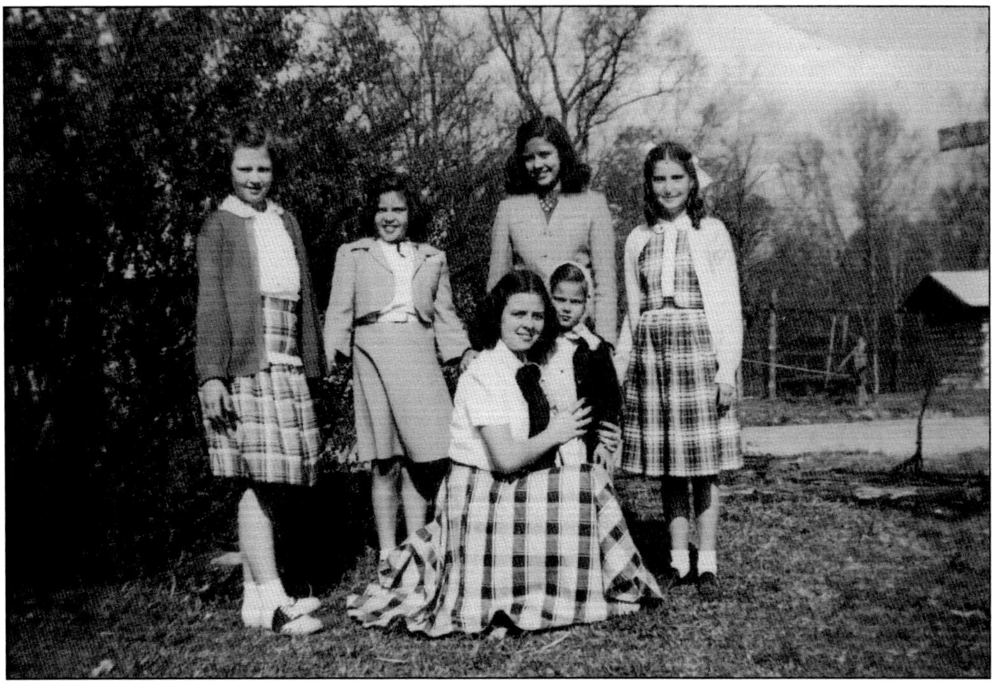

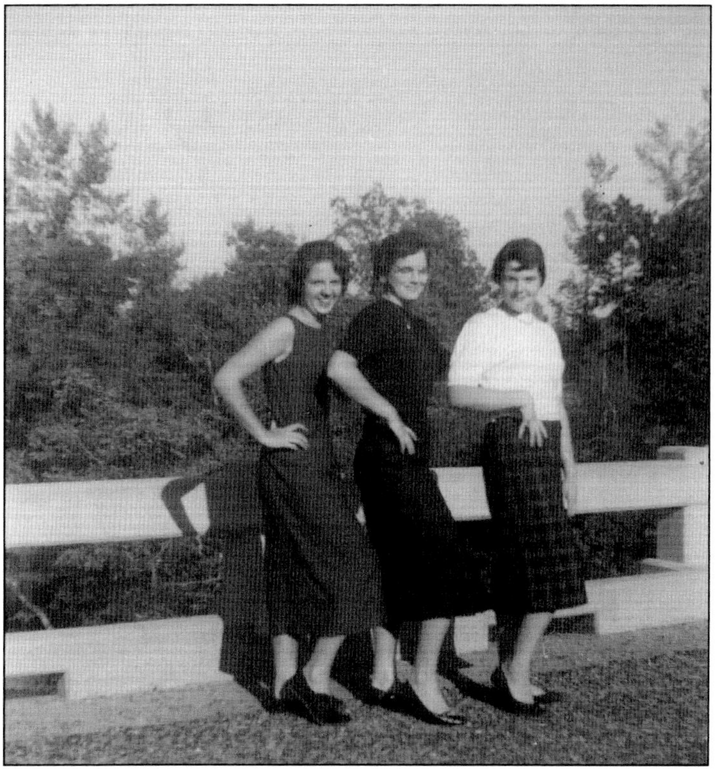

Spending a typical Sunday afternoon at the Pea Ridge Bridge are, from left to right, Joyce Jones (Cotten), Betty Roberson (Whitt), and Joyce Ashe (Thrift). Per Joyce, it was something for the locals to do on a Sunday afternoon. They would go to church, come home and help their mother with lunch, wash the dishes, and then walk to the bridge. It was a tradition and a favorite pastime. They enjoyed walking, talking, and laughing until it was time to go home. (Courtesy of Joyce Jones Cotten.)

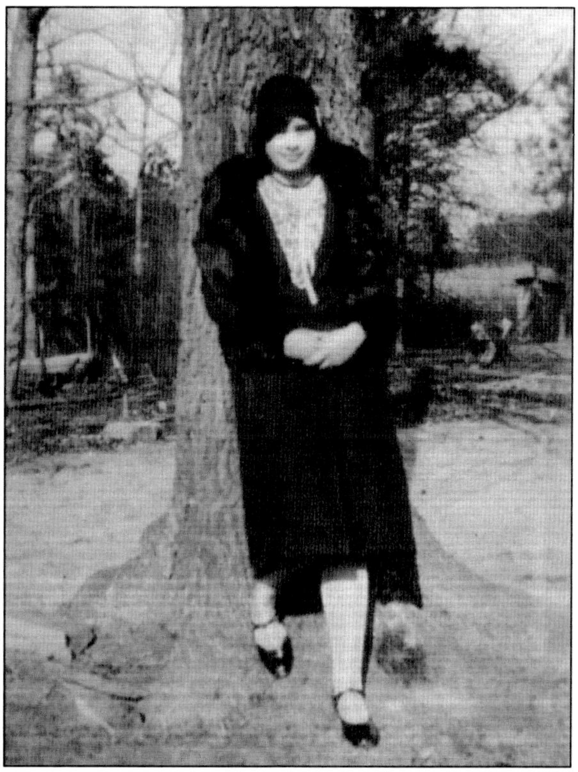

Note the absence of grass in the yard. A yard with grass to mow was discouraged, since older hand mowers, which were difficult to push, were the only means of cutting the grass. Pansy Jones of the Pea Ridge community is pictured in 1927, the year after she was married. Her outfit was very typical of the time period. Her coat was made with real animal fur. (Courtesy of Joyce Jones Cotten.)

The location is the Mitchell farm in the Pea Ridge community. Bob Mitchell is on his knees with John Lewis, a cousin to the Jones family, on his shoulders. An unidentified Mitchell family friend is on the right. (Courtesy of Joyce Jones Cotten.)

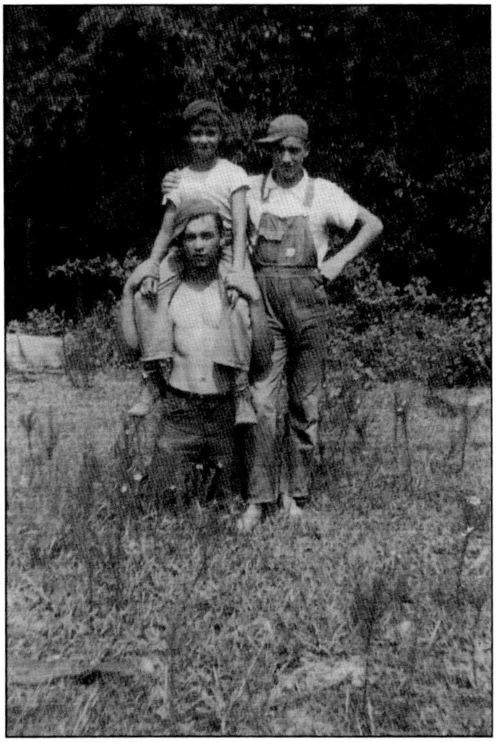

Stanley Jones is displaying results of a good coon hunt in Pea Ridge in 1957. Since Stanley was the only boy in the family, he spent a lot of time learning to hunt with his father. Stanley's sister Joyce proved that she could keep up with her brother and father and was sometimes invited to join the duo. When Stanley's father, Sam Jones, was no longer able to roam the woods at night hunting, he participated in coon dog shows and would drive all over the state to participate. His dogs would often win trophies, which cover an entire wall. Sam's dogs won state champion several times, and hunters would come from far away to trade or buy coon dogs from him. (Courtesy of Joyce Jones Cotten.)

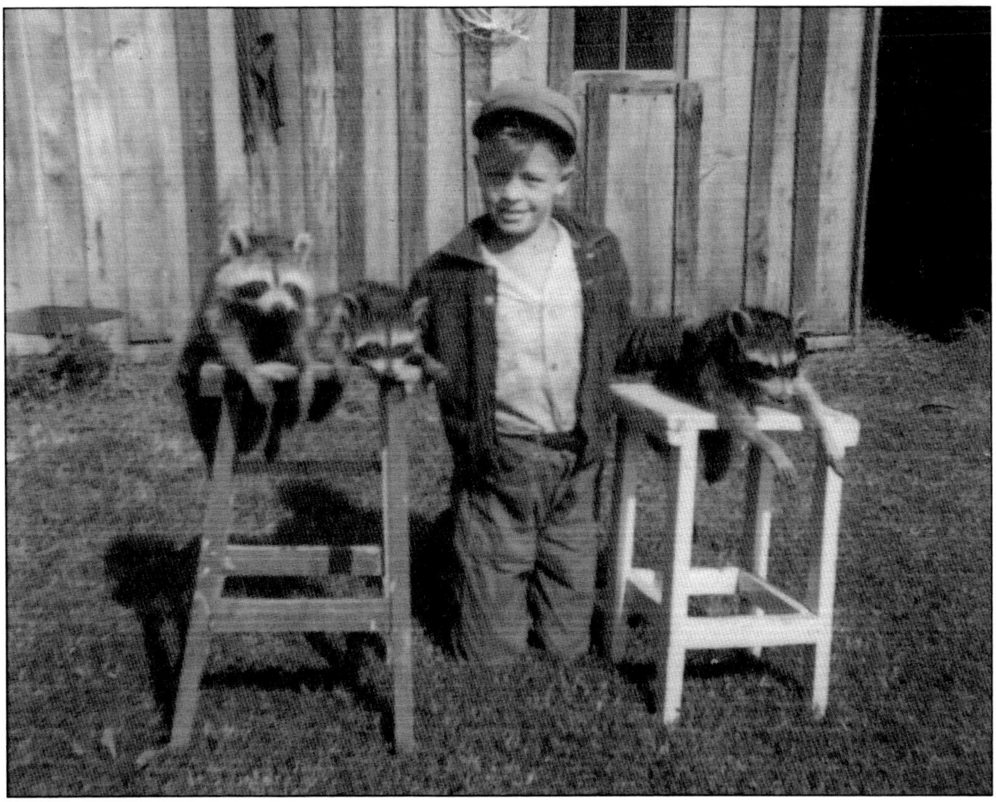

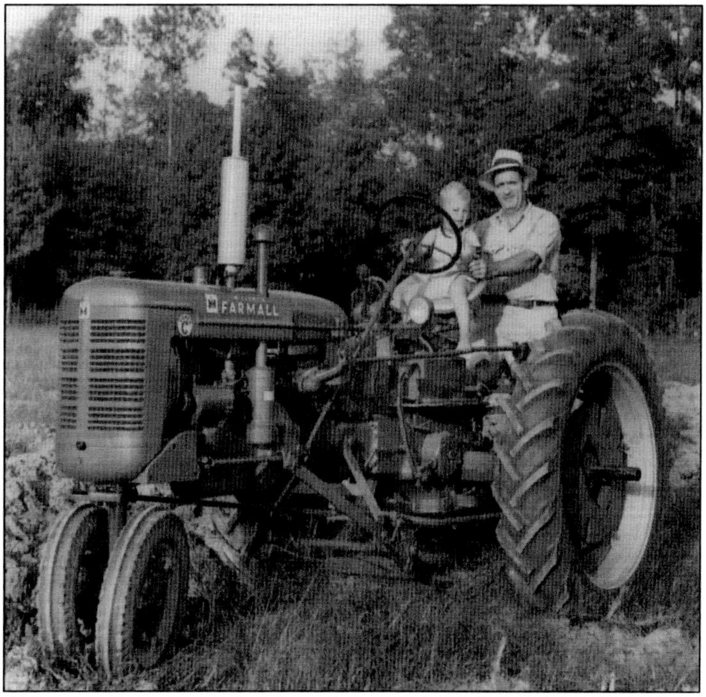

Sam Jones and his son, Stanley, are on his first tractor in 1950. Tractors in those days had separate left and right brakes, and upon getting to the end of the field and needing to turn around, Sam pressed the incorrect brake pedal, which threw the tractor up against a tree. Sam shouted, "whoa, whoa," as if he were talking to his mules instead of hitting the brakes. The tractor bounced up against the tree for several seconds before he realized he needed to press the other brake. (Courtesy of Joyce Jones Cotten.)

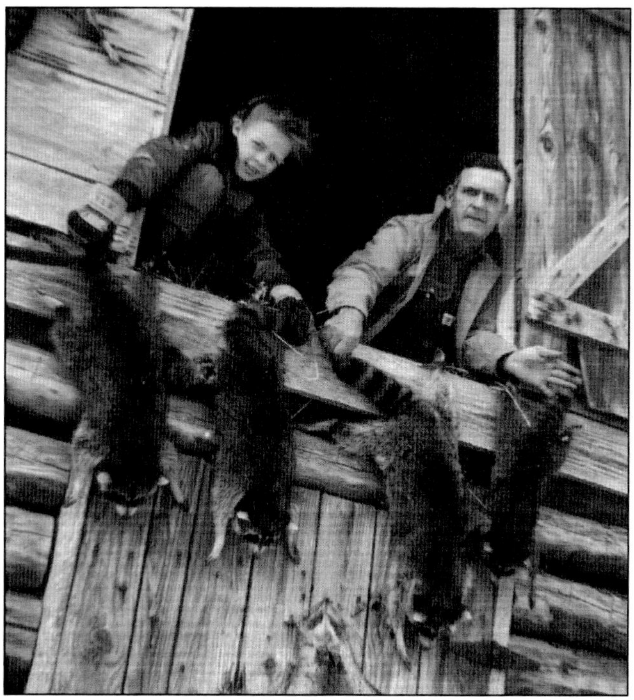

This is Stanley Jones (left) and his father, Sam Jones, in January 1959. Sam was a big coon hunter and was well-known for his hunting skills. He had a reputation for training hunting dogs, and men would travel from far away to hunt with him. Sam was proud of his hunting skills and loved to show the hides on the front of the barn. He would clean them and give the meat to someone in the neighborhood who liked to cook. The front of the barn was very visible from the house, and people were fascinated by all the hides hanging there, especially the hunters. (Courtesy of Joyce Jones Cotten.)

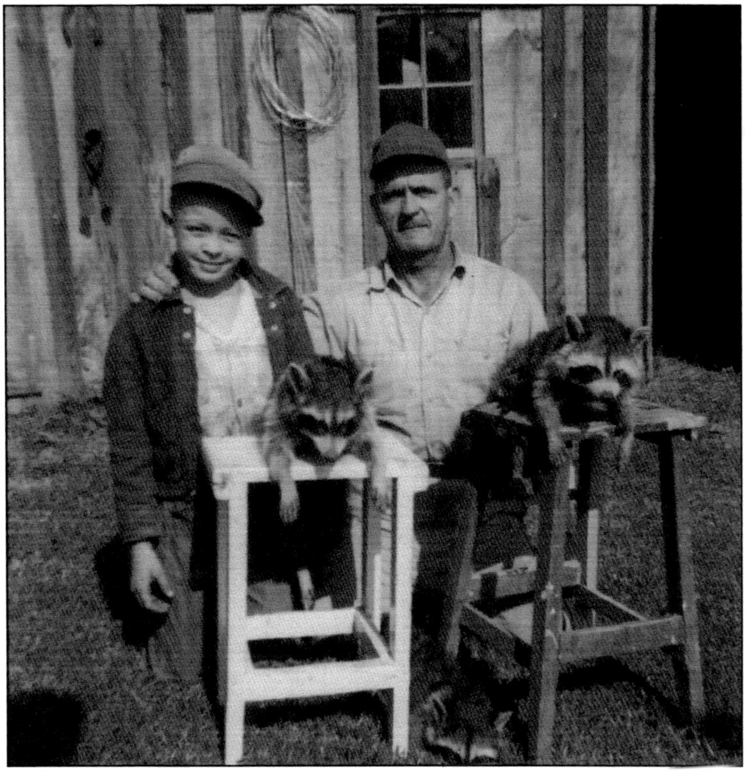

Stanley Jones is on the left with his father, Sam Jones, showcasing their coons. Sam would hang the hides on the front of the barn. Sam was such an avid hunter that he would climb a tree in the dark to flush out coons so the dogs could run them. On one occasion, he fell out of the tree and broke a couple of ribs. This photograph was taken in 1957. (Courtesy of Joyce Jones Cotten.)

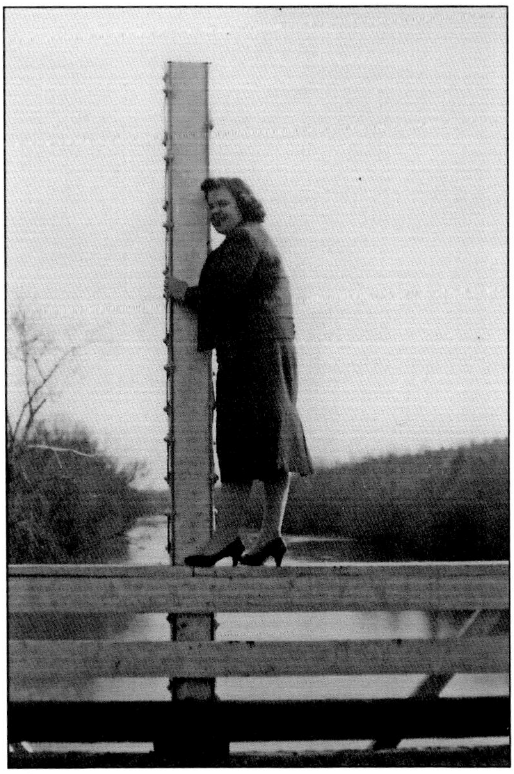

Marie Jones (Stone) is on the Pea Ridge bridge in her heels in 1956. She was quite the adventurous woman. Marie was born in 1937 and loved her family very much. She passed away in 2006 due to illness. The 2009 Pittsboro High School reunion book was dedicated to her. (Courtesy of Joyce Jones Cotten.)

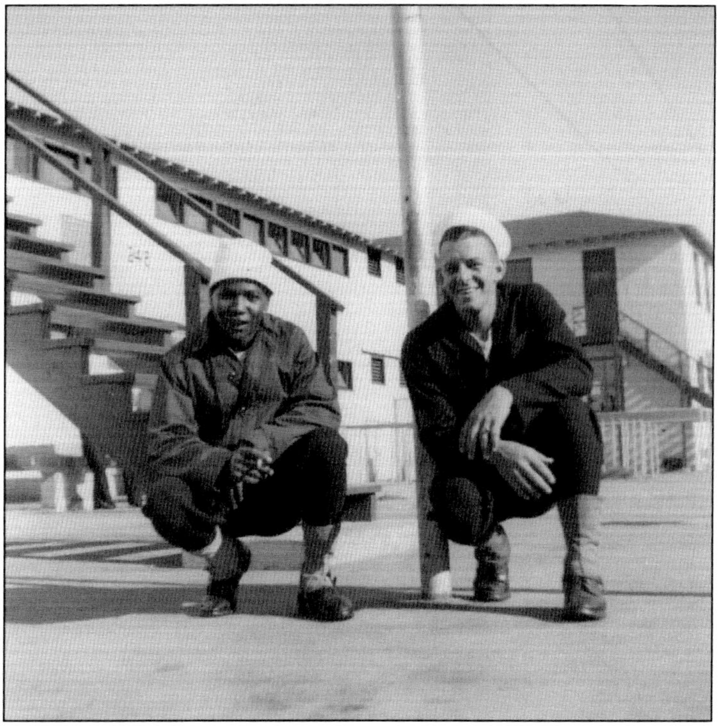

Jimmy Cotten (Joyce Jones's husband) is on the right with his good friend Nathan Green from Alabama at Navy boot camp in San Diego in 1959. (Courtesy of Joyce Jones Cotten.)

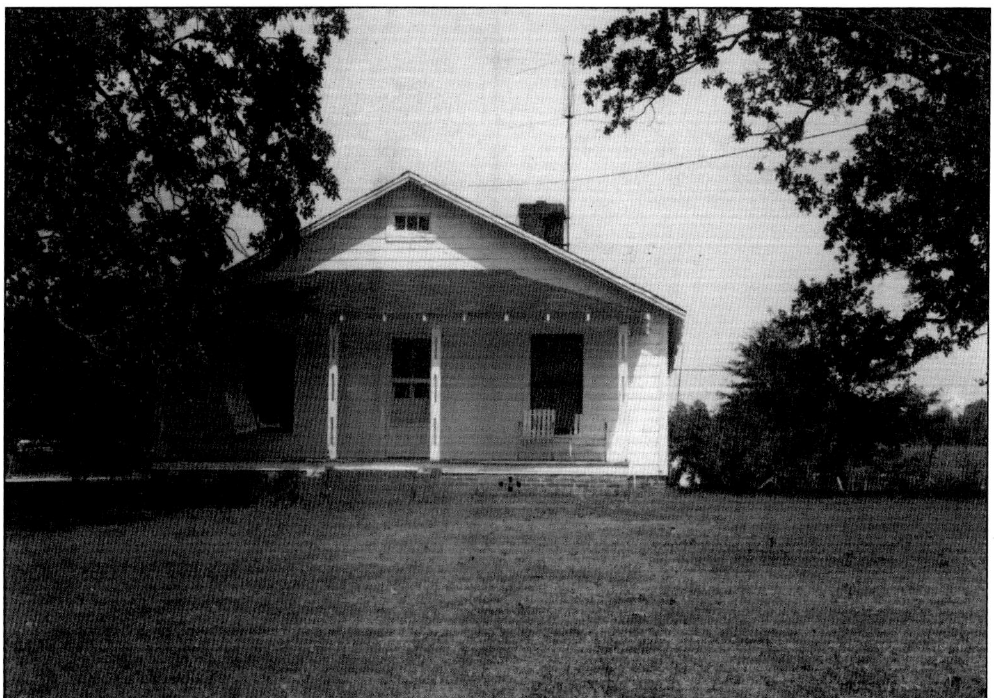

Built in 1942, this is Sam and Pansy Jones's home on Pea Ridge. This home was permanently moved to the Merry Oaks community just south of Jordan Lake. The family lost all of their land (232 acres) due to the construction of Jordan Lake. (Courtesy of Joyce Jones Cotten.)

Joyce Jones Cotten is shown here at the age of six on a swing made with cable at the Jones house. The swing was high off the ground, and when Joyce was little, her sister had to lift her up to get into the swing. When there was not anyone there to help Joyce get into it, she would twist it around. She found it fascinating to watch it unwind. Unfortunately, one day, it went in a different direction that what Joyce thought, and the corner of the seat hit her on the side of her head. It knocked her out, and the next thing Joyce could recall was her mother holding her wanting to know what happened. To this day, Joyce has a small indentation on the left side of her head where the corner of that swing hit her. (Courtesy of Joyce Jones Cotten.)

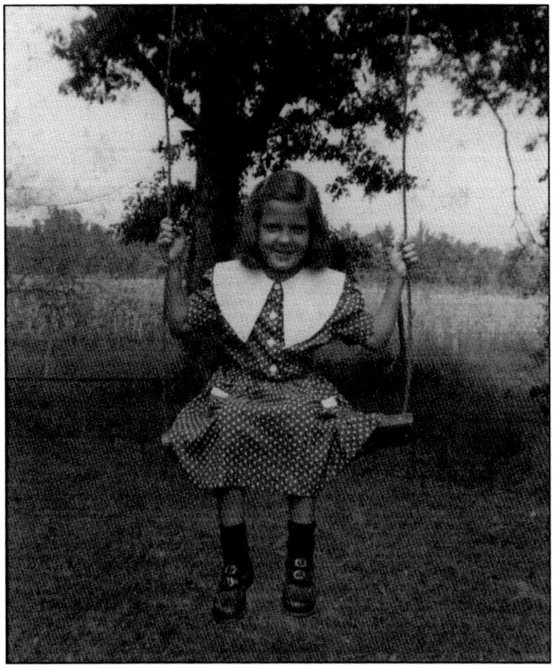

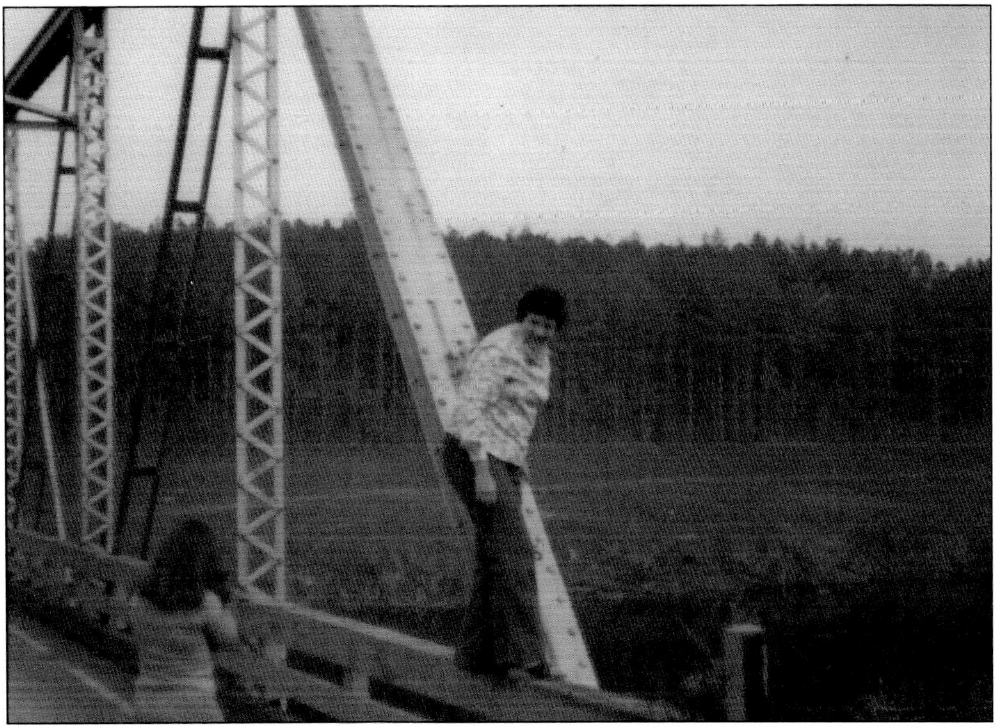

On the Sunday prior to the destruction of the Haw River Bridge, Joyce Jones Cotten, observed by her daughter Kim, climbed on the bridge one more time. Both the New Hope Bridge and the Haw River Bridge were meeting places for a Sunday afternoon stroll for years. It was typical for young people to climb on this bridge and take a picture if a camera was available, which was very rare in those days. (Courtesy of Joyce Jones Cotten.)

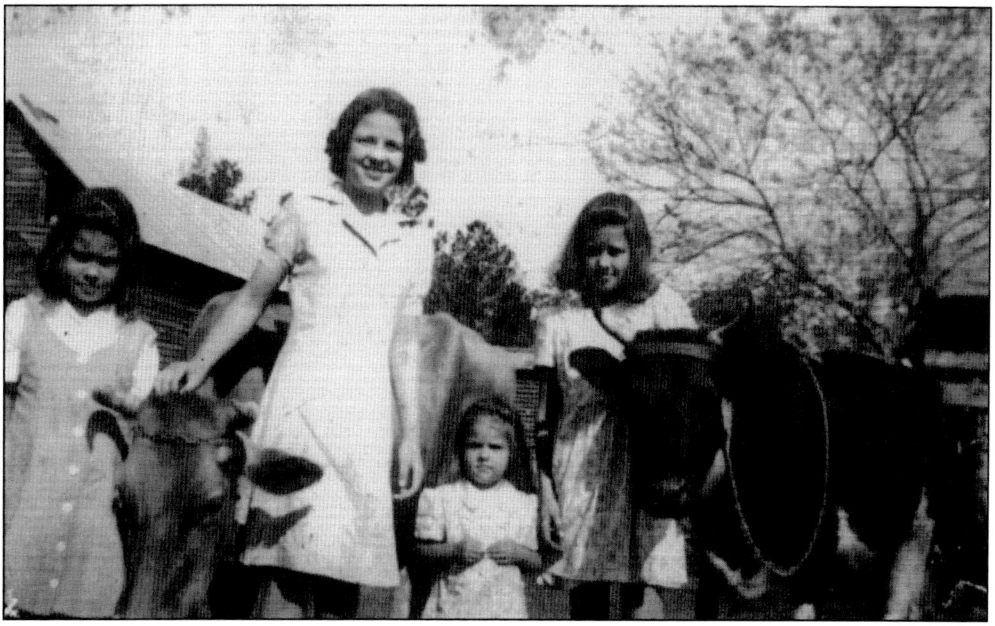

The Jones daughters had this photograph taken with the family milk cows. Traditionally the oldest child milked the cows until he or she left home, and the task was passed on to the next-born child. Joyce Jones Cotten really wanted to share this photograph, as it showed what life was like on the farm in the Pea Ridge community. Joyce and her sisters were very close. (Courtesy of Joyce Jones Cotten.)

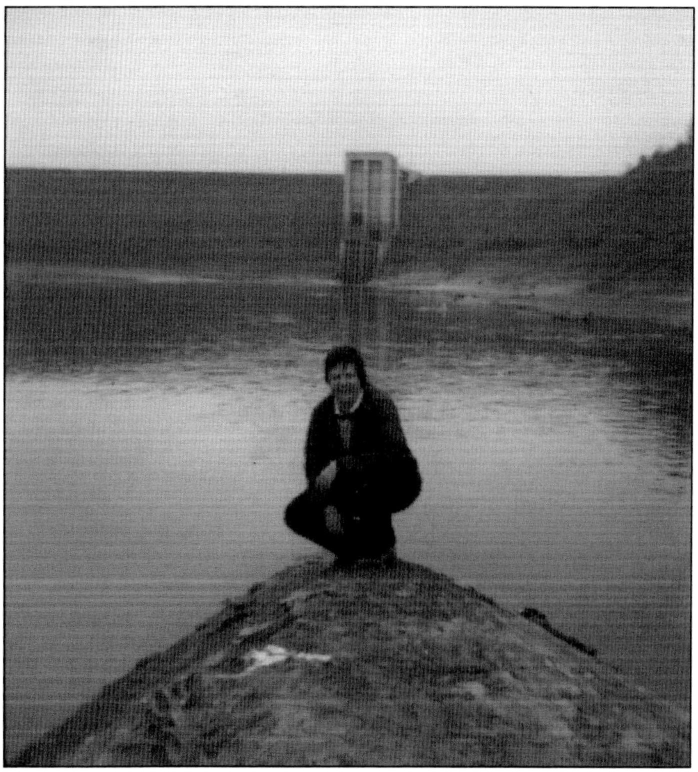

Joyce Jones Cotten is at the junction of the Haw and New Hope Rivers with Jordan Dam in the background. Joyce made her way to this area on her dirt bike in order to take this photograph. The photograph was taken several years before water was allowed to fill the lake due to court proceedings that held up the process. (Courtesy of Joyce Jones Cotten.)

This is the wedding portrait of Marie Jones (Stone) on February 14, 1959. This is her son Scott's favorite photograph of his mother (Marie is now deceased). Scott spends time with his aunt Joyce Jones Cotten, reminiscing about his mother while they enjoy looking through old photographs. (Courtesy of Joyce Jones Cotten.)

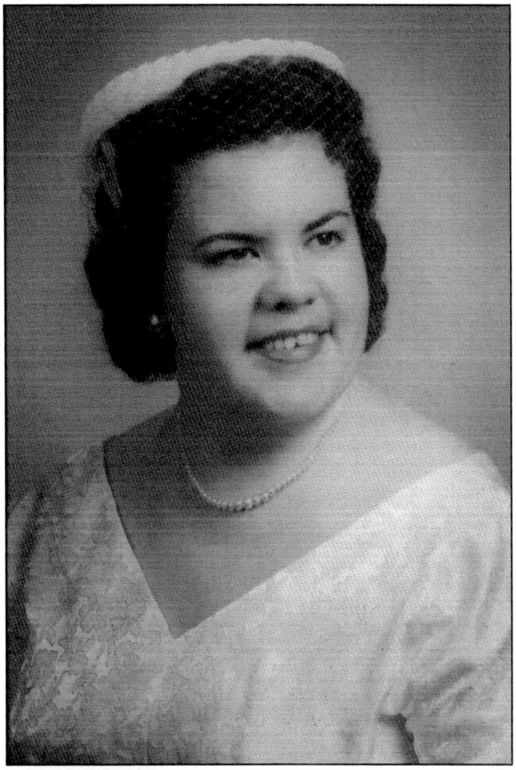

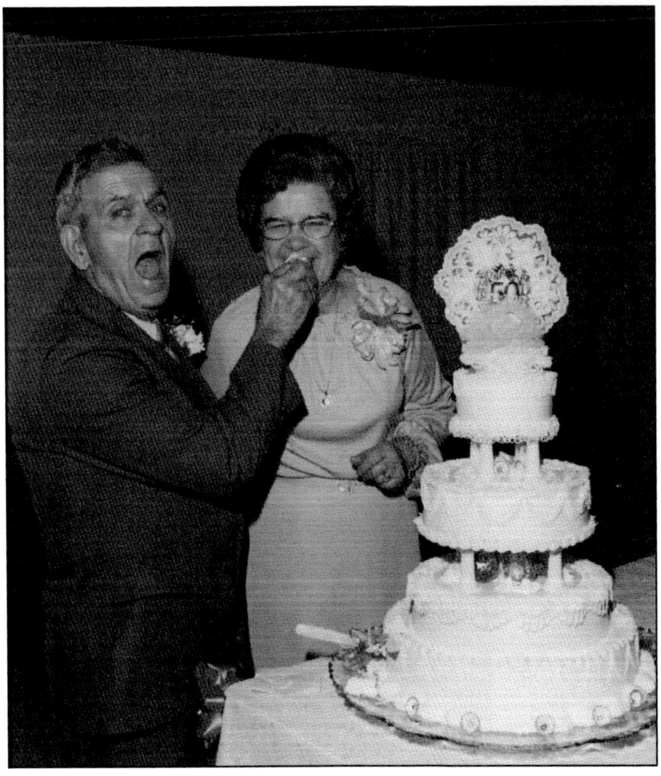

During Sam and Pansy Jones's 50th wedding anniversary party in 1977, Sam starts to feed Pansy cake and instead opens his own mouth. (Courtesy of Joyce Jones Cotten.)

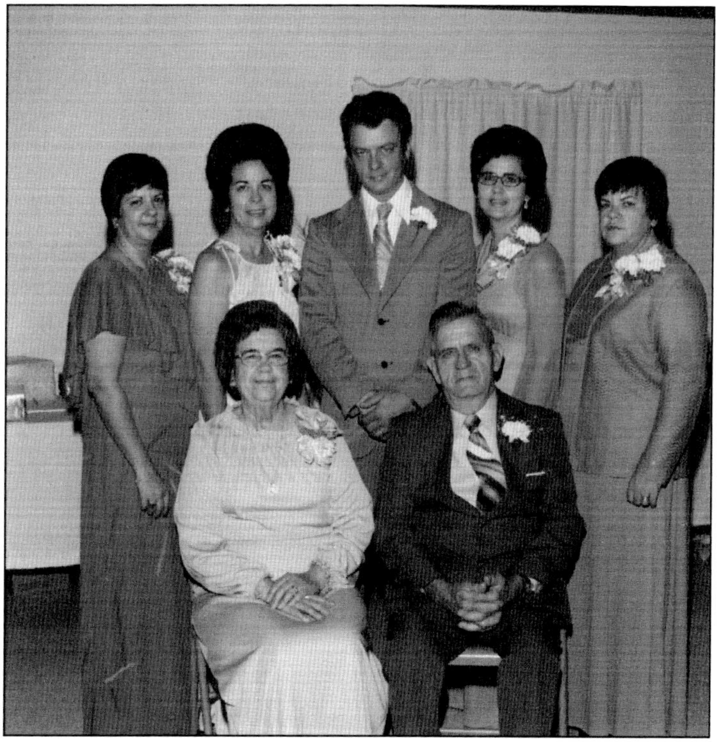

Pictured here are, from left to right, (first row) Pansy and Sam Jones during their 50th wedding anniversary; (second row) Joyce Jones Cotten, Betty Jones (Livingston), Stanley Jones, Patsy Jones (Reynolds), and Marie Jones (Stone). Joyce Jones Cotten recalls that they were all a happy and close-knit family with strong family values that they were taught to use as they grew up and continued to influence their adult lives. (Courtesy of Joyce Jones Cotten.)

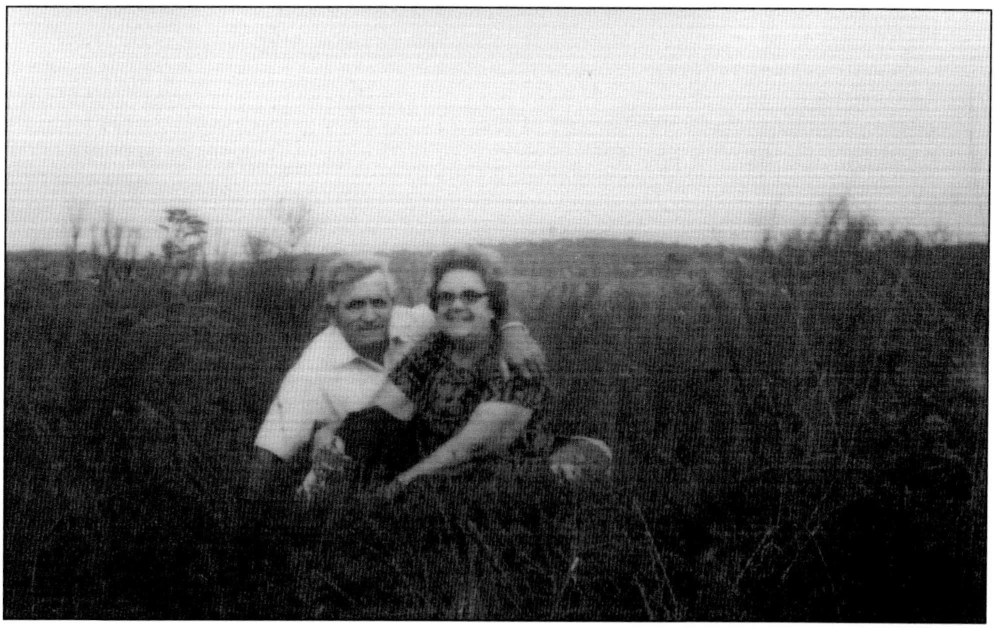

Sam and Pansy Jones are visiting their home for the last time on the Sunday prior to the destruction of the Pea Ridge bridge on September 17, 1978. The loss of their farm and home was very traumatic for them, as it was for all families in the community. They had spent their entire lifetime cultivating this farm and making a living and then suddenly, just a few years before retirement, they lost it all. They would have been 56 and 59 at the time of this picture, taken in 1978. (Courtesy of Joyce Jones Cotten.)

Eight

The Locals Then and Now

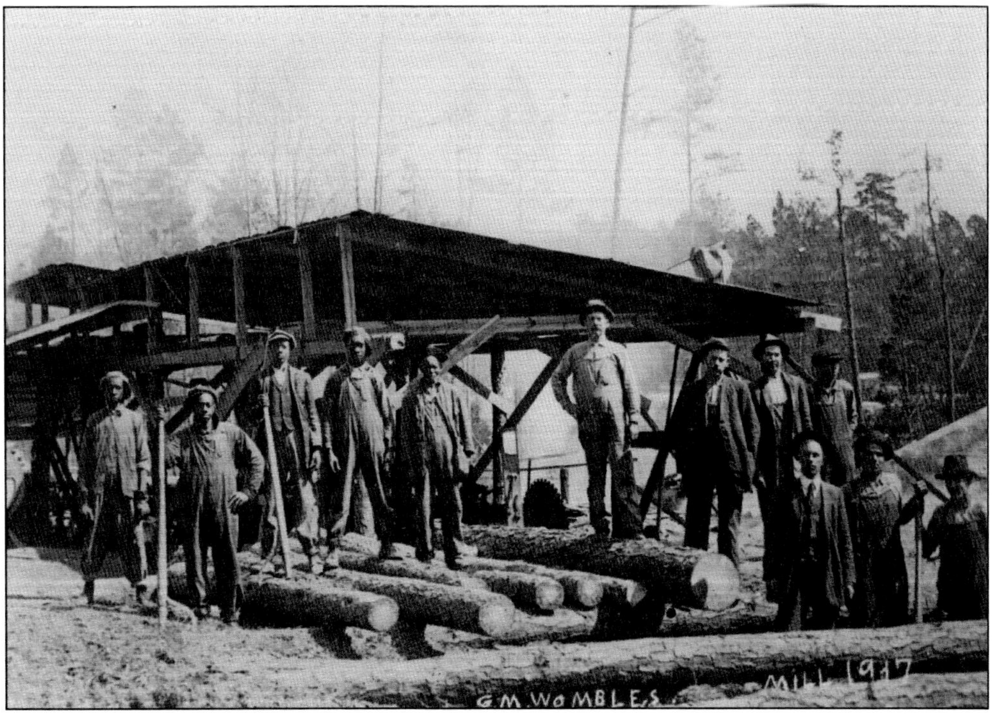

This is George Moody Womble Sr.'s rough lumber mill in 1917. The location was New Hill, North Carolina, next to Jordan Lake. (Courtesy of Joyce Jones Cotten.)

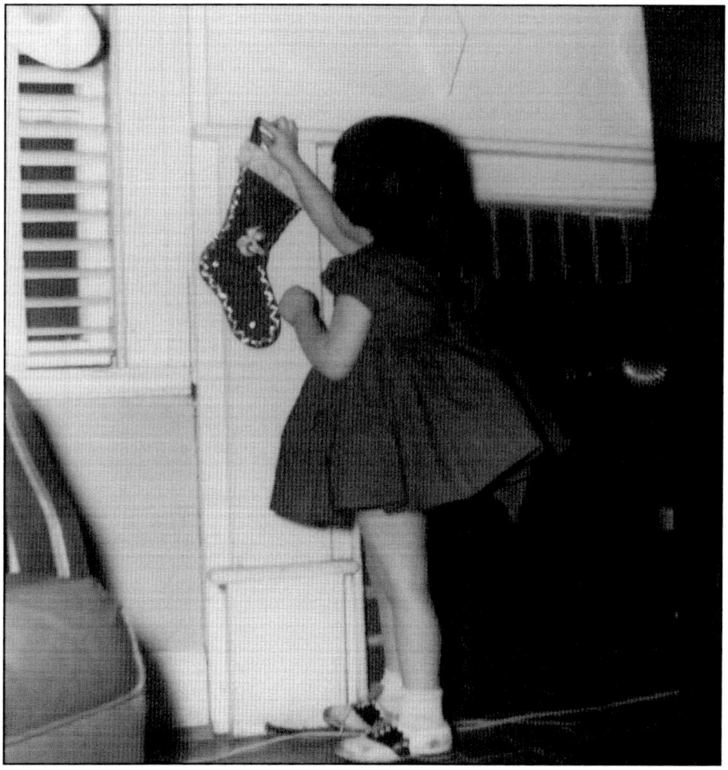

Joan Wilson Frazier's adorable daughter, Renee Krombach, is hanging her stocking in December 1962. Joan and her family love Christmas and have always spent a lot of time with one another over the years and kept up with traditions. (Courtesy of Joan Wilson Frazier.)

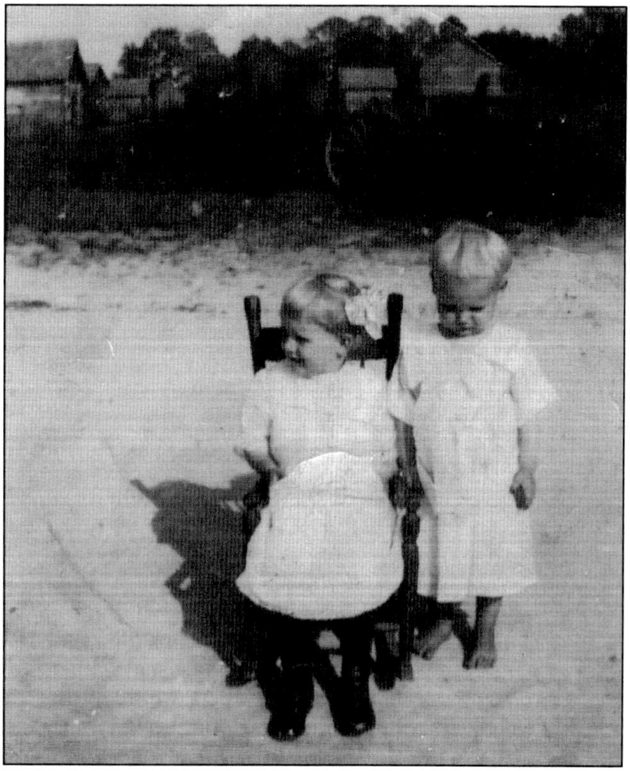

Katie Johnson Wilson is on the left and her brother, Junious Johnson, is on the right in 1920. There were no lawn mowers back then, so they discouraged grass, which is why this area appears so plain. (Courtesy of Joan Wilson Frazier.)

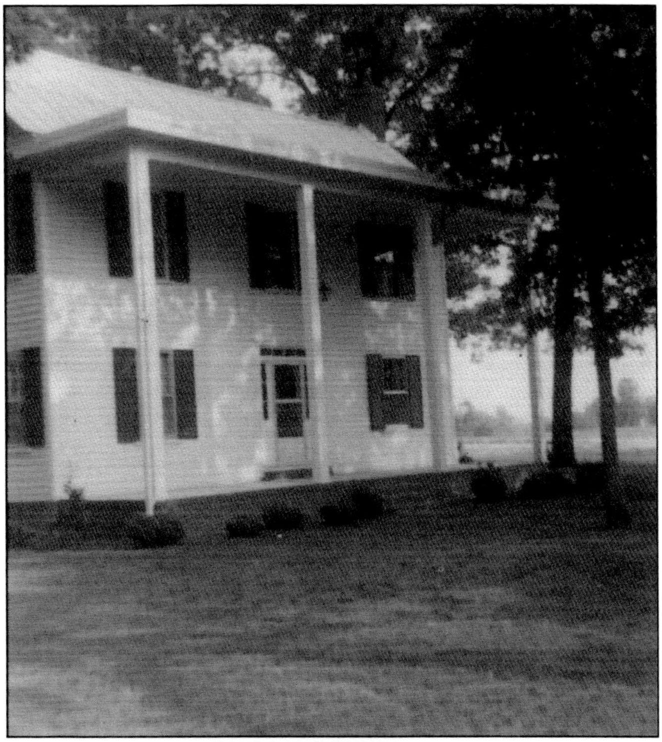

This is the original Aaron Wilson place in June 1965. The Wilson family originally owned approximately 600 acres that was split up amongst the family. Aaron Wilson gave approximately 125 acres to his nephew Roscoe Wilson. Roscoe lost 75 acres to the Jordan Lake project. This is now the home of Aaron Wilson's great niece, and Roscoe Wilson's daughter, Joan Wilson Frazier. In 1982, this home succumbed to a bad fire. Today the southern beauty Joan Wilson Frazier keeps the home and the ground absolutely stunning, as if Clark Gable himself would come out to greet visitors. (Courtesy of Joan Wilson Frazier.)

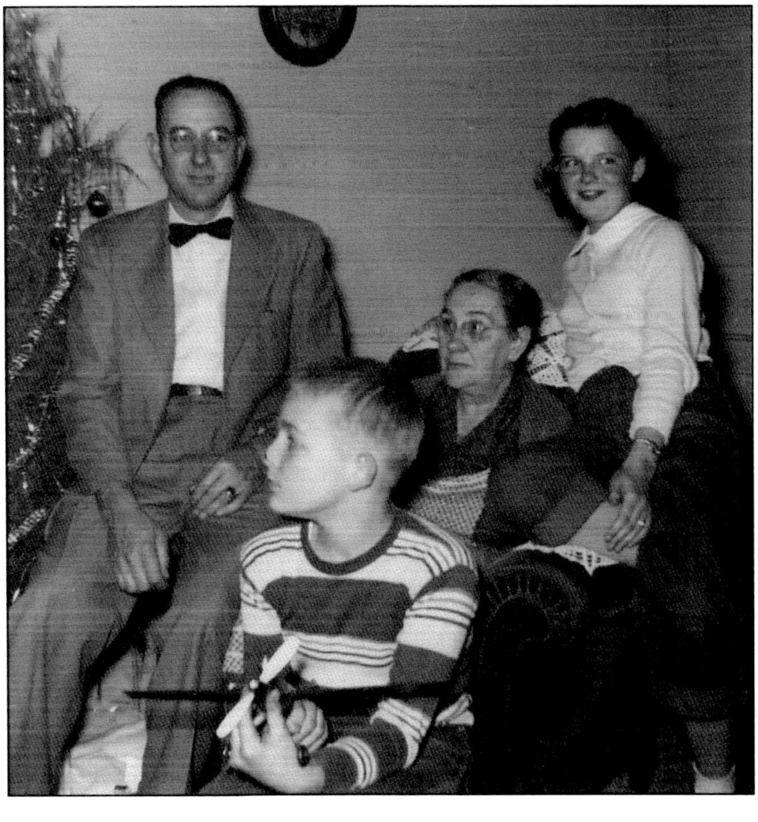

On Christmas Day 1954, pictured here are, from left to right, Roscoe Wilson, Bobby Wilson (holding toy plane), grandmother Mary Wilson, and Joan Wilson. (Courtesy of Joan Wilson Frazier.)

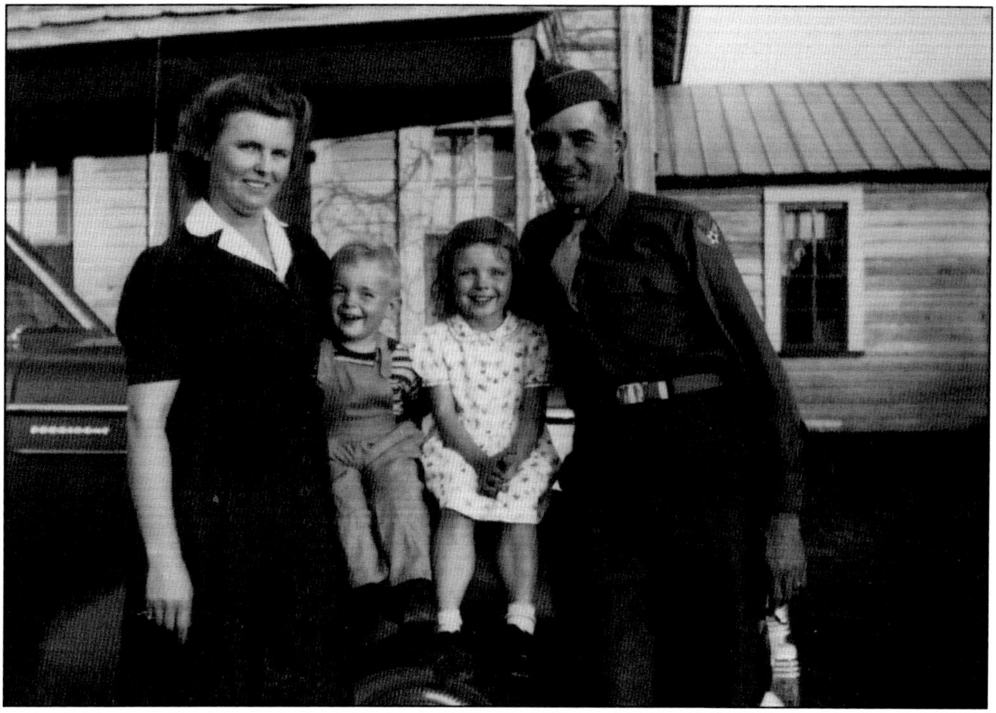

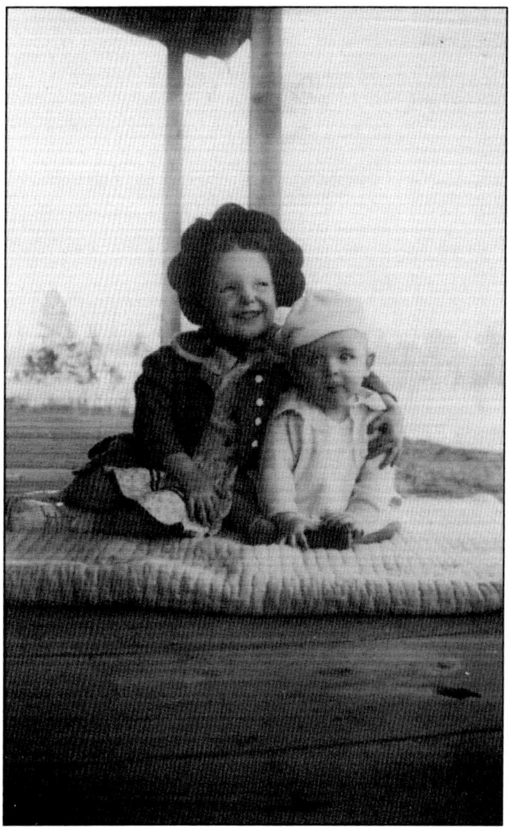

These are the Wilsons of Wilsonville in 1947. From left to right are Katie, Bobby, Joan, and Roscoe. Roscoe would come home on leave to always find Joan playing as a tomboy. On a surprise visit home, Roscoe picked up Joan, who unbeknownst to him had injured herself while playing, and she bled on his uniform. (Courtesy of Joan Wilson Frazier.)

Joan Wilson (left) and Bobby Wilson (right) are seated as babies in 1945 in front of the Naomi Wilson place. As young children, Joan was typically seen holding her brother's arm or hand. She was doing this to prevent him from sucking his thumb. Bobby went to North Carolina State University, where he met his wife, Helen. He became a geologist and unfortunately died at a very young age due to cancer. (Courtesy of Joan Wilson Frazier.)

This is a snowman made in 1954 by Bobby Wilson (left) and Joan Wilson (right). Bobby is wearing an eye patch after an accident while playing with his sister. Experiencing snow this deep in North Carolina is a rare event, and when it comes, it does not last very long. (Courtesy of Joan Wilson Frazier.)

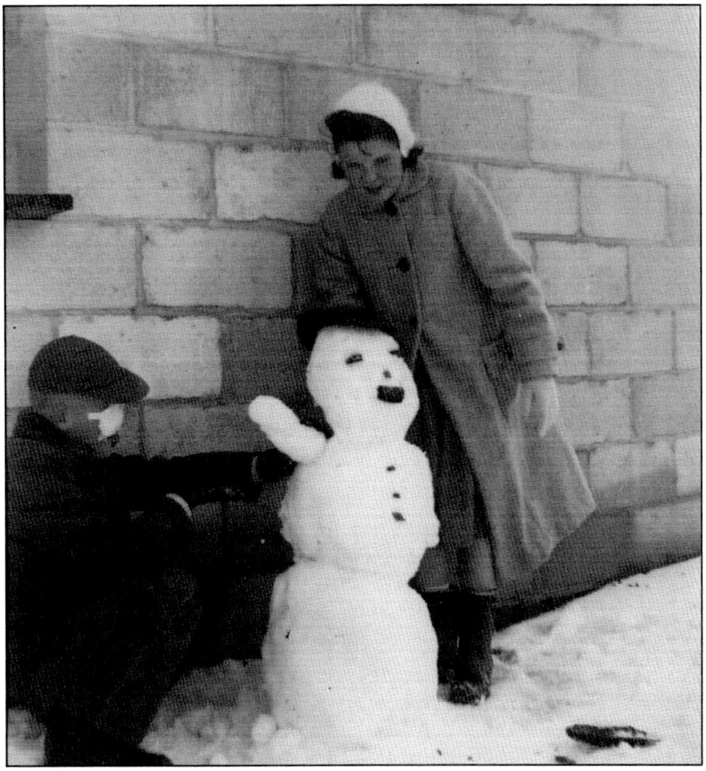

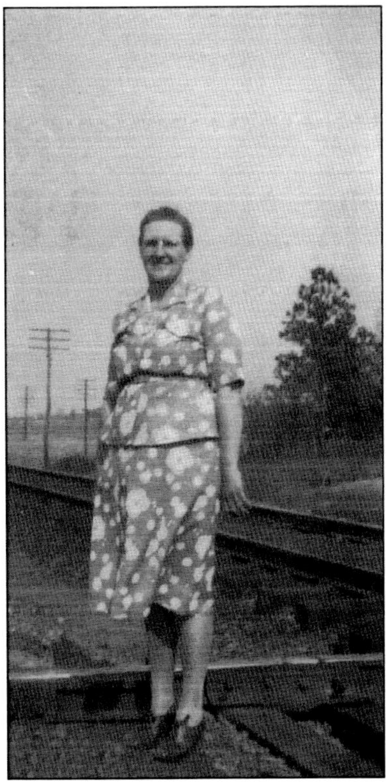

Katie Johnson Wilson's mother, Ocie Johnson, is standing on a New Hope Valley railroad spur. This part of the track led into the area of the railroad that was frequently flooded by storms and eventually was permanently retired and sits under Jordan Lake. The U.S. Army Corps of Engineers paid to have a new railroad connection created for the railroad company, which did not even want a new railroad. The new railroad was used only once. (Courtesy of Joan Wilson Frazier.)

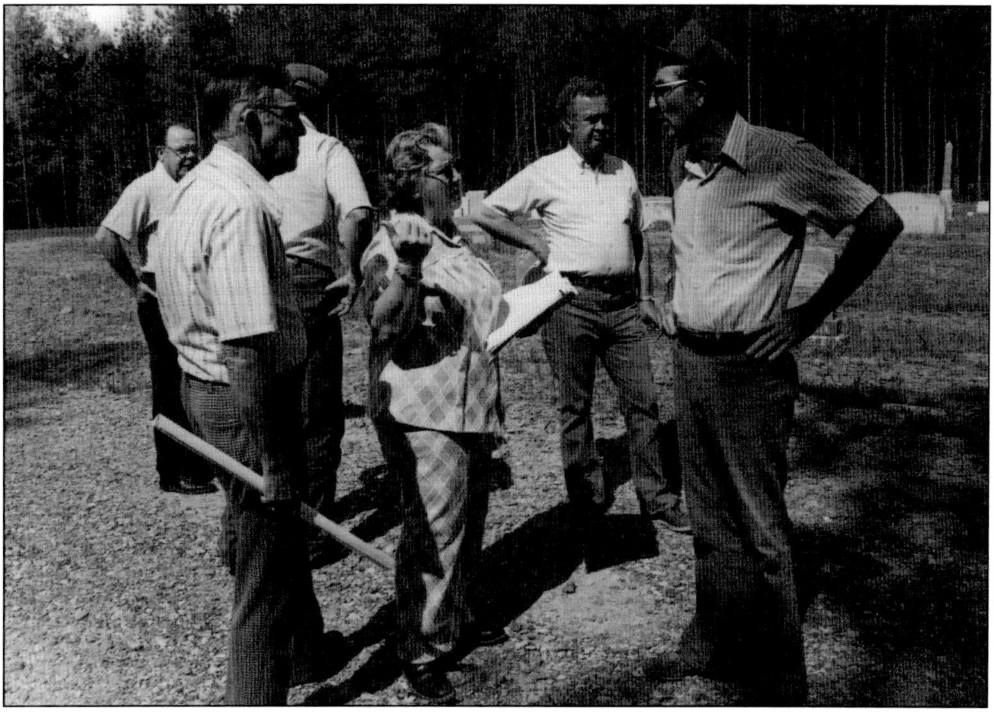

These are photographs that made headlines in the *Pittsboro Herald* on April 27, 1977. From left to right are Ebenezer Church trustee R. E. Truelove holding plans; corps inspector Kitty Mullis in center; contractor Randolph Richardson; and Paul McCoy on the right. Paul McCoy did the voiceover for the DVD *Land Beneath the Waters*, a dedication to the former owners of the land before Jordan Lake. Below, from left to right, are Randolph Richardson, Paul McCoy, R. E. Truelove learning over a family member's grave, and Kitty Mullis. A U.S. Army Corps of Engineers official, a cemetery relocation contractor, and church trustees hold a dispute in the cemetery of the Ebenezer Methodist Church regarding relocation efforts. (Both, courtesy of Jeff Starkweather.)

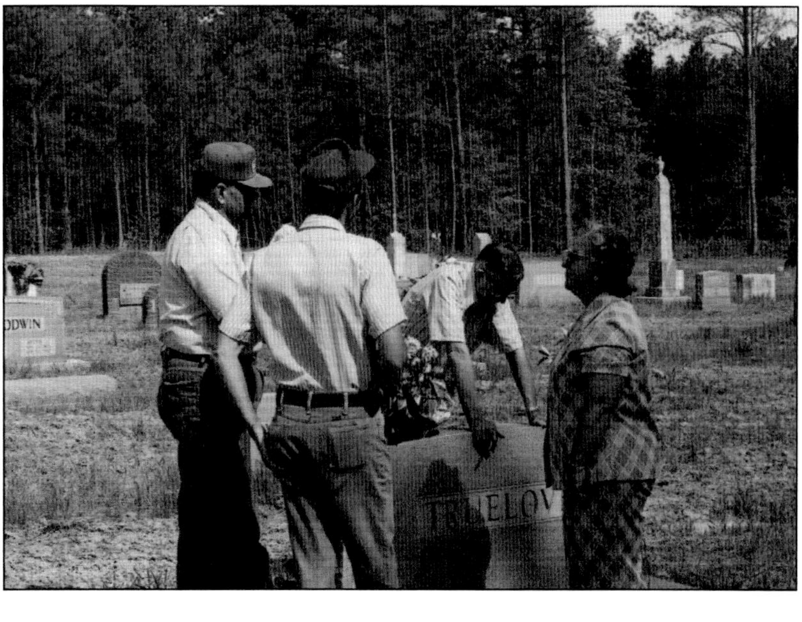

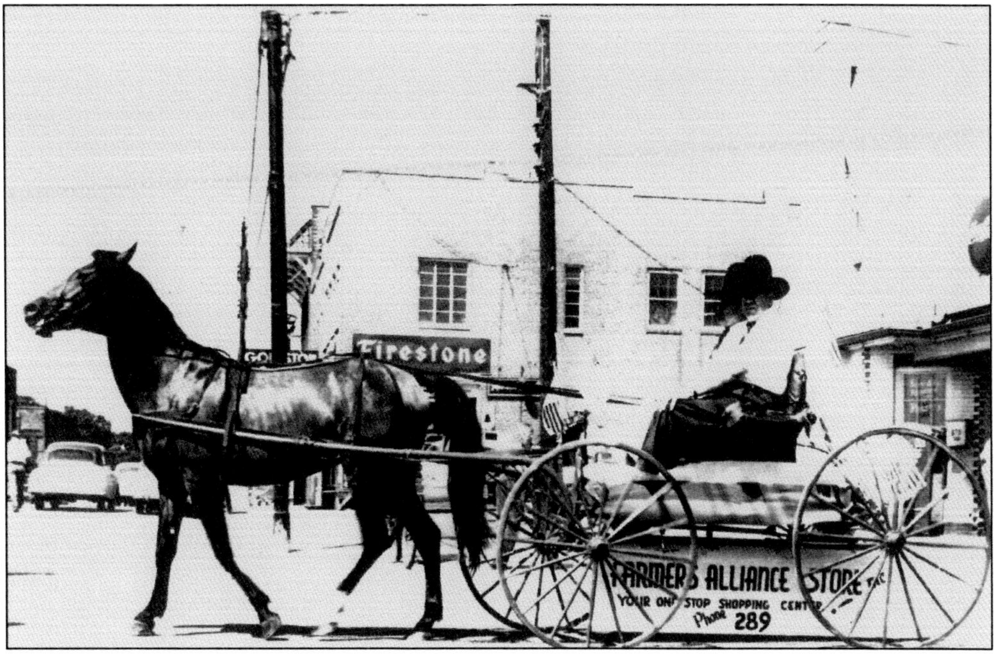

The Farmer's Alliance store has been in existence for more than 120 years and is located at 134 South Chatham Avenue. Sam Clapp and Lester Murray are seen in the buggy. Note that the phone number is only three numbers. This photograph was taken in the late 1930s or early 1940s during a Fourth of July parade. The store previously operated as a barter store for many years and today still has everything from garden supplies to hoop cheese. The store owners also keep a local history museum inside. The store appeared in *Our State* magazine in November 2007. (Courtesy of Chatham County Historical Association.)

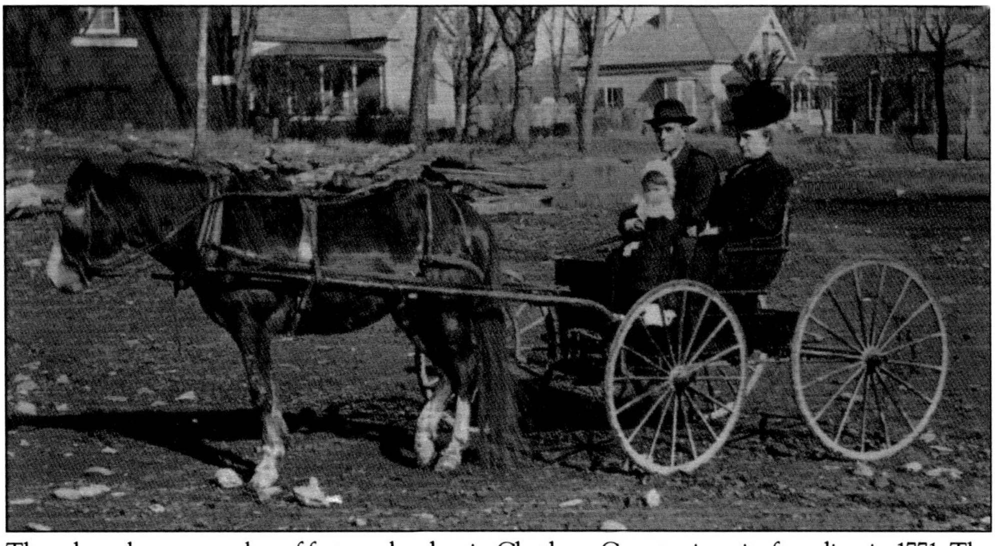

There have been a number of fraternal orders in Chatham County since its founding in 1771. The order with the most members has always been the fraternal order of the Masons. Henry Fike was a deacon for the Beaumont Lodge No. 160, which was chartered on December 6, 1854. Mrs. Henry Fike is pictured with him on East Street in Pittsboro in the 1800s. (Courtesy of Chatham County Historical Association.)

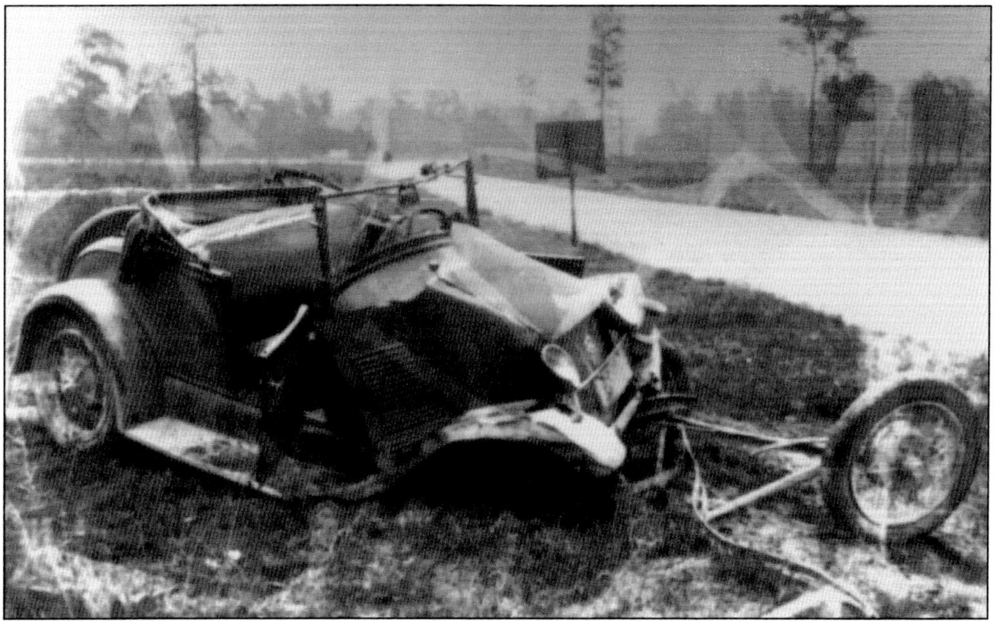

This is an early 1900s (possibly 1924) photograph of a car pulled to the side of the road after a crash with a Norfolk Southern train at a railroad crossing at Seaforth. This area is now under Jordan Lake. This intersection was found to be one of the deadliest in North Carolina, as train warning signals were not put in place. (Courtesy of Chatham County Historical Association.)

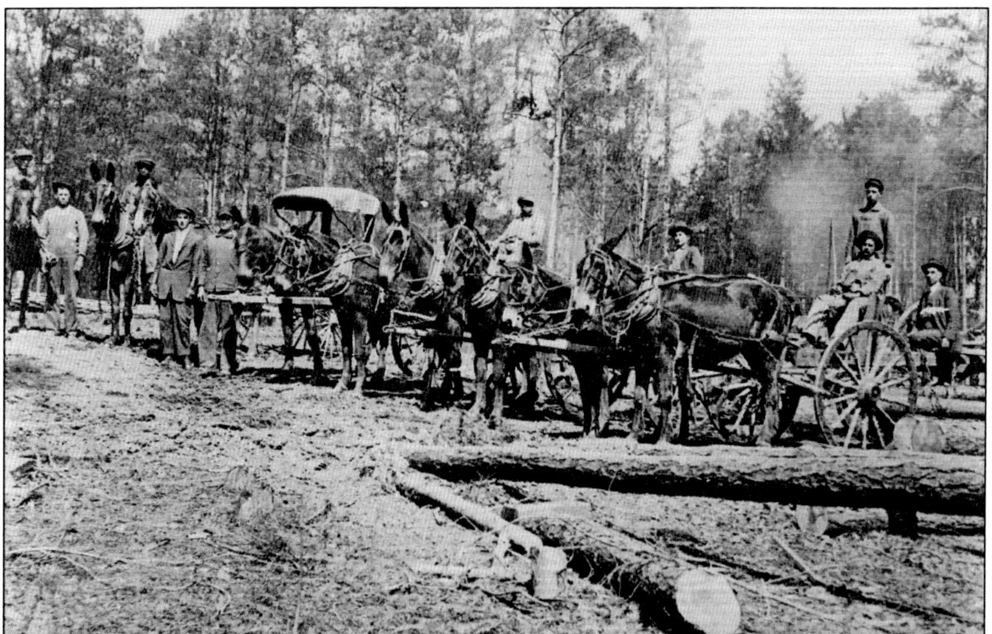

The George Moody Womble mill is pictured in 1917. The Womble family lost 163 acres to the Jordan Lake project. Four hundred acres are left in the family. (Courtesy of Teresa Yarborough, granddaughter of George Womble.)

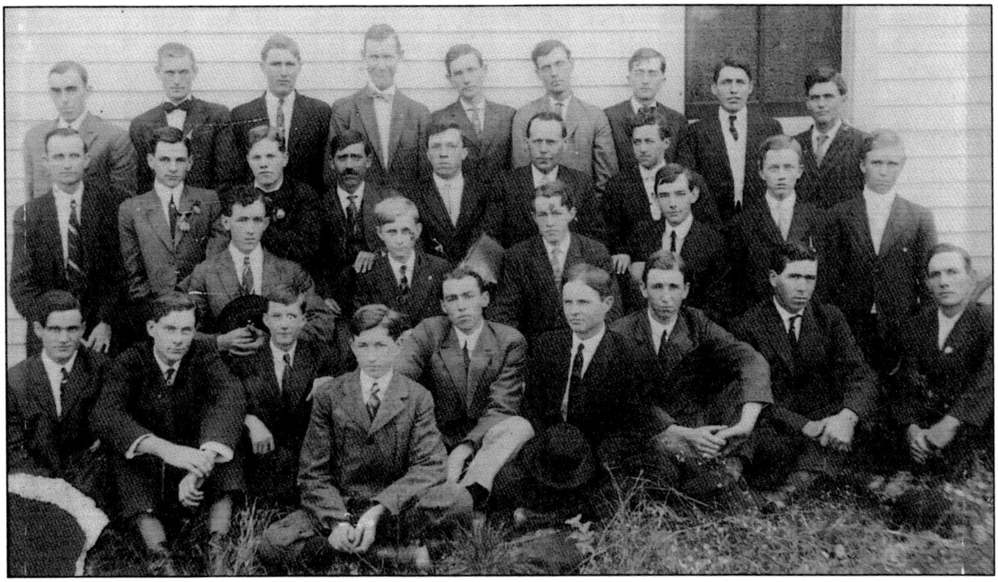

Pictured here are Bells Sunday school men around 1916. From left to right are (first row) Earlie Hunt, unidentified, John Stone, Phil Fearrington, Charlie McCoy, Lennie Bryan, C. Goodwin, Coy Johnson, and Jim Horton; (second row) Allie A. Johnson, Roy Howard, ? Bryan, J. Holleman, Troy S., and Earley Goodwin; (third row) G. Ellis, Jack Horton, John Horton, Tom Ellis, two unidentified, and Charlie Bryan; (fourth row) Luther McCoy, unidentified, V. Goodwin, Will Morgan, Jay Horton, Edgar S., Edmund Hart, and two unidentified. (Courtesy of Chatham County Historical Association.)

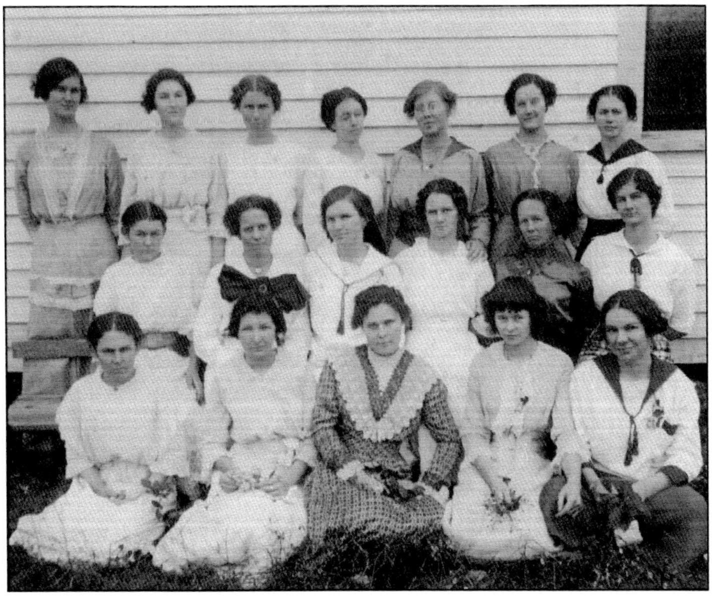

Pictured here are Bells Sunday school women around 1916. From left to right are (first row) V. Holleman, Etna M., R. Hunt, Clara Goodwin, and Ava Horton; (second row) L. Holleman, Alta Horton, Emma Horton, Paulina Stone, Berta Horton, and Bert Stone; (third row) Mita W., Gertie M., Pearl Goodwin, F. Bryan, Haitie Morgan, Edna Stone, and Annie Bryan. (Courtesy of Chatham County Historical Association.)

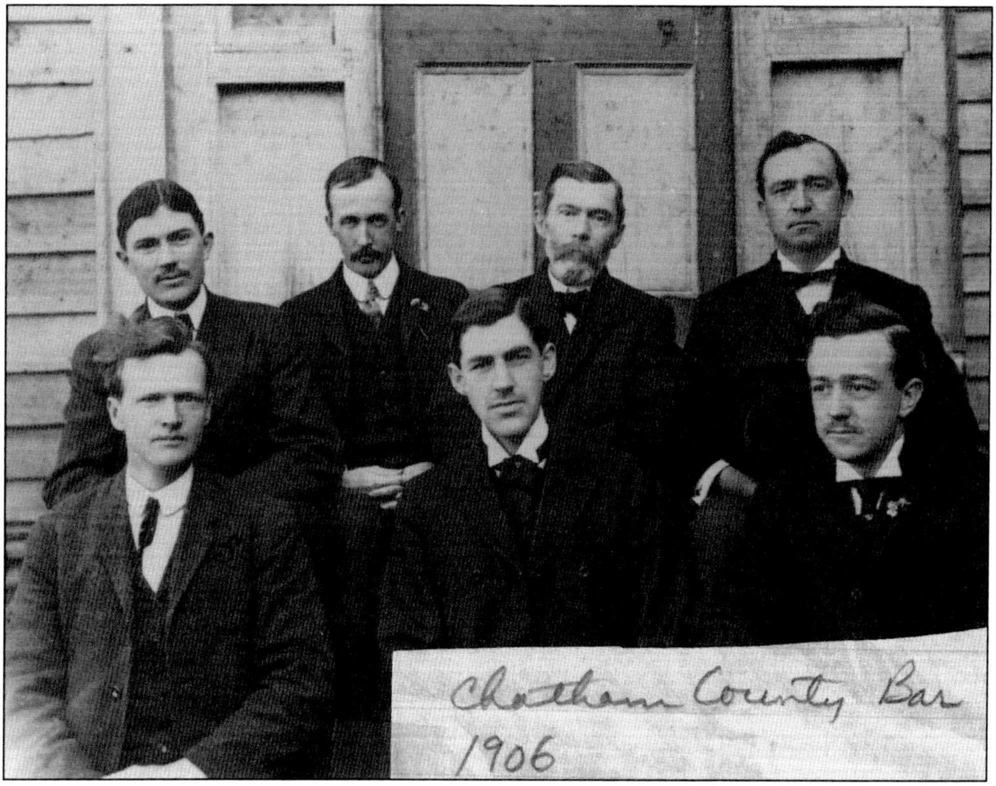

This is the Chatham County bar in 1906. Pittsboro was founded in 1787 as the capital of the newly formed Chatham County (1771) and was originally named "Pittsborough" after the Earl of Chatham. Many of the original founding families of Chatham County came from areas of Eastern North Carolina in the early 19th century and built large homes in town. (Courtesy of Chatham County Historical Association.)

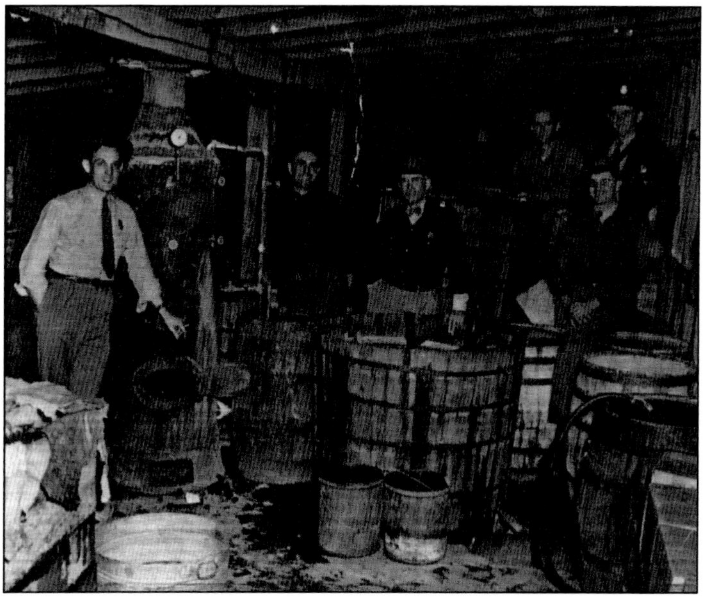

William Farrar of Seaforth, North Carolina, which is now under Jordan Lake, was a revenue man and raided illegal moonshine stills in North Carolina. This is a photograph taken after a raid at a still in 1956. From left to right are Russell Poole, William Farrar, sheriff George Andrews (Ike Andrews's uncle), Sam Tysor, J. A. Farrell, and unidentified. (Courtesy of Bryan Farrar.)

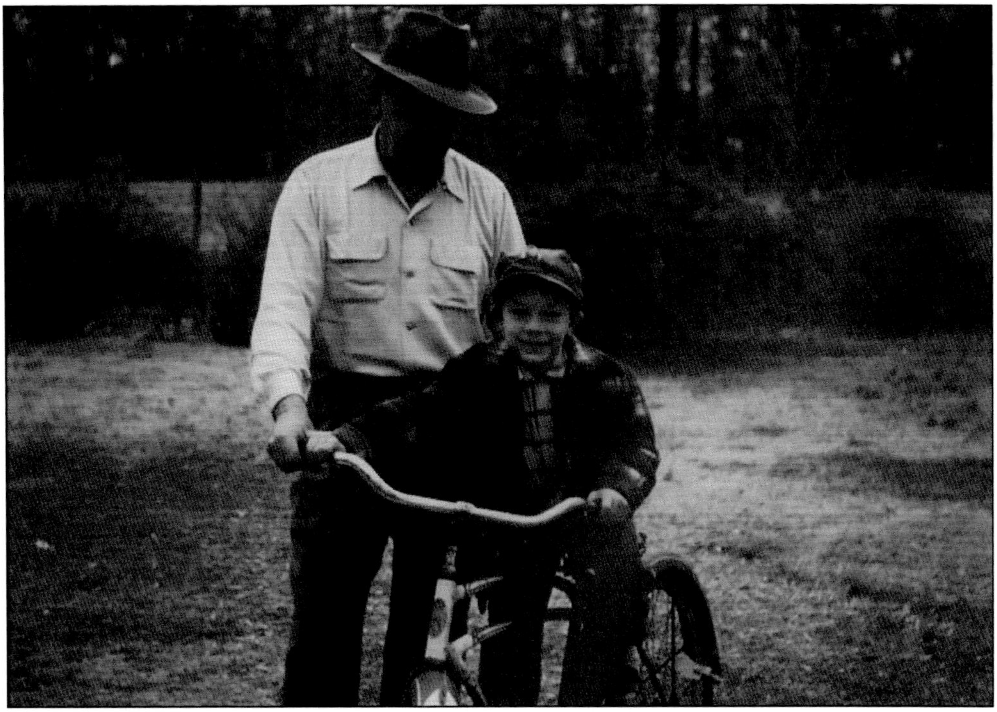

William Farrar is on the left with his son Bryan Farrar of Seaforth, North Carolina. The photograph was taken on Christmas Day in 1956. William Farrar was teaching Bryan how to ride a bike. His sons, Jack and Bryan, remembered their father most as always being a family man. The Farrar family lost all 35 of their acres to Jordan Lake in the summer of 1966. They could see the Seaforth pond, which was the family pond, from their back window, which is now the center of Jordan Lake. (Courtesy of Bryan Farrar.)

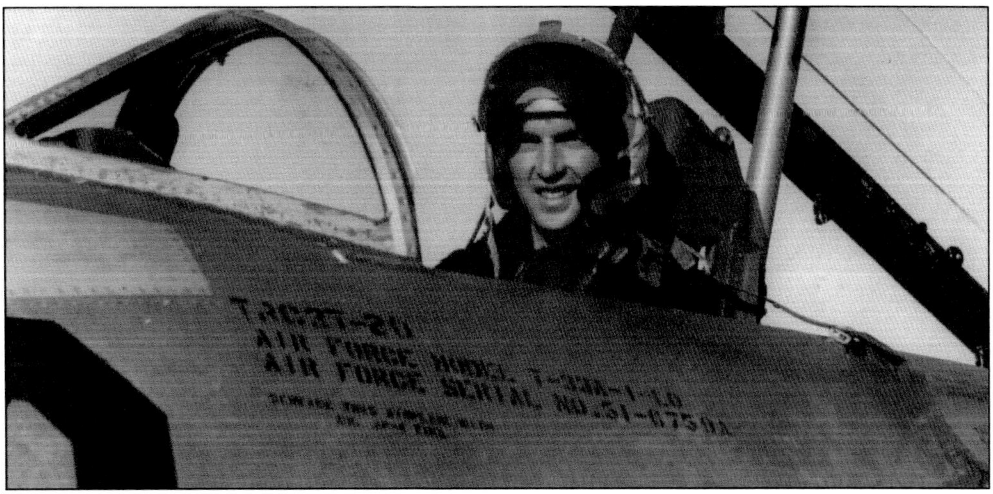

Jack Farrar of Seaforth, North Carolina, is in a T-33A jet. Jack was in the U.S. Air Force as a flight instructor for T-33 jets. Jack has since passed away, but his brother, Bryan Farrar, noted that Jack loved the New Hope Valley very much and would be honored to be a part of the *Jordan Lake* book. (Courtesy of Bryan Farrar.)

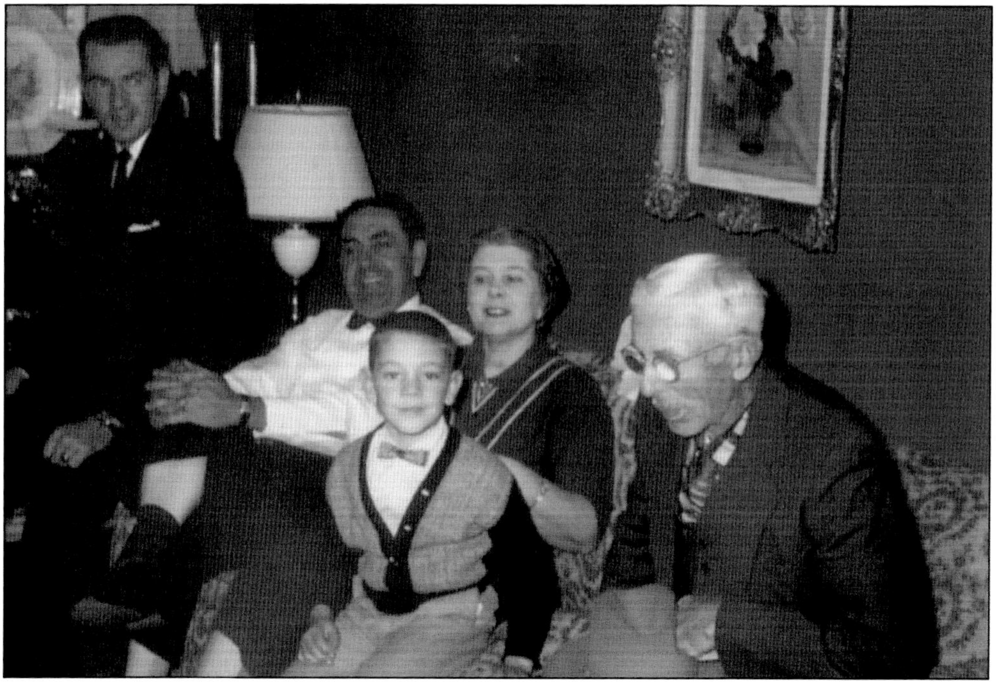

Pictured here are, from left to right, Jack Farrar, William Farrar, Bryan Farrar, Ruth Farrar, and Ruth's father, Jessie Newton Bryan. Maggie (not pictured), who ran the Seaforth store, was Jessie's daughter and sister to Ruth Farrar. Bryan Farrar said that unfortunately there are no known photographs of the Seaforth store. (Courtesy of Bryan Farrar.)

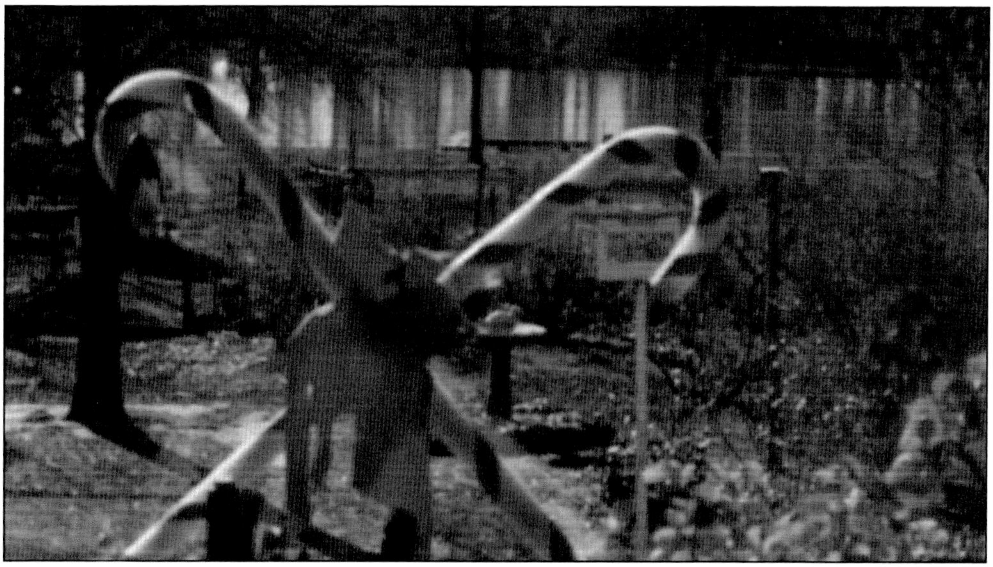

This is the view of the former Seaforth Pond from the Farrars' window. This view and pond are now in the center of Jordan Lake, under the water. The photograph was taken during Christmas 1956. Bryan Farrar, who is now the rental manager at the Cary C. Jones Memorial Park, does not go to Jordan Lake, as it brings back too many memories. Today Bryan feels that Jordan Lake has been a good thing for the county as a whole, but it was unfortunate for the families who owned land in the area. (Courtesy of Bryan Farrar.)

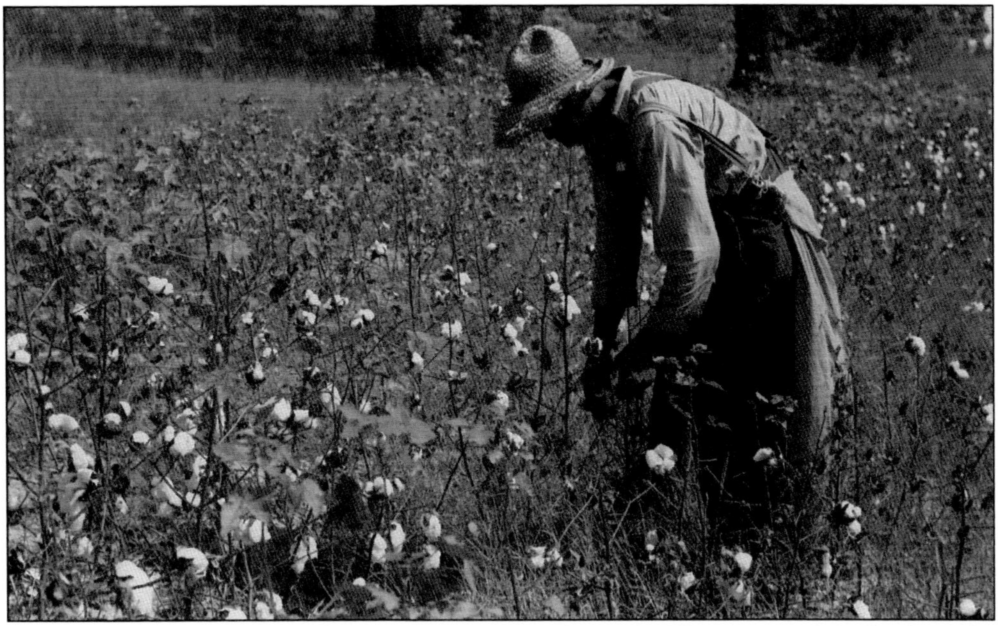

Sharecropper Will Cole is picking cotton in September 1939. The owners of the land are the Rigsbys. The photograph was taken in Chatham County near Fearrington. (Courtesy of Library of Congress, Prints and Photographs Division, FSA/OWI Collection [reproduction number LC-USF33-030519-M2].)

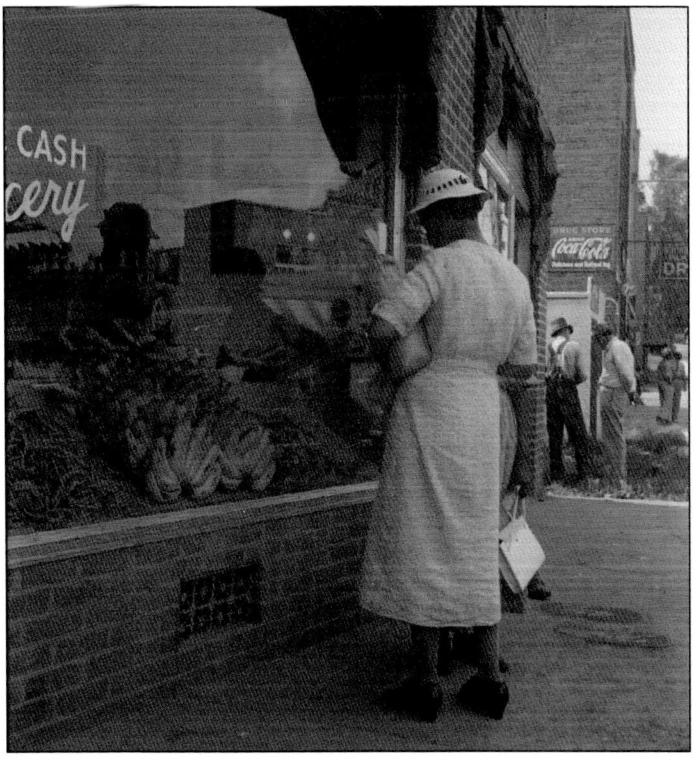

This is an unidentified local shopper on a Saturday afternoon in July 1939 in Pittsboro. Historic downtown Pittsboro has always been the main shopping hub for Chatham County. Today this historic district is lined with stores like the General Store Café with prime outside seating, an equestrian store called Blue Sky, an antique store called Beggars and Choosers, and much more. (Courtesy of Library of Congress, Prints and Photographs Division, FSA/OWI Collection [reproduction number LC-DIG-fsa-8b33871].)

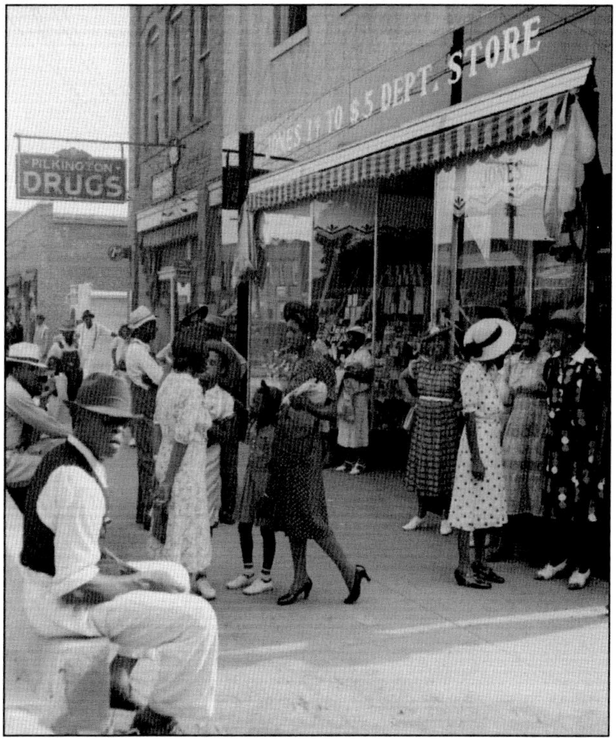

Locals are shopping in the heart of Pittsboro's historic district on a Saturday in July 1939. One of the local stores on this street still has this photograph in their window. Today it is still the hot spot where locals love to shop and meet. (Courtesy of Library of Congress, Prints and Photographs Division, FSA/OWI Collection [reproduction number LC-USF34-019846-E].)

Pictured are Patrick Barnes II and his friend Smith. Barnes and Smith were civil engineers. The photograph was taken in the 1920s. Patrick is the rodman shown in the photograph using the tripod, which has been kept in pristine condition by his son Patrick Barnes III. Barnes Sr. was hired by Henry Flagler to design the city of Sarasota in Florida. (Courtesy of Patrick Barnes.)

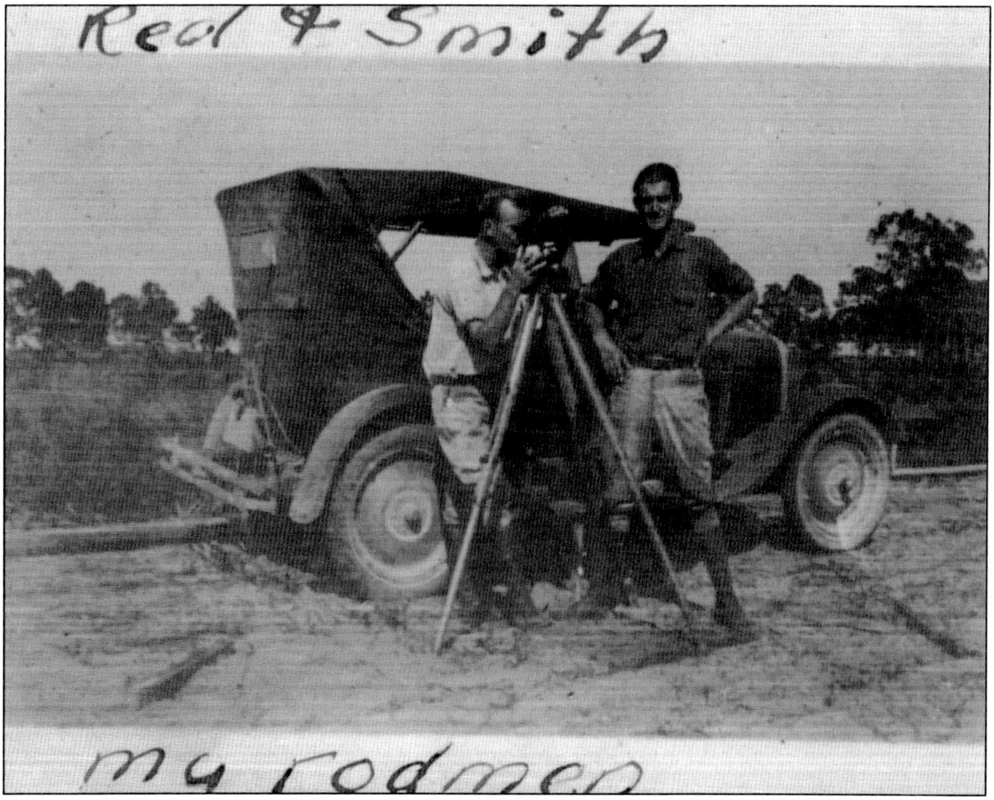

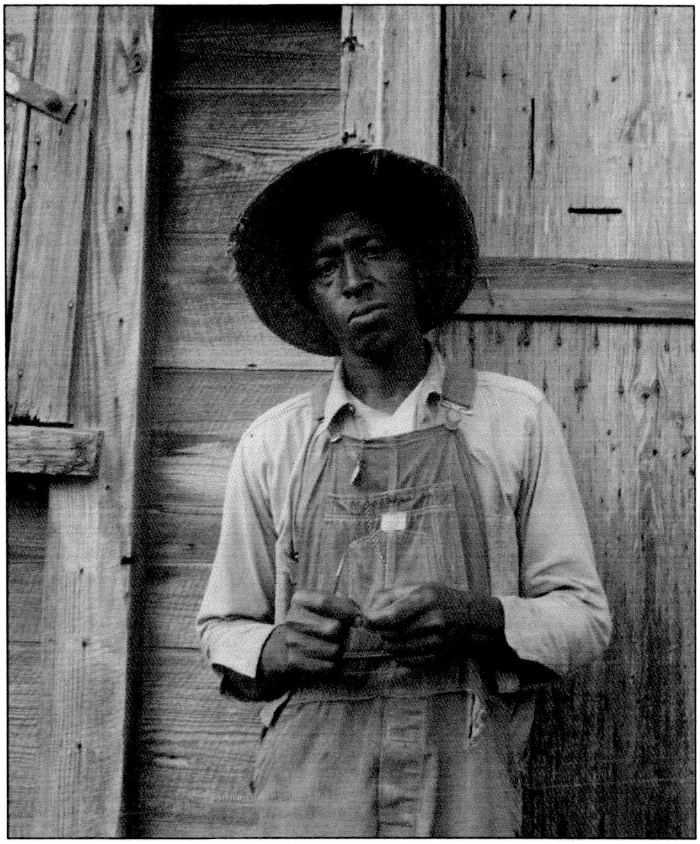

This is a photograph of a tenant farmer in Chatham County near Farrington in 1939. Landowners would rent out a portion of their land to folks called tenant farmers who might farm and reside on the land. The tenant farmers would pay for their section of land with a portion of their produced crops, cash, or both. (Courtesy of Library of Congress, Prints and Photographs Division, FSA/OWI Collection [reproduction number LC-USF34-9058-C].)

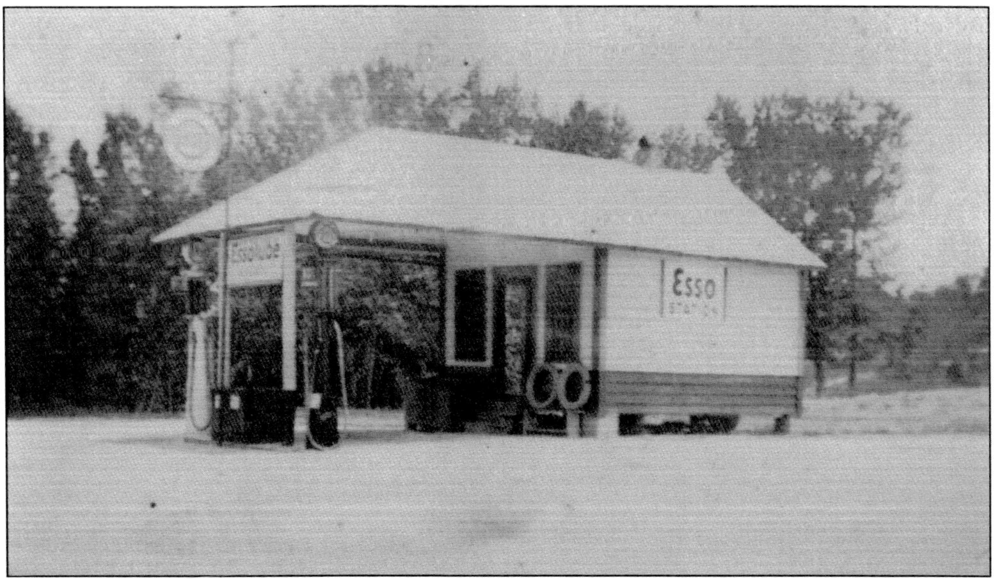

This a 1920s photograph of the original Wilsonville General Store, located at 10508 Highway 64 at the intersection leading to Crosswinds Marina. Vossie Horton, along with John Arthurs, are the current owners. Vossie Horton purchased the Wilsonville General Store in 1979. (Courtesy of Vossie Horton.)

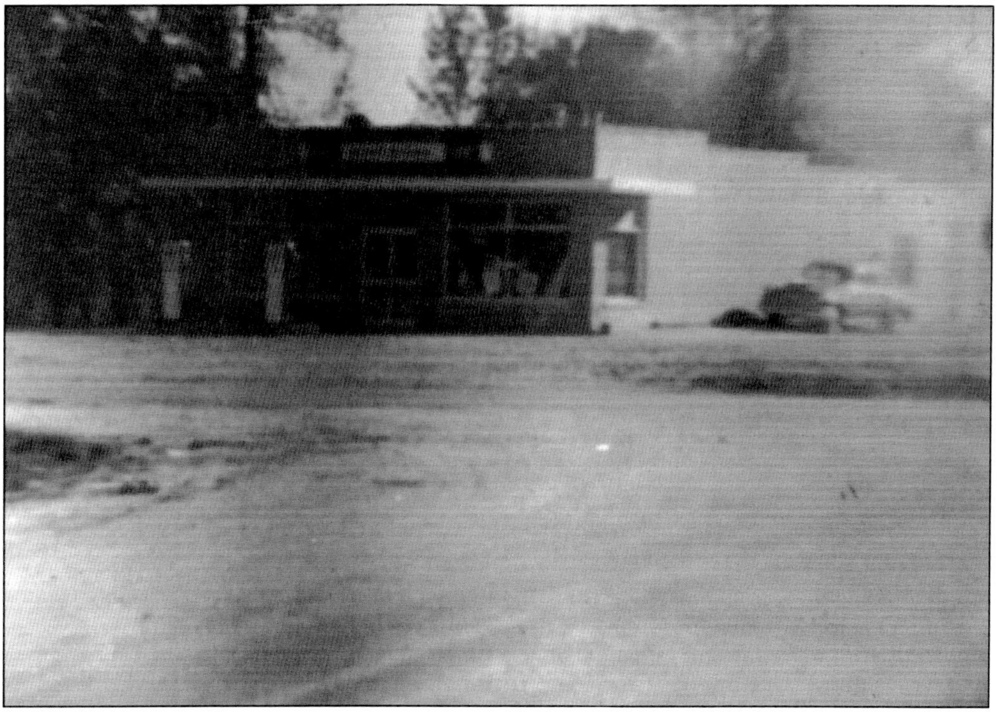

This is the Wilsonville General Store in 1950. Vossie loved his days at the general store, as he says he met new people everyday, including some famous race car drivers that came through town. The general store is now part of the Exxon chain, but the old-fashioned business is still there, and the locals are very dedicated to going there. (Courtesy of Vossie Horton.)

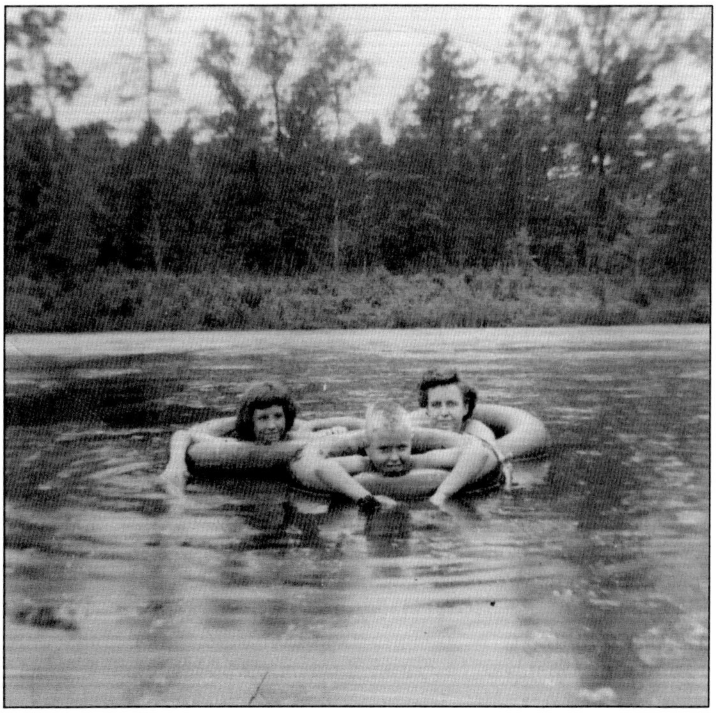

From left to right are young Minnie Bell Barnes, an unidentified cousin, and Minnie Bell Barnes, the mother of Patrick and Minnie. They are floating on inner tubes in an area that now belongs to Jordan Lake. The Bell family was kin to the Earl of Chatham, and the family held original land grants from the 1700s. (Courtesy of Patrick Barnes.)

Minnie Bell Barnes, age five, is on the left holding her doll, and Patrick Herndon Barnes III is on the right at age eight. The photograph was taken in 1945. (Courtesy of Patrick Barnes.)

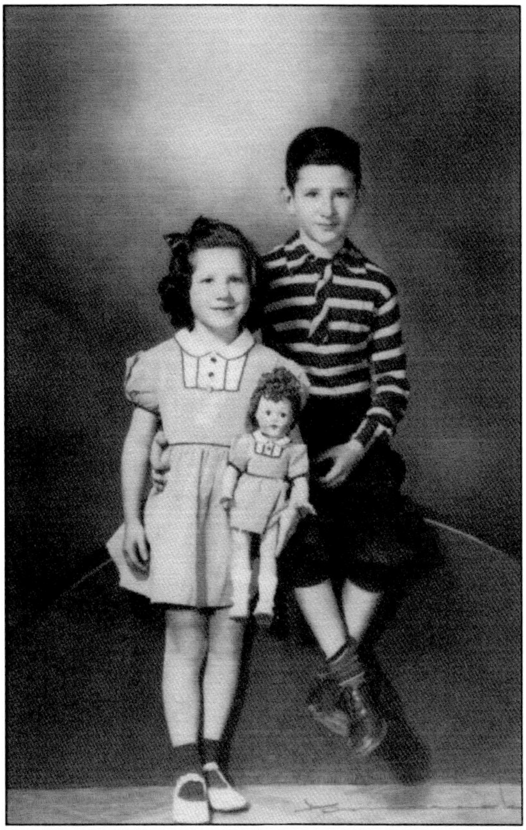

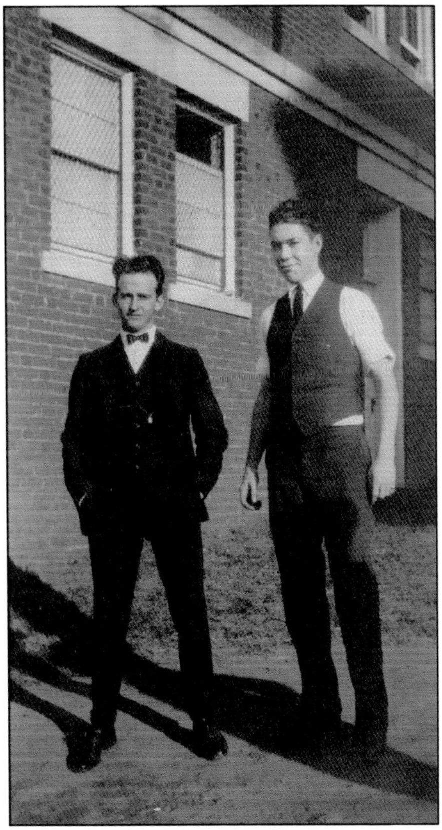

Patrick Barnes III received a civil engineering degree from Harvard and then received a baseball scholarship to North Carolina State University, where he received his master's degree. The photograph was taken at North Carolina State in 1925 with his friend Bob. The dress code for attending a university was a suit and tie. In the 1930s, Patrick Barnes II received $60 per month as a bridge engineer. (Courtesy of Patrick Barnes.)

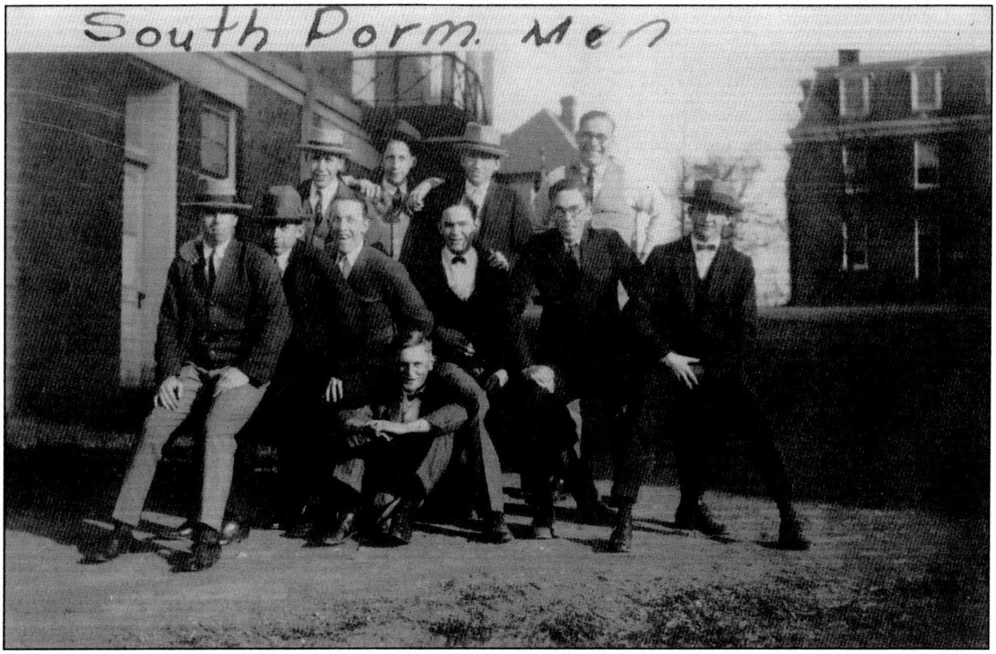

This is a photograph of the South Dormitory men at North Carolina State in the late 1920s. The South Dormitory was renamed Syme Hall for G. F. Syme, an 1898 alumnus and distinguished engineer. The men in the photograph were also engineering students. (Courtesy of Patrick Barnes.)

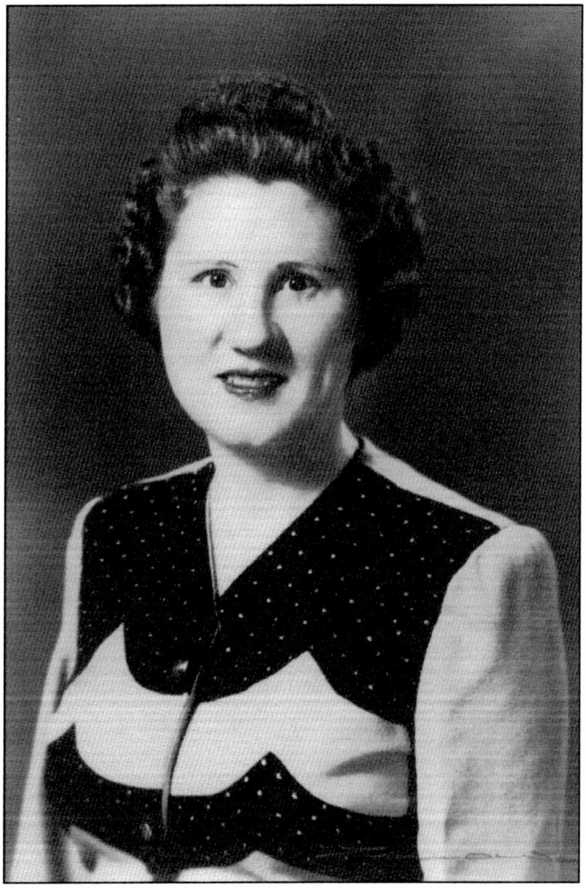

This is Minnie Bell in 1940. She finished college at age 19 and received an "open" teaching degree. Minnie Bell taught math and chemistry for 30 years and also taught at the Bells School, which was torn down for a fishing pier. In the 1930s, Minnie Bell received $20 a month to teach, and her room and board was $2.50 per month. (Courtesy of Patrick Barnes.)

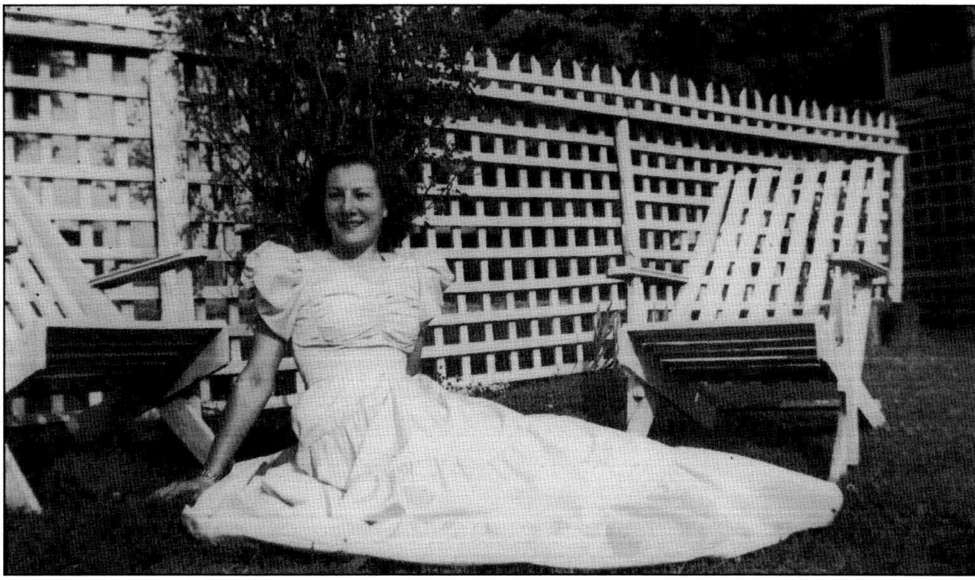

The striking Jesse Bell Utley is pictured in the 1940s in the Bells community, which is now mostly part of the Jordan Lake Project. This is Patrick Barnes's favorite aunt. The Bells community was named after this Bell family, who donated land from their original land grants for the Bells Church and School. The original Bells Church was torn down, and the area is now a fishing pier. A new church was built in its place. (Courtesy of Patrick Barnes.)

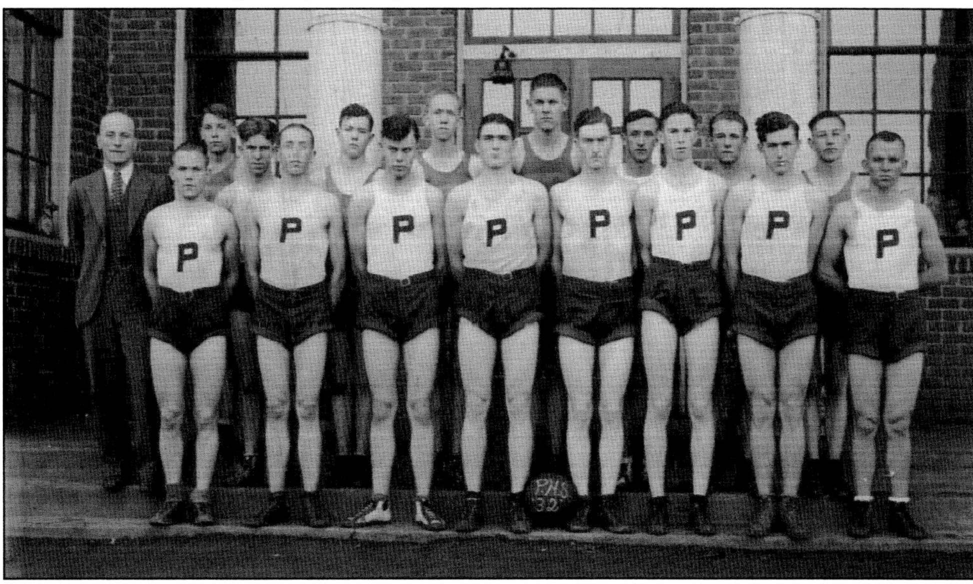

This is the 1931 Pittsboro High School basketball team. In 1901, a two-story wooden structure was built called Pittsboro School on Hillsborough Street (U.S. Route 15-501) that included grades 1 to 11. In 1923, a brick school was built in the 200 block of West Street (Route 64). In 1946, the school added the 12th grade. In 1954, the Bells High School closed. In 1965, Moncure High School merged with Pittsboro High School. Most students in Chatham County attended Pittsboro High School, since high schools were rare in the area during the first half of the 1900s. Horton High School was merged with Pittsboro High School in 1970 to form Northwood High School. (Courtesy of Joyce Jones Cotten.)

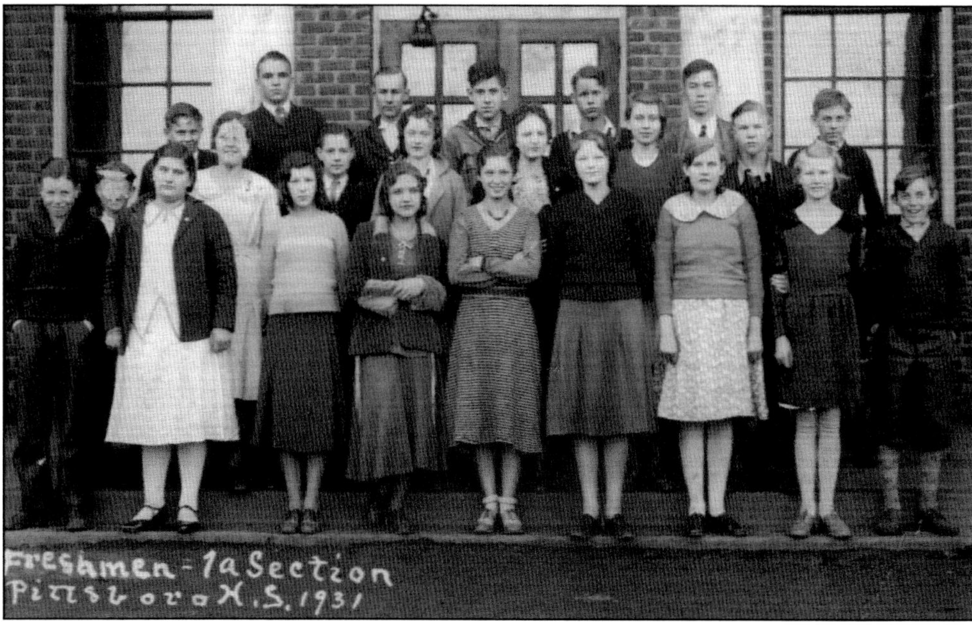

Pictured is the Pittsboro High School class of 1931. Pittsboro High School still frequently holds reunions. The student alumni database is kept by Joyce Jones Cotten. (Courtesy of Joyce Jones Cotten.)

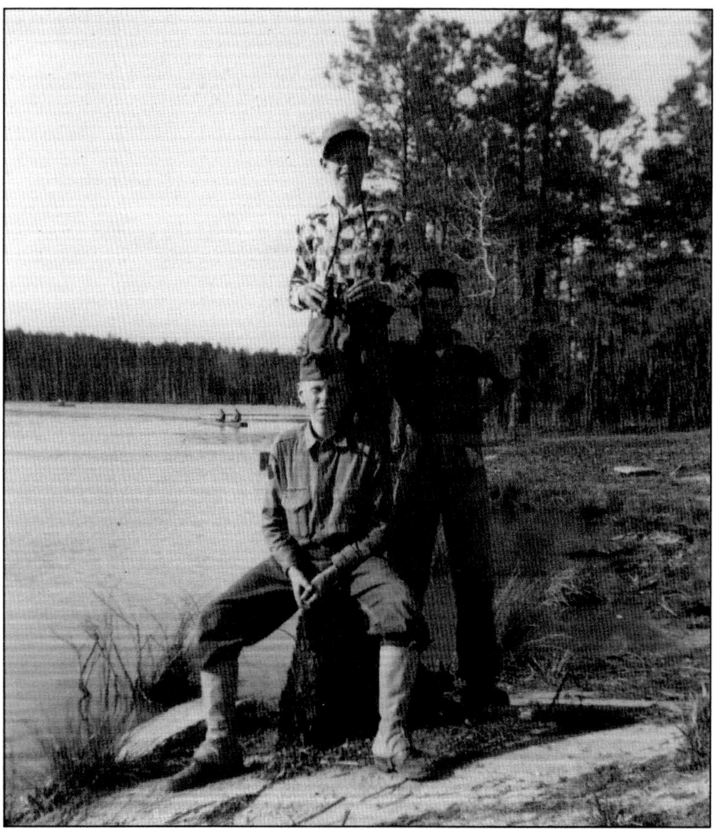

The photograph was taken in the 1950s on Horton's Pond, which is now part of the Jordan Lake Project. Pictured here are Phillip Fearrington (left front), Vossie Horton (right), and Ronald Copeland. The three of them are well-known in Chatham County. (Courtesy of Patrick Barnes.)

This is Patrick Barnes's Scout photograph. He became an Eagle Scout and was very active in the Scouting community. His troop number was 910. (Courtesy of Patrick Barnes.)

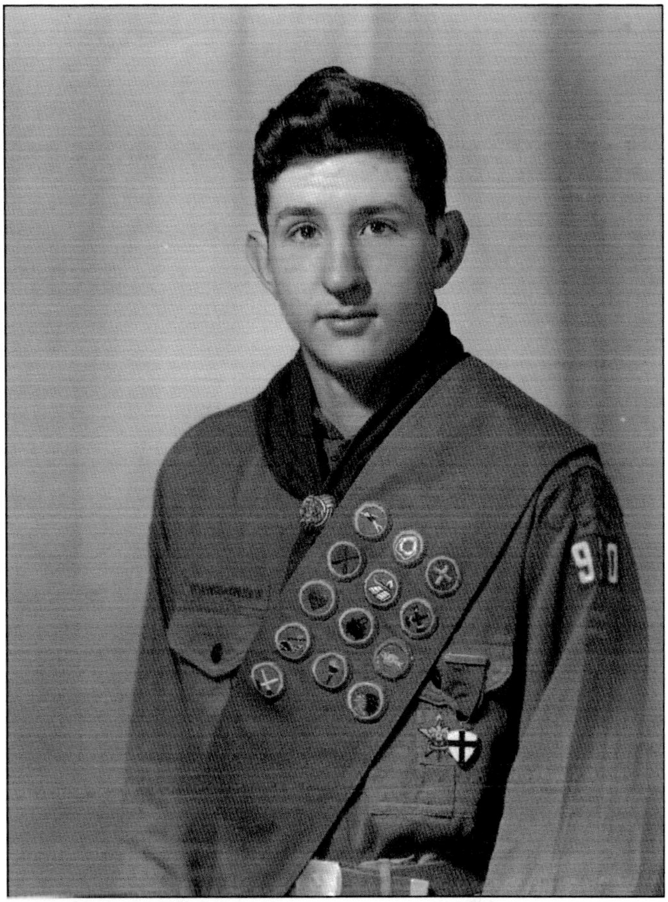

Former commissioner Patrick Barnes used to be a race car driver for fun. He loves fine cars and motorcycles. Barnes and his wife, Becky, often take long motorcycle trips around the region. Barnes looks forward to taking the motorcycle trips with his wife. This photograph was taken during his final race in 1991. (Courtesy of Patrick Barnes.)

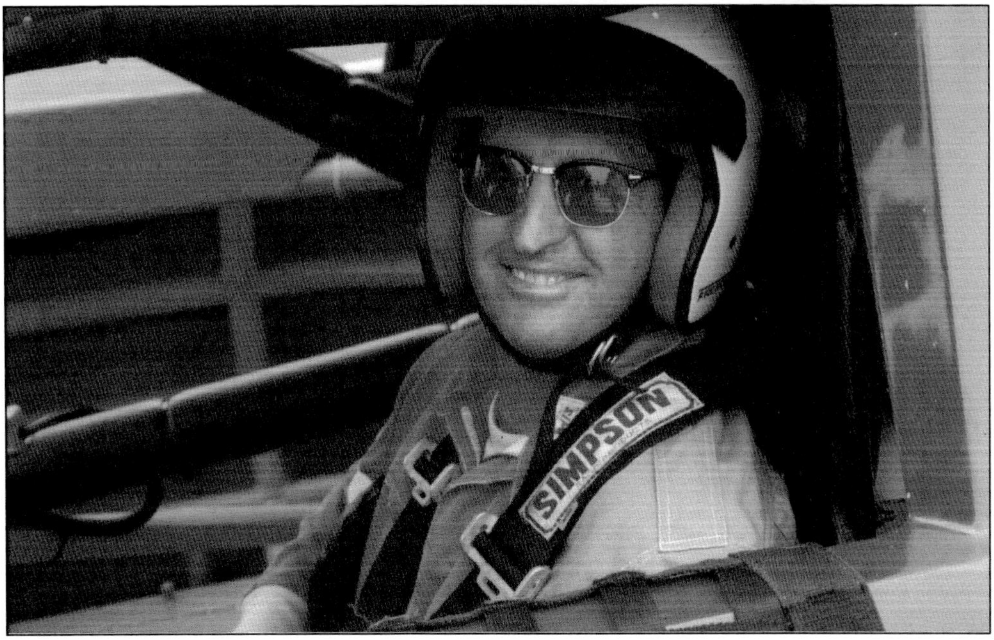

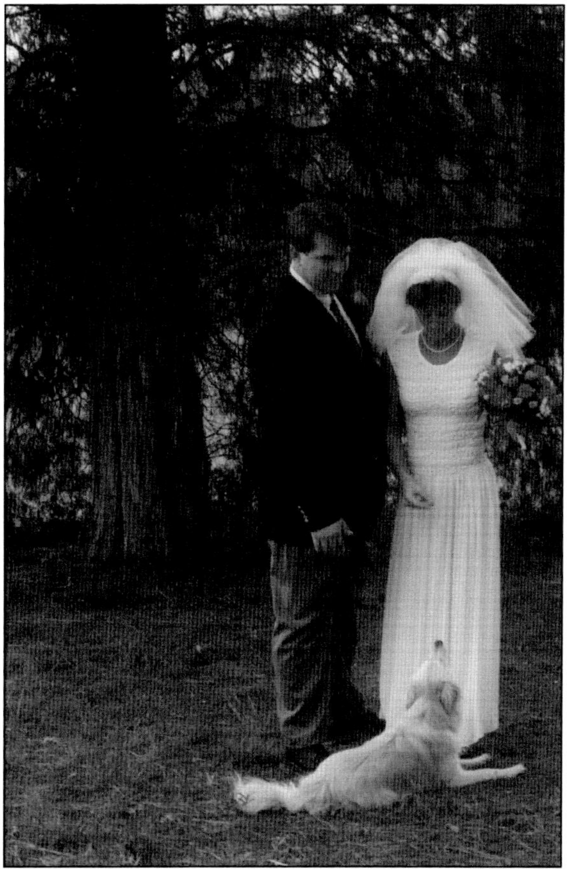

Patrick Barnes's lovely daughter, Mindy Barnes, was married to Ed Scammon on August 28, 1999, on the porch of the Barnes property next to Jordan Lake. Barnes is very fond of his daughter and says he has three daughters and "a whole bunch more" that he mutually adopted and loves very much. Mindy was one of four family members who have gotten married on the original Bell/Barnes property. (Courtesy of Patrick Barnes.)

The Patrick Barnes Construction Company was hired to protect Bayer's building in 2003 after the terrorist attacks on U.S. soil on September 11, 2001, resulted in heightened security issues around the United States. Bayer is located in Research Triangle Park, which has brought many jobs and businesses to the Chatham area. This photograph also shows the creative sidewalk in front of Bayer, which was also created by the Barnes company. The concrete styled structures weigh a couple of tons and are anchored into the ground. (Courtesy of Patrick Barnes.)

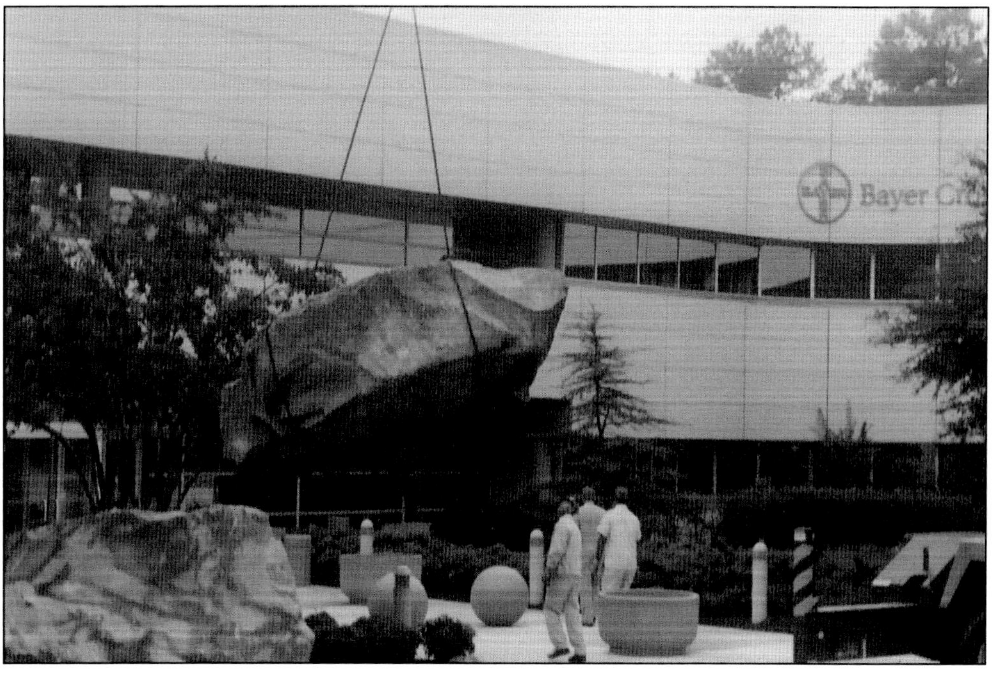

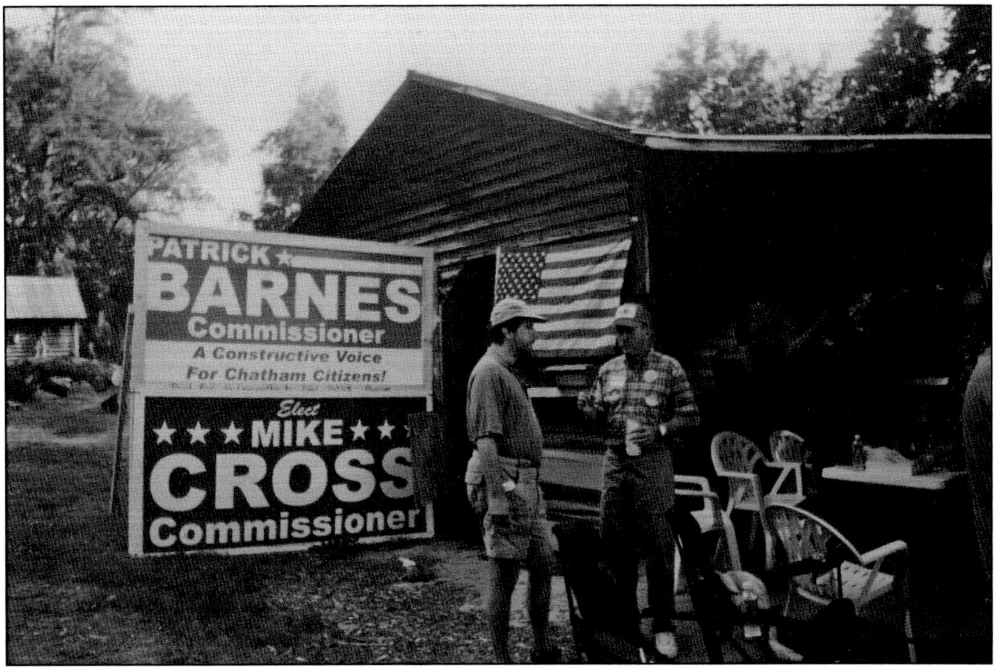

Patrick Barnes is speaking with a guest during the 2004 campaign. Both Patrick and Mike Cross were elected as commissioners. Patrick Barnes posted the following announcement in 2009: "It has been an honor to serve you. I believe I have been very successful in setting the tone of change necessary to brighten Chatham's future. I am hopeful that whomever takes up the reigns will continue to focus on the entire county and not just the northeast. Chatham County's success can only be defined by the success of all regions within Chatham." (Courtesy of Patrick Barnes.)

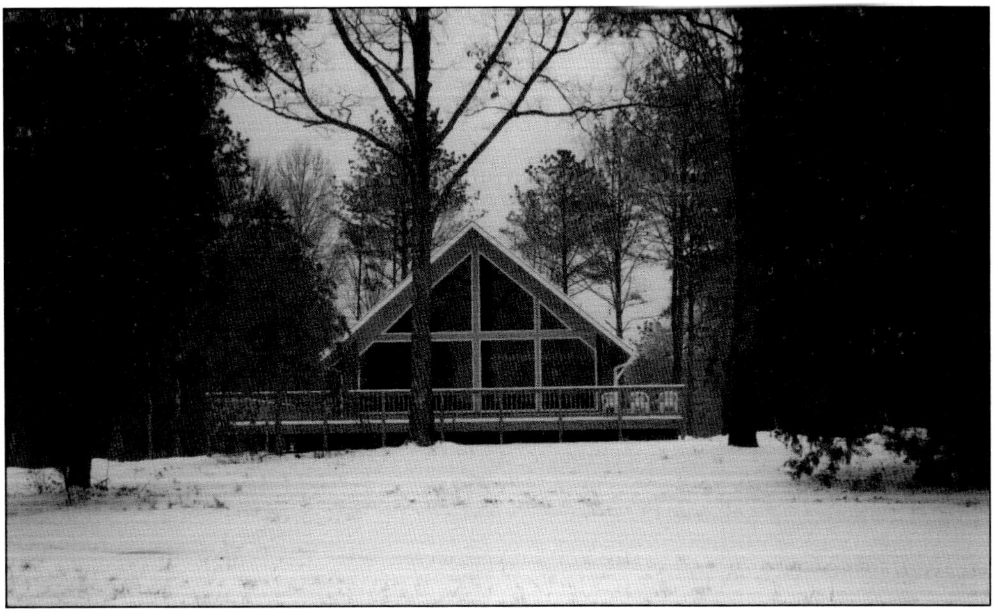

The Barnes family (descendants of the Bell family) built a new home next to Jordan Lake in 1994. (Courtesy of Patrick Barnes.)

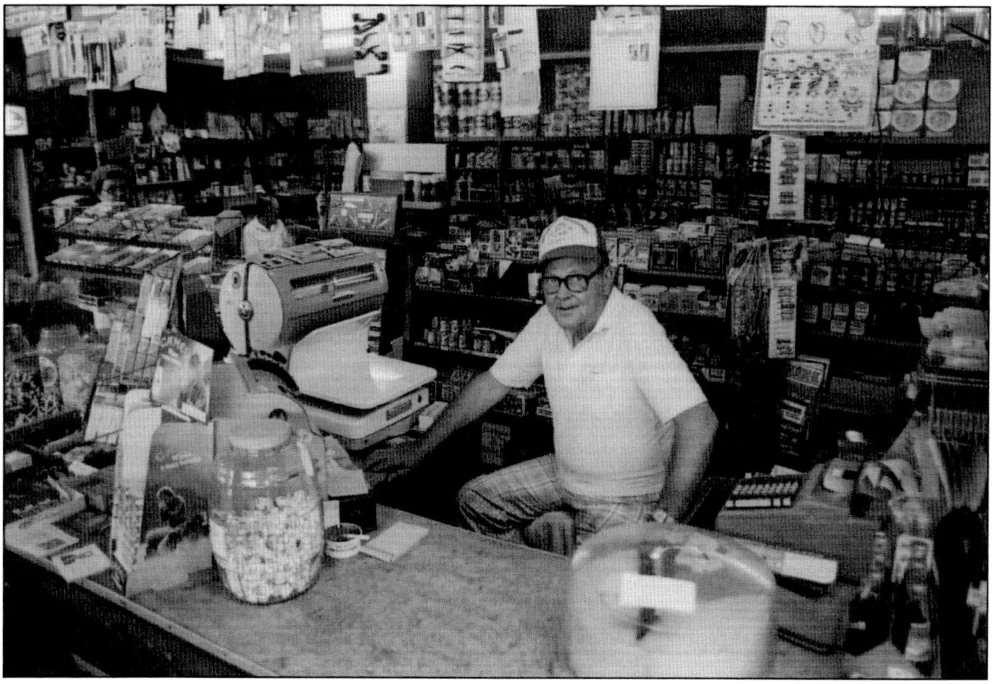

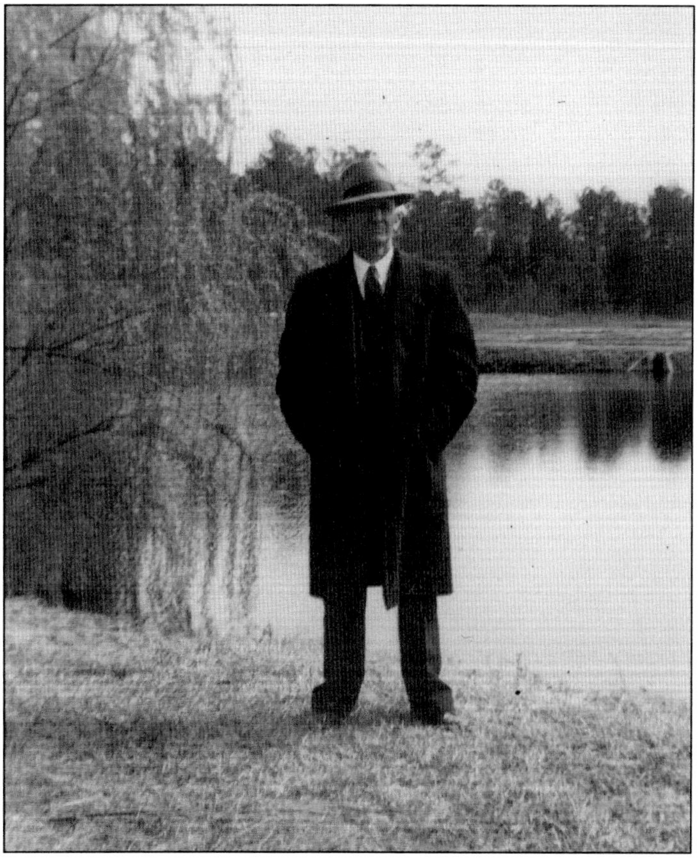

The Farrington Store and part of the Farrington community are now part of the Jordan Lake preserve. In the 1940s, the store would give free haircuts on Saturday mornings. (Courtesy of Jeff Starkweather.)

Patrick Barnes II is in front of the Moncure pond, which is now part of the 47,000 acres belonging to the Jordan Lake Project. This photograph was taken in the 1940s. Barnes passed away in 1981, but he left a part of himself behind in the significant structures he helped design and build as a civil engineer across the country. (Courtesy of Patrick Barnes.)

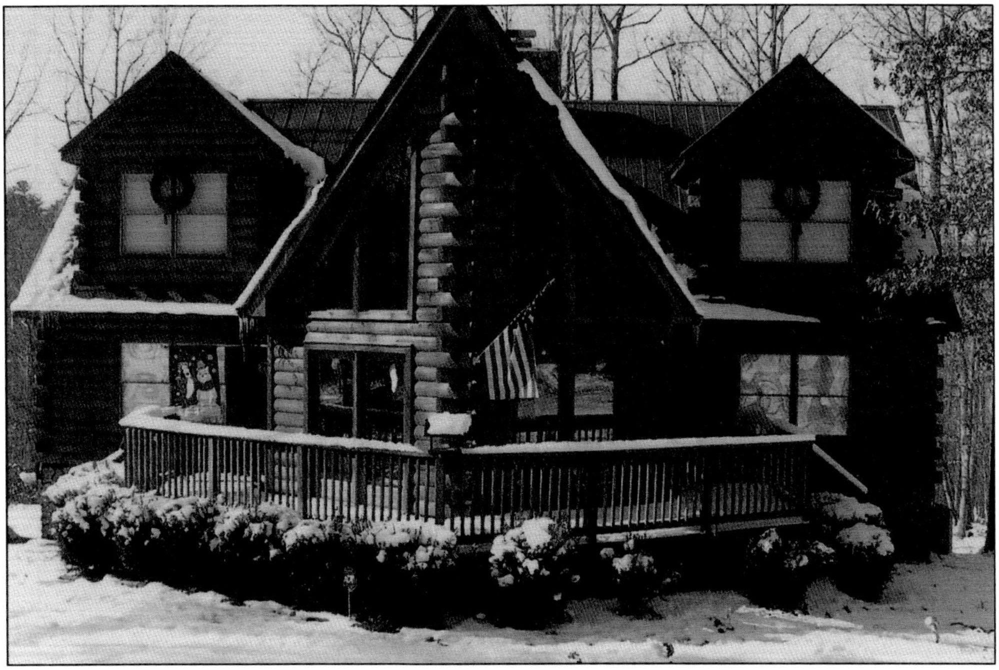

Above, Dwayne Duquette built a log home on property adjacent to the Jordan Lake gamelands. Benny, Dwayne's father, always had a boat when Dwayne was growing up, so right after Jordan Lake was open to the public, they started fishing at Jordan Lake. Dwayne would get home from high school and prepare the boat for his favorite pastime with his father. Dwayne loved the beauty of the hills surrounding the lake and knew one day he would buy a home there. Later Dwayne Duquette and his wife, Joy, purchased 5 acres near the Robeson Creek boat access. Below, Jordan Lake has thousands of acres of land open to the public via the Jordan Lake game lands. Part of the Duquettes' property connects to the game lands. Dwayne, pictured in the photograph, is checking his corn feeder hanging from a deer stand. (Both, courtesy of Dwayne Duquette.)

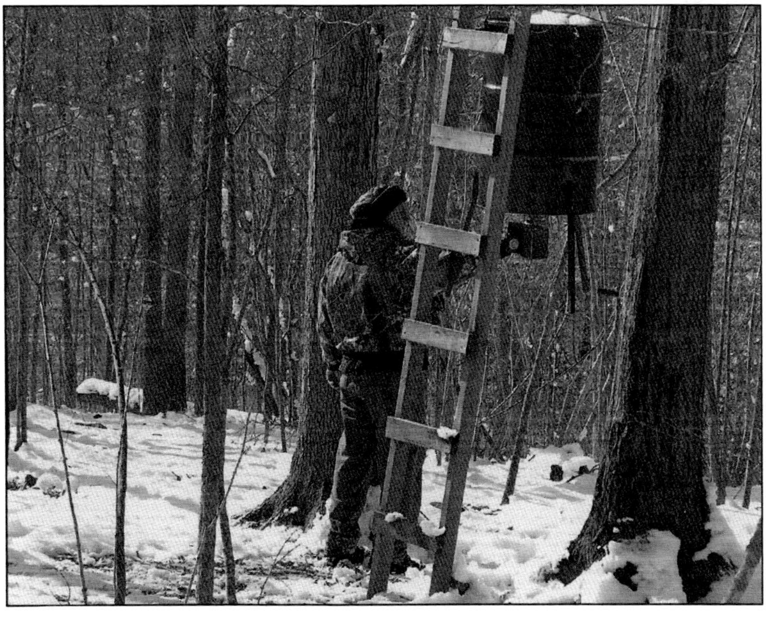

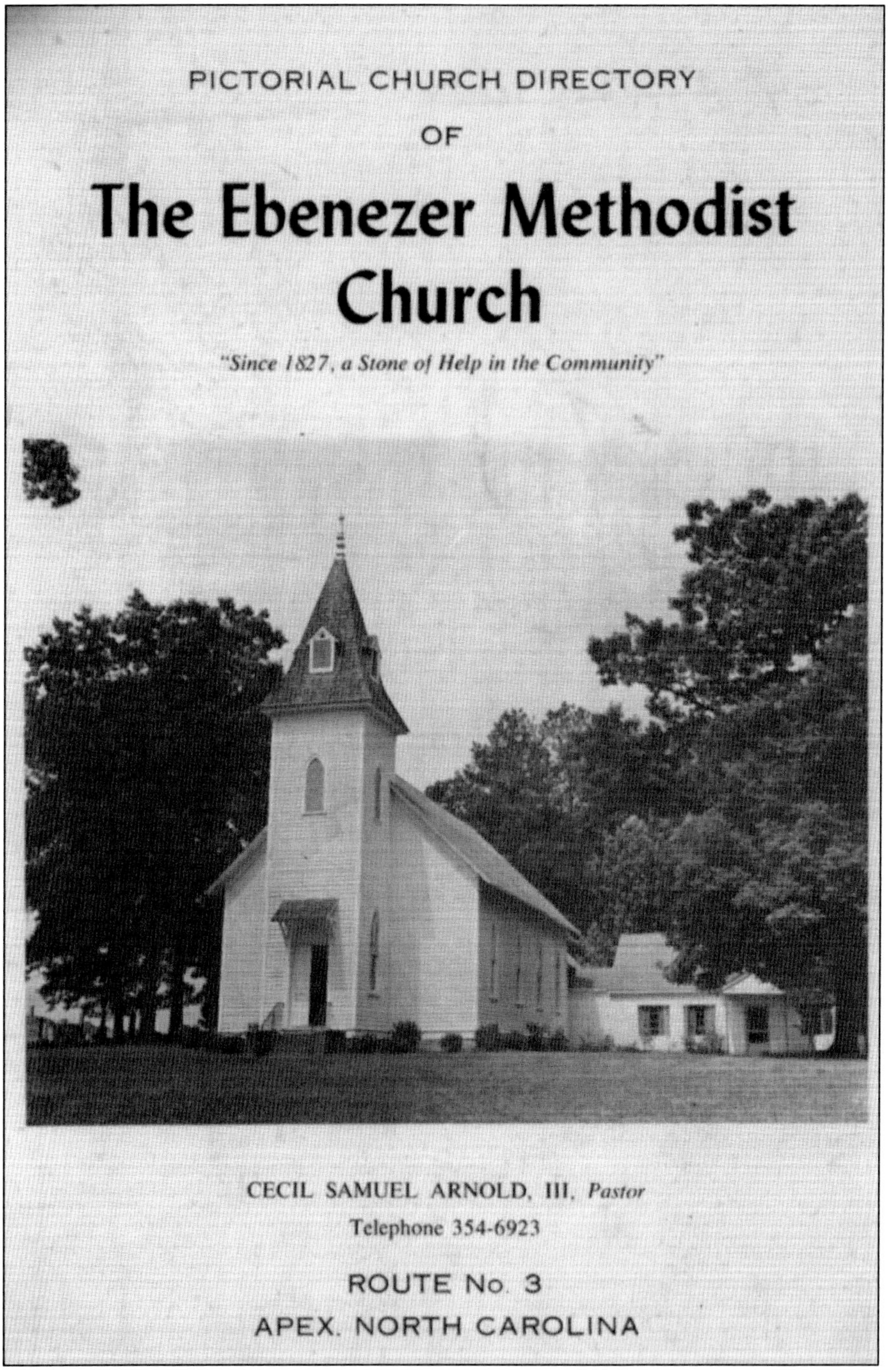
PICTORIAL CHURCH DIRECTORY

OF

The Ebenezer Methodist Church

"Since 1827, a Stone of Help in the Community"

CECIL SAMUEL ARNOLD, III, *Pastor*

Telephone 354-6923

ROUTE No. 3

APEX, NORTH CAROLINA

This sanctuary's stunning windows, altar rail, handmade pews, horizontal grooved paneling, wainscoting, chair railing, and heavy doors are all from the late 1800s. The Ebenezer Methodist Church was placed on the National Register of Historic Places in 1985. In 1867, after the Civil War, the church's African American members withdrew to form the Ebenezer African Methodist Episcopal Church. One hundred years later, the church again lost significant membership when locals were moved due to Jordan Lake. (Courtesy of Joan Wilson Frazier.)

This is a photograph of the Ebenezer Church being moved from its original site on Beaver Creek Road to a site 2 miles north on Beaver Creek Road. The original location is now the location of the Ebenezer boat ramp. The church, with approximately 100 parishioners, is known as the "church of help" and pledges 10 percent of its annual budget to mission support. It has also been recognized as one of the top churches in the Sanford district in per capita donations. (Courtesy of Joan Wilson Frazier.)

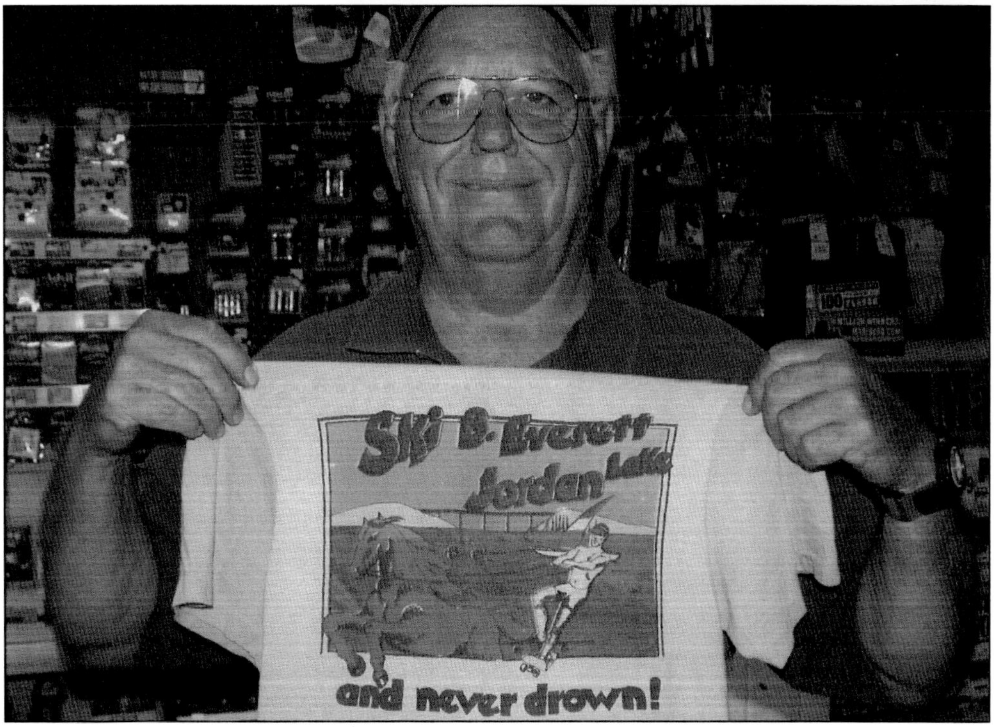

Vossie Horton, who owns the Wilsonville General Store, holds up one of the t-shirts he sold in the 1970s. The t-shirts were so successful that even members of the U.S. Army Corps of Engineers purchased them. The locals felt that the lake would never open, since construction originally began in 1967. The shirt says "Ski B. Everett Jordan Lake and never drown." (Courtesy of Vossie Horton.)

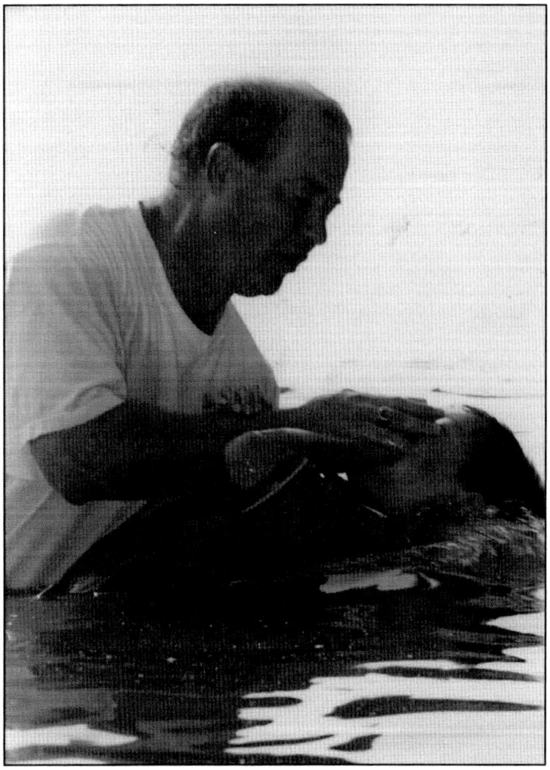

Pastor Don Brown of the Village Church draws a child out of the waters of Jordan Lake after he is baptized by full immersion. As a father and family man, the Village Church knew that Anthony Esquivel of Middleman Photography would grasp the essence and heartfelt moments of the day. (Courtesy of Middleman Photography.)

Pastor Don Brown baptizes a mother in Jordan Lake while her newly baptized son looks on. (Courtesy of Middleman Photography.)

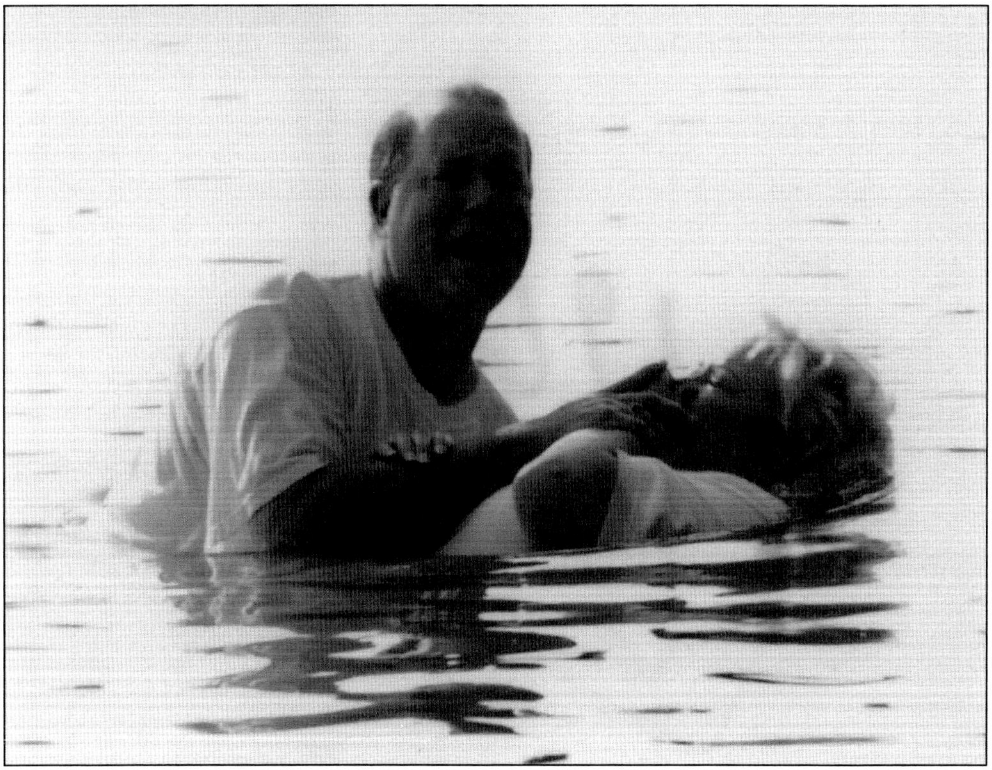

At right is a beautiful close-up of two children at the Parker's Creek area of Jordan Lake. Below are, from left to right, Aaron (15), who was baptized at Jordan Lake at age 7 and still enjoys a good swim there; Kyle (7) who is Filipino by birth but North Carolinian by adoption, as this is the only home he knows; Nikki, a homeschooling mother who has found this part of North Carolina to be a fantastic place to lay down roots and raise a family; Lemuel (11), who came to North Carolina at age 8 via international adoption and considers North Carolina the best place in the world; Elliana (12), who was baptized in Jordan Lake at age 5; and Anthony, who is a husband, father, and photographer who came to North Carolina in 2000 and has not looked back. He loves this state, where the beach and the mountains are all a short drive from his Triangle-area home. (Both, courtesy of Middleman Photography.)

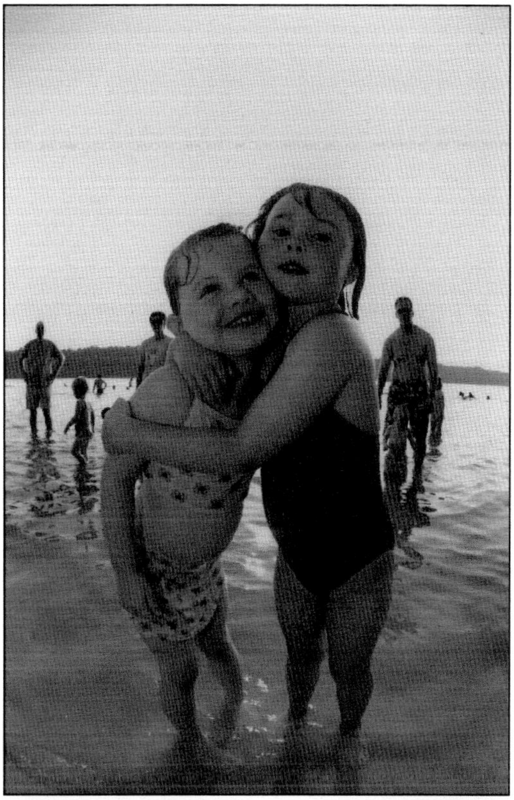

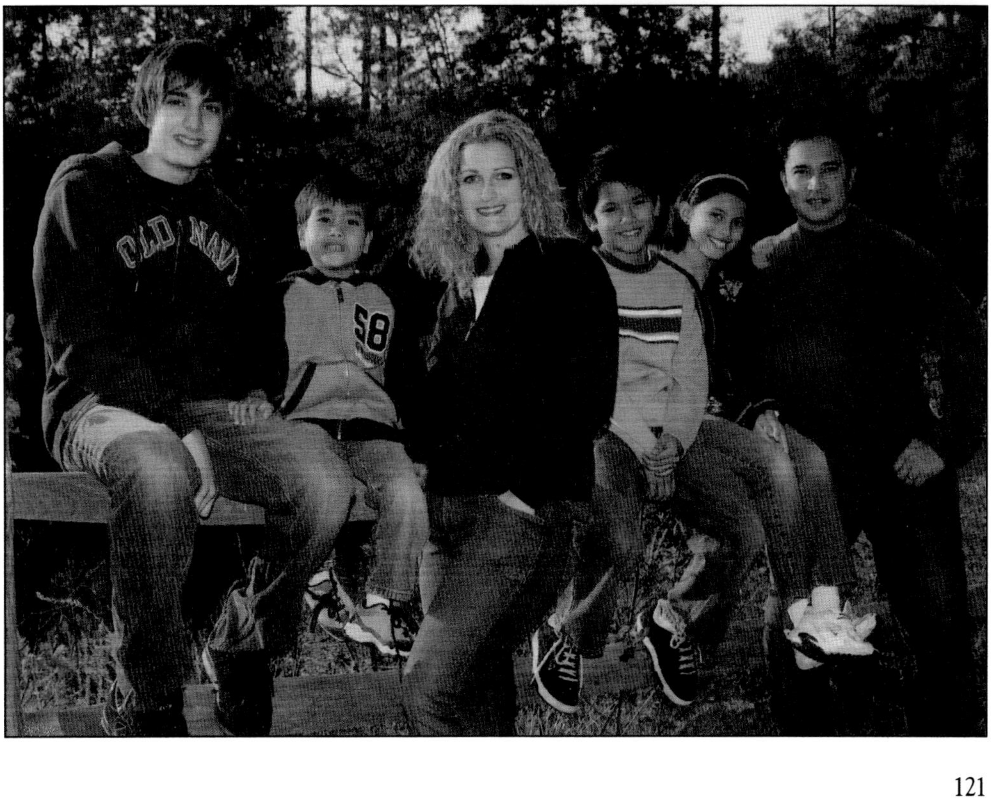

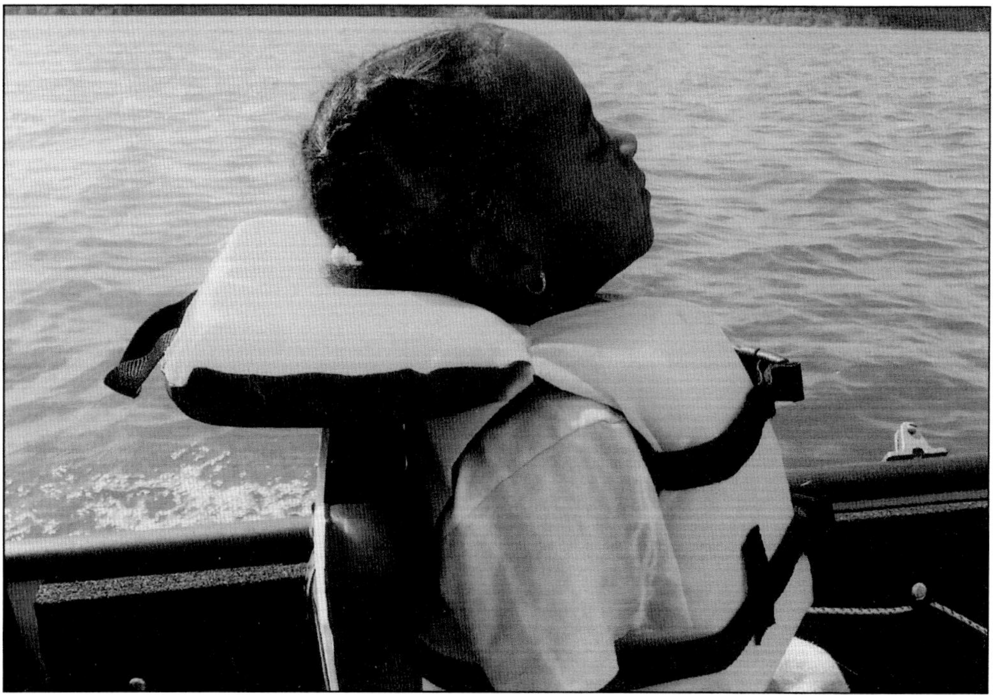

Ivan Watkins captured the special moment above of his daughter enjoying the sun during her boat ride on Jordan Lake. There were many times when Ivan's little girl fell asleep with her head on his lap as the family fished to a full moon during the night. Aside from capturing images of his children, Ivan also enjoys photographing memories for others. Ivan feels his passion for video and photography allows him to preserve precious slices of time that would be forever lost. Photographs possess the ability to restore memories or remind people of events that their minds have forgotten. Ivan feels that each family should try to take pictures. Not only do they provide enjoyment for the present, but they also serve as historical records that will be appreciated by generations to come. Below, at the Jordan Lake boat ramps, Ivan Watkins taught his youngest son how to catch shad baitfish using a cast net. (Both, courtesy of Ivan Watkins.)

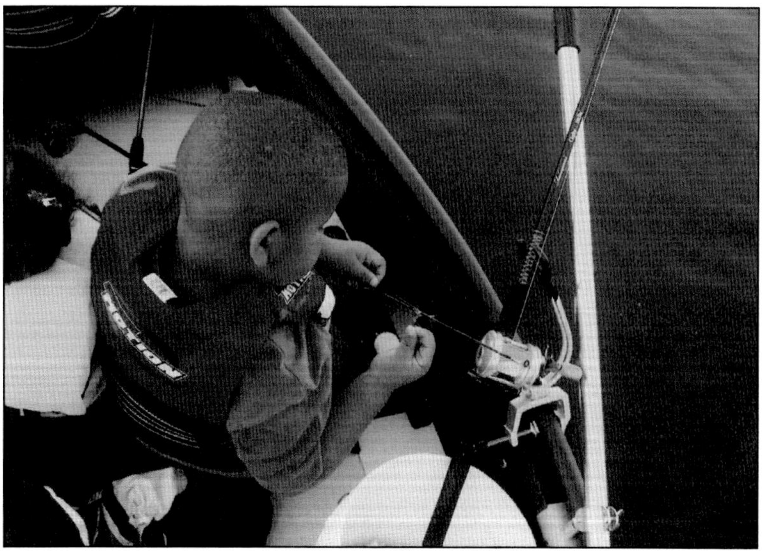

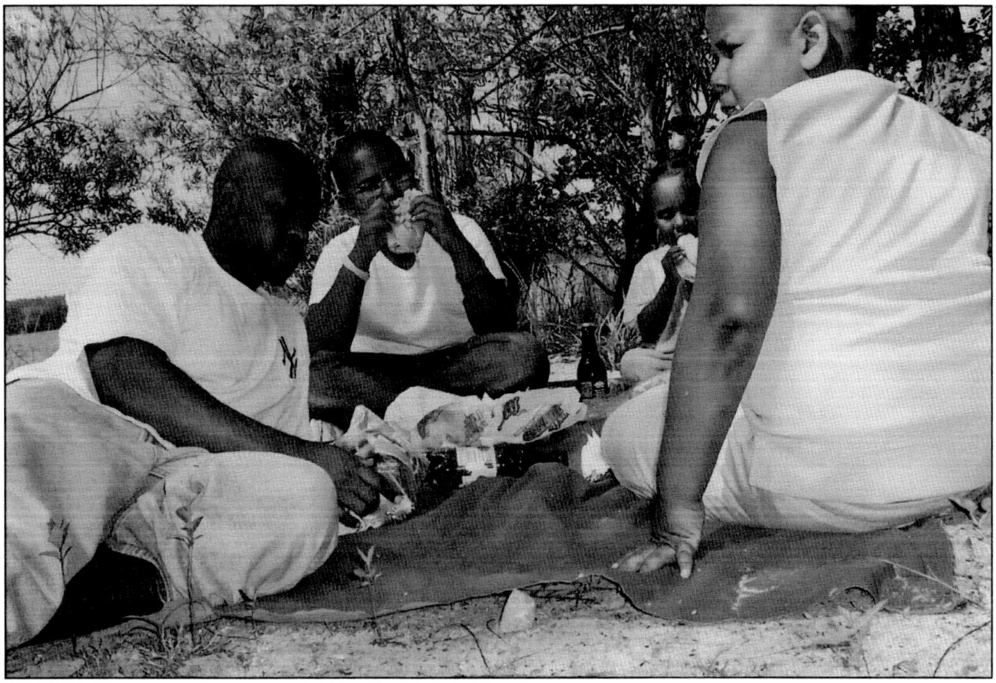

The Watkins family enjoys spending time at Jordan Lake. They take part in boating, fishing, sightseeing, and just relaxing on one of the several islands that can be found. Ivan Watkins will never forget the time he told the children that they were going to "Watkins beach." They had never been to a beach at the lake before. They played in the sand until the sun started to set. Another favorite memory was when the family packed a lunch and ate it on one of the islands at the lake. For them it was an adventure to be the only humans on a single plot of land that was surrounded by water. Watkins said he would never forget seeing his oldest boy explore the island with their dog. There were many nights filled with catching catfish and crappie. Jordan Lake was also the place where the Watkins family taught their dog to swim. Jordan Lake provides many fond memories for them. (Both, courtesy of Ivan Watkins.)

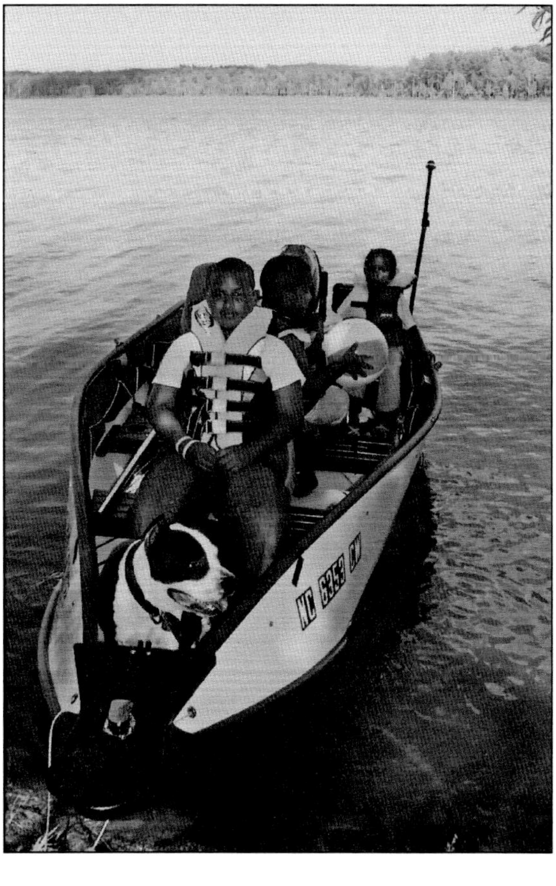

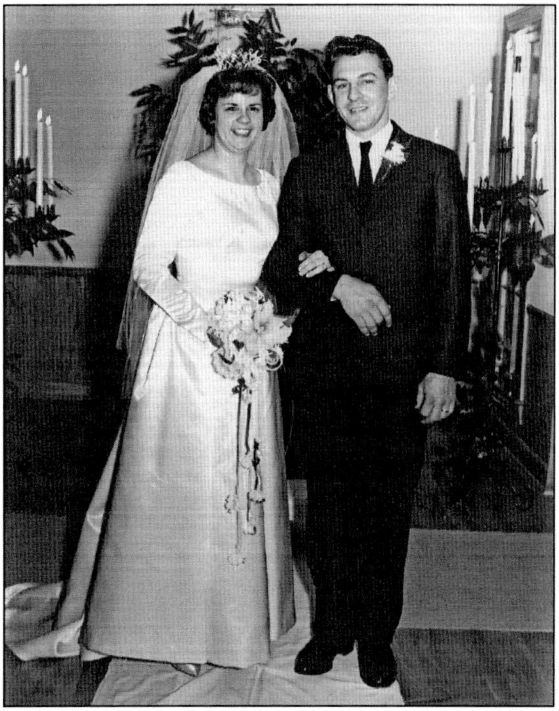

Per Joyce Cotten, Jimmy Cotten is a kind and gentle person and husband and a wonderful partner. He is slow to anger and is extremely dependable. He is not a big conversationalist and not full of loving words. He can, however, select some of the sweetest cards that say the things he cannot seem to put into words. He is always by her side through the good and the difficult times. They work hard together to have a loving home based on faith and trust, and they have grown older together. He is quick to support and defend her. He is a wonderful father to their daughter Kim—kind, considerate, supportive, gentle, loving, and always there for her. They have been married for 46 wonderful years. There were lots of good times and also difficult times, but they were always together. He is the love of her life. (Courtesy of Joyce and Jimmy Cotten.)

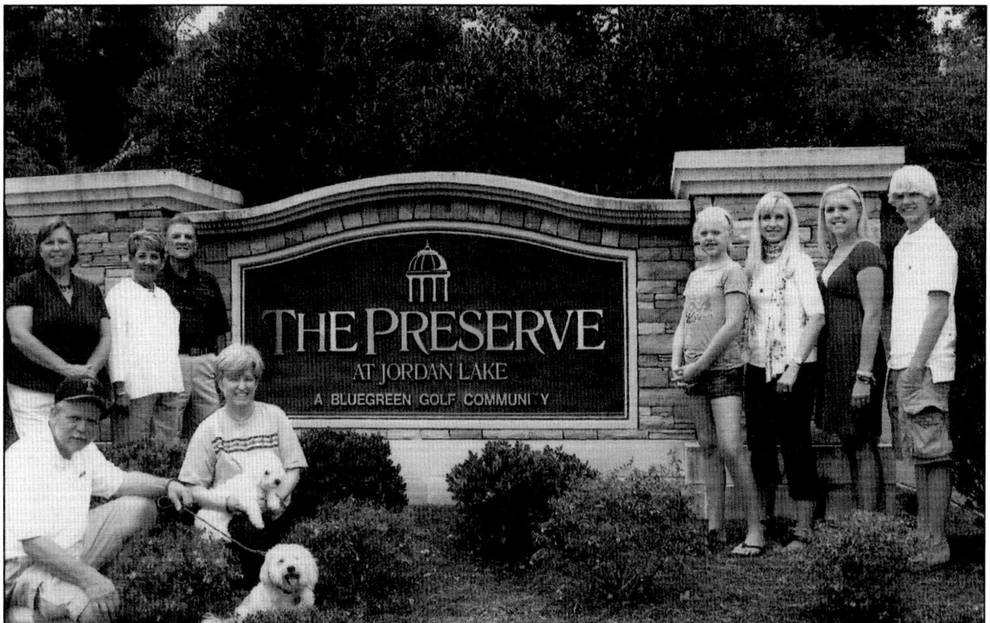

The Preserve at Jordan Lake is a golf community with outstanding homes. Pictured here from left to right are (first row) Tom Shafer with his dog Eli and Tom's wife, Bonnie Shafer, with her dog Bentley; (second row) Lauren Roberts, Sharon Carfora, Joe Carfora, Olivia Knuth, Dawn Knuth, Megan Knuth, and Chad Knuth. Located at the shores of Jordan Lake, just south of Chapel Hill and west of Raleigh, the Preserve at Jordan Lake golf club is a semiprivate golf course offering one of the best golfing experiences in the area. (Courtesy of Lauren Roberts.)

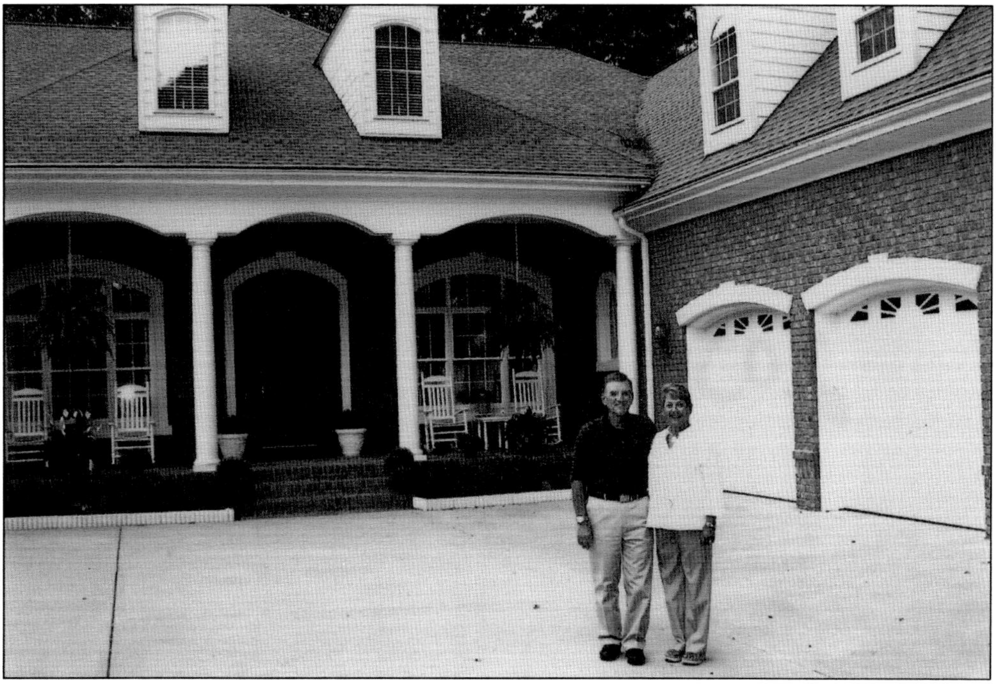

Joe Carfora (left) is standing with his lovely wife, Sharon Carfora. *Golf Week* magazine rated this community as one of America's top 100 residential golf courses and among the top 40 for new golf course communities. (Author's collection.)

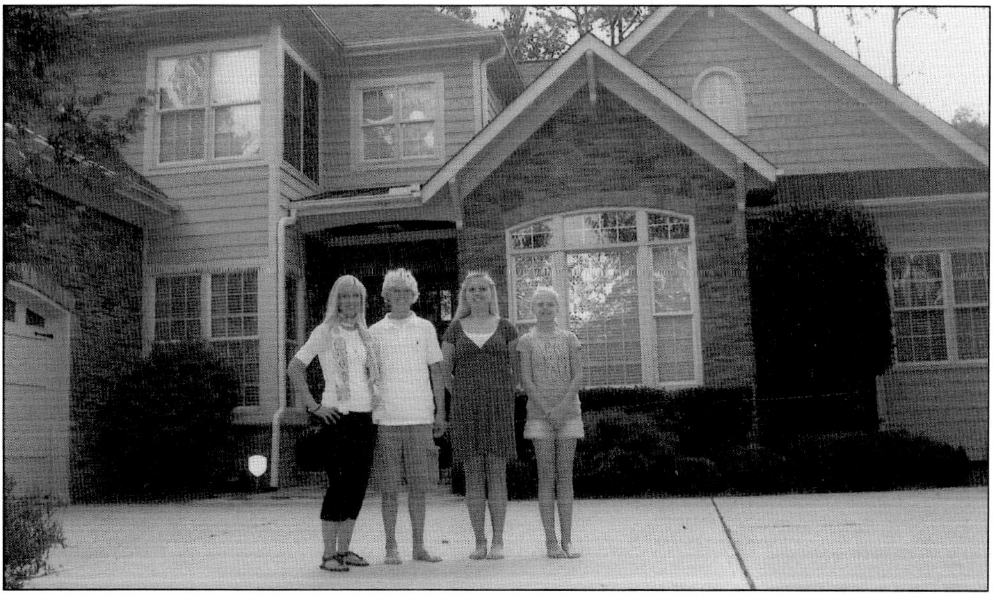

The Knuth family is standing outside their home on Davis Love Drive in the Preserve at Jordan Lake. The Knuth family found the preserve while taking the children to an educational forest event several years before. They saw the new golf course community nearby and fell in love. Dave Knuth (not pictured) runs the trails of Jordan Lake for exercise. The children love Jordan Lake so much that they have even held their birthday parties there at the picnic sites. From left to right are Dawn Knuth, Chad Knuth, Megan Knuth, and Olivia Knuth. (Author's collection.)

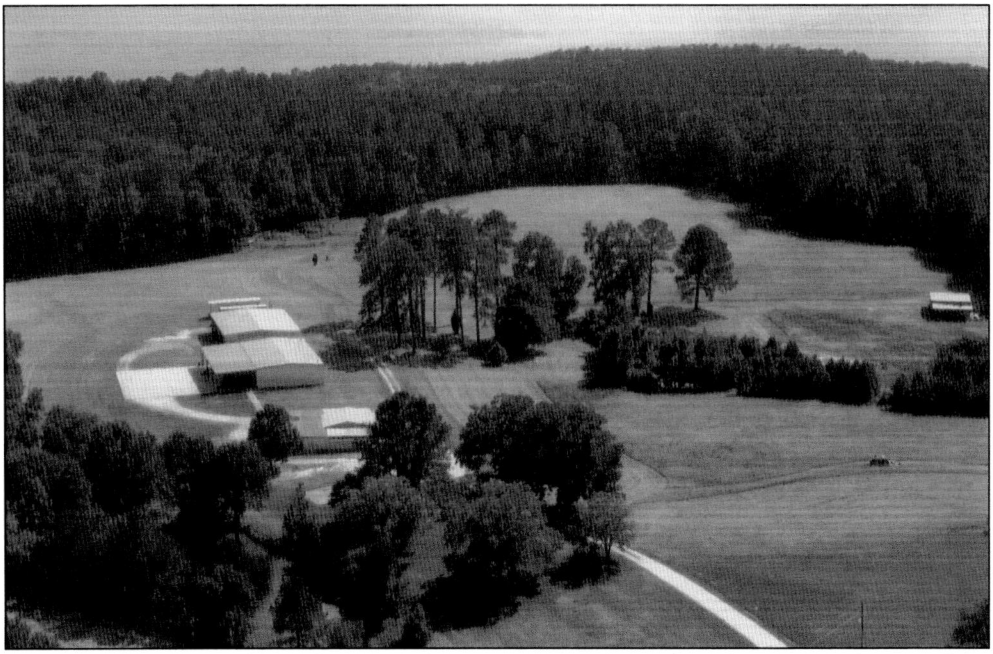

This is an aerial view of Patrick Barnes's home next to Jordan Lake. The water at the top of the photograph was all previously part of the Barnes family land. The government purchased the land through eminent domain for Jordan Lake. The lake has significantly increased the value of local real estate. (Courtesy of Patrick Barnes.)

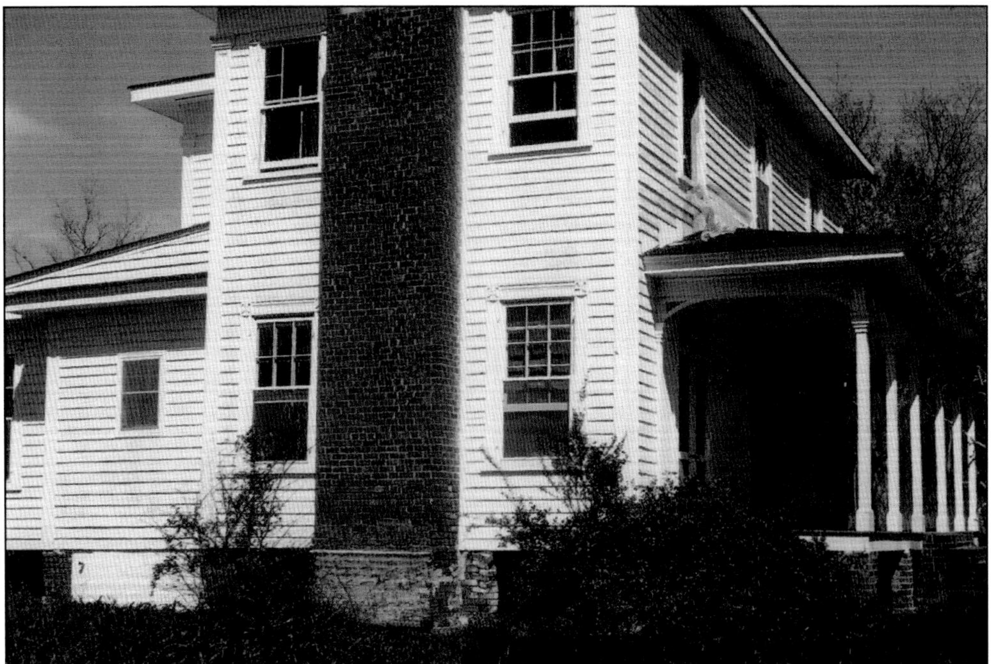

This is the John Acree Mason house in 1977. The home is a two-story Greek Revival dwelling. It was built in the early 1800s and was lived in by John Acree Mason, a soldier in the War of 1812 and a very wealthy farmer. (Courtesy of U.S. Army Corps of Engineers.)

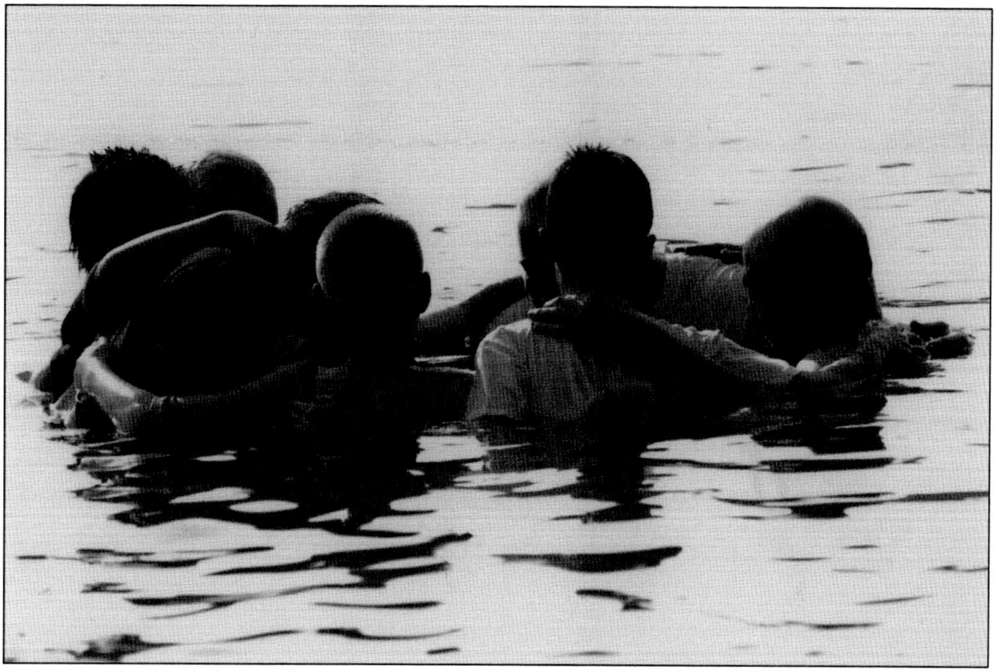

A group of baptismal candidates from the Village Church at Holly Springs have a word of prayer and thanksgiving after being baptized in Jordan Lake at the Parker's Creek area. (Courtesy of Middleman Photography.)

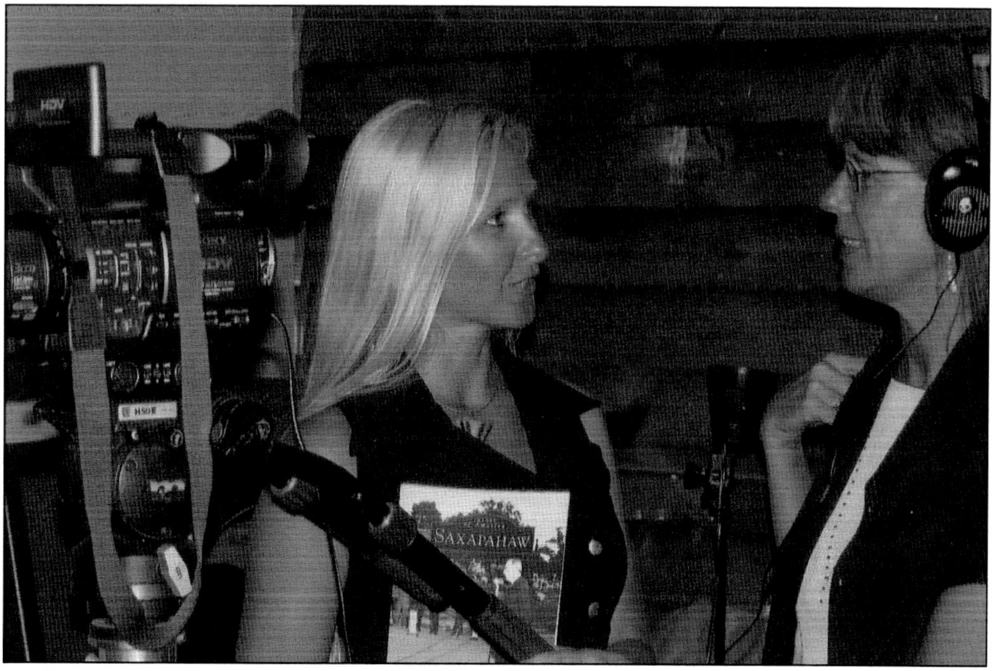

Studio production manager Donna Buskirk of the People's Channel in Chapel Hill is interviewing author and medical writer Heather Leigh Wallace. Donna is also the author of the book *How to Make Money While You Look for a Job.* The interview was about the release of *Saxapahaw* and the upcoming *Jordan Lake*, both for Arcadia Publishing. (Courtesy Donna Buskirk.)

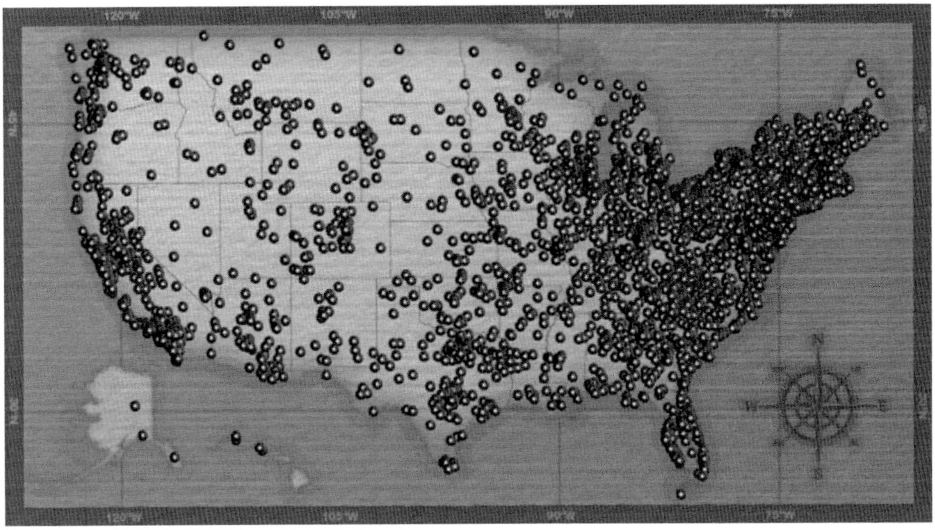